US Labor and Political Action, 1918–24

A Comparison of Independent Political Action in New York, Chicago and Seattle

Andrew Strouthous
Associate Lecturer in American History and Politics
Colchester Institute
Anglia Polytechnic University
and
Associate Lecturer
Open University

First published in Great Britain 2000 by
MACMILLAN PRESS LTD
Houndmills, Basingstoke, Hampshire RG21 6XS and London
Companies and representatives throughout the world

A catalogue record for this book is available from the British Library.

ISBN 0–333–73571–4

First published in the United States of America 2000 by
ST. MARTIN'S PRESS, INC.,
Scholarly and Reference Division,
175 Fifth Avenue, New York, N.Y. 10010

ISBN 0–312–22185–1

Library of Congress Cataloging-in-Publication Data
Strouthous, Andrew, 1948–
US labor and political action, 1918–24 : a comparison of
independent political action in New York, Chicago and Seattle /
Andrew Strouthous.
p. cm.
Includes bibliographical references and index.
ISBN 0–312–22185–1 (cloth)
1. Trade-unions—New York (State)—New York—Political activity–
–History—20th century.   2. Trade-unions—Illinois—Chicago–
–Political activity—History—20th century.   3. Trade-unions–
–Washington (State)—Seattle—Political activity—History—20th
century.   I. Title.
HD8085.N53S77   1999
322'.2'0973—dc21   98–55308
                                                                              CIP

This book is printed on paper suitable for recycling and made from fully managed and
sustained forest sources.

10   9   8   7   6   5   4   3   2   1
09   08   07   06   05   04   03   02   01   00

Printed and bound in Great Britain by
Antony Rowe Ltd, Chippenham, Wiltshire

In memory of my mother
Ellen Strouthous 1918–93
and my father
George Strouthous 1913–93
who believed in education and travel in equal
measure

Contents

Acknowledgements

This book is based on research completed at University College London – indeed it would not have come to fruition without the UCL History Department's award of a Postgraduate Teaching Studentship. Thanks are due to the Heads of the History Department, past and present, who believed in this project.

Thanks are especially due to Rick Halpern for his support and encouragement as my supervisor, and his subsequent advice on publishing this book. I would also like to thank Neville Kirk, without whose urgings and encouragement this manuscript may have remained in my desk drawer.

I would like to thank the following for the provision of funds for research trips: The Central Research Fund, University of London; John F. Kennedy Institute, The Free University, Berlin; The Hale Bellot Fund, University College London; Arthur and Mary Burchell Fellowship, British Association of American Studies; and The Royal Historical Society. Also my late parents gave extra financial support for trips abroad, and provided finance for writing this book. Thanks are also due to my sister Christella for providing furniture that has made the long hours in the author's garret comfortable.

Special thanks are due to Peter Alexander for reading the manuscript of this book, and for his valuable and much appreciated comments. Ian Birchall read the original research that this book is based on, providing perceptive comments and corrections. The Seminars of Comparative Labour and Working Class History; the New Approaches to Socialist History; and the Northern Marxists Historians Group all provided a useful forum in which to discuss the ideas contained in this book.

Lesley Bogden, Inter-Library Loans Librarian, University College London, made the *Seattle Union Record* possible. I would also like to thank the staff at the following: the Tamiment; the Library of Congress, Manuscripts Division; the Chicago Historical Society; the National Archives, Washington DC; and the Library of Congress (Manuscripts Division).

I received much generous hospitality on my visits abroad. In particular from Ronnie Geller, Pete Gillard, Phil Naylor, Jim Portnoy and Debbie Seaborn. The following provided comments and support, or just good company: Phil Taylor, Rachael Walker, Jim Cronin, Neil A.

Wynn, Farhang Morady, Jon Olley, John Page, John Walker, Anne-Marie Vincent, Phil Long and Caroline O'Reilley. Thanks to Paul Buhle, Roger Horowitz and Stanley Shapiro for papers, essays and articles.

Finally I would like to thank my nephew James Daniel Walker, whose visits stopped me from slaving for too long over the word processor, and whose sense of fun and mischief enlivened the writing process.

Abbreviations

ACW	Amalgamated Clothing Workers
AFL	American Federation of Labor
AI	Associated Industries
ALP	American Labor Party (New York)
CCFLP	Cook County Farmer Labor Party
CCLP	Cook County Labor Party
CFL	Chicago Federation of Labor
CFU	Central Federated Union (New York)
CLU	Central Labor Union (Brooklyn)
Con Con	Constitutional Convention
CPPA	Conference for Progressive Political Action
CTLC	Central Trades and Labor Council (Greater New York)
CWTUL	Chicago Women's Trade Union League
FFLP	Federated Farmer Labor Party
FLP	Farmer Labor Party
IAM	International Association of Machinists
ILGWU	International Ladies Garment Workers Union
IWW	Industrial Workers of the World (also called Wobblies)
KCFLP	King County Farmer Labor Party
KCLC	King County Labor Council
KCTA	King County Triple Alliance
NAACP	National Association for Advancement of Colored People
NPL	Non-Partisan League
NWLB	National War Labor Board
NWTUL	National Women's Trade Union League
NYFLP	New York Farmer Labor Party
NYSP	New York Socialist Party
NYWTUL	New York Women's Trade Union League
SLC	Stockyards Labor Council
SCLC	Seattle Central Labor Council
SPA	Socialist Party of America
TA	Triple Alliance
TUEL	Trade Union Education League
UMWA/UMW	United Mine Workers of America
WSFL / WSF	Washington State Federation of Labor

Introduction

This comparative study of independent working-class politics in New York, Chicago and Seattle between 1918 and 1924 is inspired by the debate over the absence of a working-class party in the USA. Ever since Werner Sombart asked 'Why Is There No Socialism in the United States?' historians and social scientists have contested the answer.[1] The weakness of socialism is not a problem unique to the USA. Indeed mass socialist parties are a rare phenomenon which only exist in a few countries. Seen in this light the American situation is not particularly unusual. However, Sombart was questioning the absence of a working-class party in a country he considered to have an advanced working class.[2]

Compared to the situation in other advanced capitalist countries such as Britain and Germany, the political accomplishments of American organized labour were limited. However, at the time of Sombart's treatise the future of labour parties in Britain and Germany was by no means certain. When the German and British parties did finally develop they were reformist, believing in change through utilizing the existing political and economic system. Although not particularly radical, they did represent the working class through direct links with the unions. It is the absence of this type of labour party in the USA that concerns this study.[3]

Even today, in the USA, millions are discontented with the two main parties, as the flirtation with Ross Perot and recent attempts to launch a labour party demonstrate.[4] However it is not the intention of this book to consider this question in a general sense, or in relation to the whole of US political history. Rather a key conjuncture in US working-class political history is examined. The period chosen starts with the end of the First World War which saw the USA engulfed in a wave of mass strikes.[5] This raises the question 'why was it that, in the period that followed the First World War, US labour's attempt to establish its own party failed?' For this is the most substantial attempt by organized labour to build a labour party to date. It is this failure to build a labour party between 1918 and 1924 that is the central concern of this book.

Although this book is concerned with the 'missing workers party' it is not directly concerned with the debate over 'exceptionalism'. It concurs with Aristide R. Zolberg's view that 'the "exceptionalist" tradition and its mirror image, "the end of ideology" approach, are

1

so bound up in ideological controversy that they have outlived their usefulness as intellectual frameworks suitable for contemporary research.' In rejecting the exceptionalist framework it is not intended to deny that the American working class has its own distinctive history and development. If it did not, there would be no need for this study. It is not distinctiveness that is rejected here but, to quote Zolberg, the method of evaluating 'working-class formation by positing one national pattern as the theoretic norm in relation to which all others are treated as deviant cases'. Indeed this method drains the term 'exceptional' of all content, for every working class has its own distinct history. They are all exceptional. At the same time there are many similarities between the working classes of all countries. The existence of the working class is not conditional on the building of its own party but on its conflicts with its ruling class which take many forms.[6]

Nonetheless, it is necessary to briefly consider the way in which exceptionalist thinking shaped American labour historiography. The old school of labour history put institutions and leaders at its centre; the policies of the American Federation of Labor (AFL), and its leadership's 'pure and simple' business unionism, has stood in for the entire membership. This includes the AFL's national executive's rejection of any independent workers' party in favour of a 'non-partisan policy' of choosing between the two established parties. Thus Gwendolyn Mink claims, 'In fact American Trade Unionism explicitly rejected the idea of independent labor politics.' This is a simplification that does not correlate to the concrete evidence.[7]

The reality was significantly different for, between 1919 and 1924, the AFL was riven by civil war to determine its political policy. Major city centres of the AFL embarked on the project of building labour parties and thus Samuel Gompers battled against them for several years. Victory for the AFL's anti-labour party policy was not guaranteed in advance. Neither side believed that some predetermined theory doomed them to failure. If they had, they would not have fought a bitter struggle to control the political destiny of the AFL. In 1924, the AFL supported an independent presidential candidate for the first time in its history. This was partly a result of the political activity of those who had advocated a labour party during the previous six years. Paradoxically, the defeat of the La Follette presidential campaign in 1924 represented the final victory of those who opposed independent political action.

Yet for the most part historians have paid scant attention to this activity. There are few books that deal with the AFL and the attempts to build labour parties between 1918 and 1924.[8] The majority of accounts available consist of unpublished dissertations, some over seventy years old.[9] This dearth of material is no accident. It is the outcome of the exceptionalist approach impacting on US history. History has been utilized to map out the present. It is argued that workers do not want unions or parties, they are content with the 'Dream'. This viewpoint is read back into the past; as workers failed to build a party, those who tried wasted their time. The inevitability of history was against them and therefore the struggles of those who tried to build a party are downplayed. History is only about those who win, and other possible outcomes in history are not of importance. Thus to quote Richard White, 'We eliminate its strangeness. *We eliminate, most of all, its possibilities. History should do more than just validate the inevitability of the present*' (my emphasis). Because workers did not create a labour party, and never desired one according to the exceptionalist school of thought, important episodes in working-class history have been ignored. The political activity of workers between 1918 and 1924 is one such episode. The concerns of the present have eliminated the 'possibilities of the past'. Indeed on researching for this book I was told by the head of a major archive that no such thing as labour parties existed in the US in 1920.[10] As lamentable as this situation is, it is not the intention of this book to provide a complete history of US working-class political activity.

Rather this book is concerned with the intense conflict, over the issue of a labour party, that divided the AFL between 1918 and 1924. For those who supported a labour party, and later the independent political action of the La Follette campaign, were not an insignificant minority. Indeed many were the leaders of the AFL in major US cities. By dealing with the specific history of this period, rather than becoming lost in the vagaries of ideology this account discovers that the failure to build a party in this period has far more to do with the balance of class forces than any ideological commitment of workers to American Liberalism. Furthermore the consequences of this struggle for the ensuing La Follette campaigns have also been ignored. This has led to a minimizing of the importance of labour to the La Follette campaign. This book provides the evidence that labour was far more central to the 1924 La Follette campaign than previously recognized. It also demonstrates that the political action of workers in 1919 flowed into the progressivism of the 1924 General Election.[11]

These key concerns raise a series of secondary questions in their wake, for this book is not just a simple telling of an untold story.

Important questions are raised by the events outlined here. How substantial was support for a labour party inside and outside of the AFL? What barriers did the labour parties face? To what extent did the craft nature of the AFL preclude building a labour party? Did the nature of industry, workplace size and organization affect the possibilities? How did factors such as race, ethnicity and gender affect the movement, and how did the movement relate to these factors? What was the more important factor in failure, the AFL's leadership opposition, or lack of popular support at the polls? Did the American political system aid or hamper the new parties' development?

This book is concerned with answering these questions, and this concern infuses it from the beginning to the end. In carrying out this project it is insufficient to provide a history based simply on national events. Generalizations made from national activities can lead to an underestimating of the importance of events. A national balance sheet, from the La Follette headquarters, does not tell the full story. A closer look at the three cities in this study reveals, contrary to the established historiography, that many unions were active in the campaign. National histories that do not check general experiences with local ones are prone to such errors. Local research undermines such mistaken generalizations.[12]

However, in using local studies there is a risk of losing sight of any generalized conclusion. For the experience of the Seattle working-class movement was different from that of New York and vice versa. All localities have their own peculiarities and commonalities. How can this dilemma be resolved? Zolberg considered this problem at an international level, and his solution is well suited to the problem faced here:

> One way out of this dilemma is to treat each historical situation as a case of working-class formation – that is, as something that is akin to one of several possible states of dependent variable and that can be accounted for by reference to variation among a set of factors considered...[13]

Using this method, differences and similarities in each locality can be taken into account and tested against the overall national picture. The use of the comparative approach transcends the barrier to generalization erected by a purely local study. The use of comparison can identify the

> combination of factors that best account for the variation that is found, taking into consideration that structural factors merely deter-

mined a range of possibilities within which actual outcomes resulted from constant strategic interaction among a number of players.[14]

The reason for choosing the labour movements of the three cities as case studies is to provide a comparison that can answer the questions raised above. The questions raised are investigated in each local study and tested against the others. The choice of New York, Chicago and Seattle, in particular, is because of their centrality to labour party and independent political action between 1918 and 1924, and because their labour movements were characterized in different ways. These studies do not simply concentrate on the political or trade-union factors involved, but take into account the social and economic factors shaping working-class formation in all three cities. These particularities and differences are outlined in Chapter 1 which follows.[15] It is sufficient to note at this stage that the social and economic structure of each city was very different. In spite of this the labour movements in all three cities were, for the most part, dominated by AFL unions. In studying the relationship between difference and similarity, the main factors that defeated organized labour's commitment to independent political action emerge.[16]

Before proceeding with the case studies, Chapter 1 will detail the change in US labour relations created by the First World War. These changes at a national and local level altered the attitude of some AFL members towards the state, encouraging the belief that it could be used to carry out reform. This new optimism led to the demand for a labour party. The chapter also outlines the general economic, political, social and trade union background to each city. Chapters 2 to 4 detail the labour party movement in New York, Chicago and Seattle between 1918 and 1920. These chapters deal with the formation, and the first major election campaigns, of the labour parties. Chapters 5 to 7 deal with the subsequent decline of labour party activity between 1921 and 1924 in the three cities, and its transformation into the independent political activity of the La Follette campaign. The conclusion to Chapter 6 discusses the wider ramifications of this activity. In the final three case studies much of the evidence is published for the first time, for no historian has portrayed the grassroots activities of the unions during the La Follette campaign before. As far as possible, each chapter investigates the same range of factors as the previous one. The final chapter assesses to what extent the sum total of the case studies challenges the conventional portrayal of the US working class in regard to political action.

1 From Reconstruction to Labour Parties: the Crucible of War

> We mined the coal to transport soldiers,
> We kept the home fires all aglow,
> We put Old Kaiser out of business,
> What's our reward? We want to know![1]

Between 1918 and 1919 the postwar reconstruction of American society became an issue of importance for employers, workers and government. While President Wilson planned for 'democracy and peace' on the world stage the American Federation of Labor (AFL) formed reconstruction committees, nationally and locally, to formulate its plans. This chapter traces the process that began with the issue of reconstruction and ended with the formation of labour parties in New York, Chicago and Seattle.

The First World War boosted the American economy, creating full employment and raising labour's confidence. In 1917 and 1918 strikes took place across a wide range of industries. Workers demanded higher wages to compensate for inflation; others struck for shorter hours or union recognition. The metal trades, heavily involved in munitions production, had more strikes than any other sector. Close on their heels came the building trades, shipbuilding, mining and transportation. These were not the only areas involved, and strikes took place across a wide range of occupations, including women telegraphers. All these industries were central to the war effort.[2]

The growing disruption became of increasing concern to the government, which feared that wage increases would fuel inflation. This wartime experience was the crucible for the labour party movement. An understanding of both the American Federation of Labor's temporary break with voluntarism and the trajectory of labour party activism must begin with the corporatist experiments of the wartime administration.[3]

So that President Wilson could pursue the war effort without hindrance he obtained a 'no-strike pledge' from Samuel Gompers, President of the AFL. Gompers, however, was unable to get the Executive

Council of the AFL to agree to the pledge. To overcome AFL objections Wilson initiated the National War Labor Board (NWLB). The aim of the NWLB was to prevent strikes and lockouts for the duration of hostilities. Workers' rights to organize and bargain collectively were conceded, but this did not mean a closed shop. The employers' right to organize was guaranteed, as well as existing union conditions. The employers' right to meet with representatives of non-union employees remained in force, but it was stated that all workers had a right to a living wage. Established in April 1918, the NWLB was composed of representatives of capital, labour and the public. It became the supreme court of industry, overseeing industrial relations during the war.[4]

Prior to the war the AFL advocated 'voluntarism', the belief that workers should improve their conditions through their own economic organization, and not depend on the state for reform. However, Samuel Gompers, its strongest advocate, broke with voluntarism in order to mobilize labour for the war effort. He not only tolerated the intervention of the state through the NWLB, but, along with other leaders, also accepted nationalization of key utilities such as the railroads. After the war the rail unions and the majority of the AFL leadership continued supporting nationalization of the railroads, forcing the issue through the AFL convention of 1920 over Gompers' objections.[5]

Wartime labour shortages, coupled with the frequent intervention of the NWLB in favour of striking workers, led to an increase in union membership both inside and outside the AFL. The NWLB and its Joint Chairman, Frank Walsh, won the respect of a layer of trade-union officials and members. Union recognition, equal pay for equal work for women, a 44-hour week, and wage increases were typical of awards enforced by the NWLB to end disputes.[6] Under the Board's protection, union membership grew by nearly one million by the end of the war. The Board did not succeed in preventing all strikes; indeed the number of disputes increased. As Joseph McCartin has argued:

> By allowing workers to connect democracy in industry to democracy in Europe, the federal program had the effect of offering a potent vocabulary to labor militants who had little trouble in seizing it to attack the authority of employers.

The belief that the war was for democracy abroad saw workers take up the slogan of industrial democracy at home. Workers demanded the 'de-kaisering' of industry, rather than higher wages and shorter hours.[7]

Thus the Chicago Federation of Labor (CFL) pledged to its 'fellow working men and women of the Allied nations that we will never surrender until Labor's rights and Democracy is acknowledged the world over'.[8] This ambivalent language, while supporting the war, was concerned with the rights of labour. For shopfloor militants industrial democracy was not an abstract issue; it meant the ability to defend or improve conditions against ruthless employers. The NWLB provided a vocabulary and legitimacy for these struggles. However, for much of the AFL leadership involvement with the NWLB was merely an emergency measure; they had no desire to see such government intervention continue after the war.

The ending of hostilities raised the question as to whether the relationship created by the NWLB would continue. More conservative AFL leaders desired a return to the status quo, but more progressive leaders – and even some industrialists, statesmen and publicists – believed that the remarkable achievements of industry during the war should continue. This suited a corporate ideology that sought to strengthen and expand production by involving the trade unions, while excluding those which were antagonistic to capitalist development.[9] Nevertheless, the reconstruction programme adopted by the AFL convention did not mention shop committees or the continuance of the NWLB. The philosophy of 'voluntarism' remained intact. Workers would improve their living standards by their own economic strength; however this did not mean striking, or adopting militant, class-struggle style unionism.[10]

This attitude did not take into account the fact that the AFL had changed dramatically during the war. Before the war most AFL disputes took place on a craft or local basis; across-industry strikes were rare, as were general strikes. After the war many trade unionists in some sectors, most notably meatpacking and steel, formed joint committees to negotiate across entire industries. This new situation offered possibilities for reforming or modernizing the AFL, but the leadership opposed change. However, some sections of the AFL did take up the challenge offered by the new situation – in particular the progressive union leaders of the Chicago and Seattle labour movements.[11]

THE PROGRESSIVE OPPOSITION

John Fitzpatrick, President of the CFL, was a full-time organizer for the AFL, but he was not a typical AFL official. Under his leadership the CFL advanced a militant, class-conscious style of trade unionism.

Fitzpatrick played an active role in mass-organizing drives in meat-packing and steel during the 1917–19 era. He supported the efforts to unionize female teachers and black packinghouse workers. He had little faith in government action and believed the giant corporations were beyond its control. Indeed government was more likely to be controlled by them, hence the use of the courts and the army against striking unionists. He believed it was necessary for labour to be able to 'balance power' with the industrialists.[12]

Fitzpatrick did not believe that workers were strong enough to create that balance immediately. For organized labour to counter the power of the employers it would be necessary to extend its ranks to include the unskilled, women and blacks. But even this would not be enough: it would still have to confront the power of the state. From this he deduced that the old non-partisan politics of the AFL could no longer be used by labour; both Republicans and Democrats had betrayed the working class. Both had used the courts against the unions and carried out the bidding of big business. Workers needed their own party that could utilize the existing state to curtail the power of the employers and provide welfare for the workers.[13] Fitzpatrick's experience of the NWLB and his involvement with Frank Walsh had changed his attitude towards the relationship possible between the state and workers. Like Fitzpatrick, Walsh, a labour attorney from Kansas, had a Roman Catholic and Irish background. A progressive Democrat, he did not join the Labor Party, although he gave it much money and support.[14]

Fitzpatrick's plans were not revolutionary; he advocated that workers utilize the state by creating their own political party. The power of the employers would be balanced by a combination of independent political action and an extension of trade unionism. However, he did not propose breaking with the AFL to form industrial unions; instead he proposed an amalgamation of the trades inside each industry, and in particular the recruitment of the unskilled into the AFL. But to achieve this he did not wish to destroy the traditional structures of the AFL. Instead, he desired to expand and modernize the outlook of the AFL, making it more effective in dealing with modern industry. A process of 'federated unionism', a voluntary linking of union organizations, would be a step towards industrial unionism.[15]

Fitzpatrick's strategy also required the building of a labour party: 'to raise labor to a position from which it could counterbalance the power of industry in American Society'. Though not revolutionary, these ideas were a radical break with the voluntarism of the AFL leadership. For Fitzpatrick industrial democracy was not achievable without independent political action.

Not everyone in the CFL was of the same opinion as Fitzpatrick. Its delegates included Socialists and syndicalists, as well as 'pure and simple' trade unionists. The most cohesive group of radicals were the hundred or so grouped around William Z. Foster, the founder of the syndicalist Trade Union Educational League, an organization dedicated to industrial unionism. However, unlike the Industrial Workers of the World (IWW), the strategy of Foster's organization was to 'bore from within' the AFL rather than to establish independent unions. The endorsement of the CFL, and its financial support, made it possible for Foster and his allies to organize 'federated unionism' in the stockyards, where they formed the Stockyards Labor Council (SLC). These radicals believed in 'workers' control', which did not mean cooperation with management through committees, but workers' self-management. Industrial unionism would be a key step to achieving workers' democracy. Most of these militants paid little regard to political parties. Foster had refused to include, in an iron and steelworker strike bulletin, the advice that steel workers should join a labour party until ordered to do so by Fitzpatrick.[16] Though Fitzpatrick had political differences with the syndicalists he continued to work with them. In early 1919 the Communists and the syndicalists had no major influence inside the AFL. Therefore in this period it was the advocacy of a labour party by progressive unionists, such as Fitzpatrick, that typified the major opposition to the AFL's conservatives.

THE RACE FOR RECONSTRUCTION

The ending of the war led to demobilization and economic contraction. Employers responded by discharging labour, cutting costs and increasing hours. Union leaders were well aware that the employers wanted to rescind the concessions they had made during the war.[17]

Once again the unions expected that the law would be used against them. As for the concessions the Wilson administration had made during the war, these had been due to national necessity rather than any real interest in labour's welfare. The same party that passed the Clayton Act used injunctions against striking miners in November 1919. Though workers' confidence had grown, there was growing unease at what the postwar settlement would bring.[18]

Some sections of the AFL came to the conclusion that they could not trust either of the two old parties to carry out reconstruction. In particular they looked to the reconstruction plans of the British Labour Party. Progressive, AFL and Socialist publications carried extensive coverage of its reconstruction programme. To implement a similar reconstruction programme favourable to workers, they needed a party on the same lines as British workers. In response to President Wilson's 'Fourteen Point' programme for world peace, the CFL produced 'Labor's Fourteen Points' and went on to form an Independent Labor Party (see the appendix, 'Labor's Fourteen Points'). The formation of labour parties, or demands that the AFL form such a party, mushroomed across America.[19]

THE LABOUR PARTY IMPULSE

That there was significant support inside the AFL for a Labor Party is sustained by a survey of 285 unions replying to a questionnaire. Eighty-nine per cent favoured the formation of a labour party.[20] The survey confirmed that there was substantial support inside the AFL for the formation of a labour party. The labour progressives such as Fitzpatrick now became the most significant opposition to the AFL's conservative leadership. However, there was one other organization during this period whose attitude was significant.

That organization was the Socialist Party of America (SPA). Though its main strength was in unions outside of the AFL, especially those in the needle trades, it did have considerable influence inside the AFL, particularly in the Machinists Association. It also had a long tradition of being the main socialist electoral alternative to Republicans and Democrats. Its electoral support in some areas was substantial. It is quite common for historians to assert that the party had peaked as an electoral force by 1912. Although, this was true for the Socialists' presidential vote, the organization still got a substantial vote in areas such as New York, Wisconsin and Milwaukee. Therefore in late 1918 and early 1919 the attitude of the Socialist Party towards the Labor Party was of considerable importance. However, the Socialist Party was not a monolith, and its members had different attitudes towards the new party. In New York and Chicago they opposed the labour parties at the polls, but in Seattle they cooperated. As the experience with the Socialists varied in each city, the differences will be examined further in each of the three case studies.[21]

Labour's experience of wartime corporatism created the impulse for the formation of labour parties. For the first time the state had played a positive role in industrial relations. Many sectors of previously poorly organized workers had improved their conditions and hours, often with the help of the NWLB. Many feared that the end of the war would see the loss of the gains made. Therefore it was in a contradictory atmosphere of growing confidence and growing apprehension that the debate on reconstruction led to the logic of independent political action. The experience was not the same everywhere. As we shall see later, the Chicago movement was still defiant when it formed its party; in Seattle the movement had just suffered serious defeat. To prepare the ground for a comparison of independent political action between the three labour movements, it is necessary to sum up the main economic, political and trade-union backgrounds of each of the three cities that make up this comparison.

New York

New York City had more manufacturing enterprises in its confines than any other city in America. However, the majority of these were small scale, and the largest sector was the needle trades. New York was the nation's garment-making capital; over 160 000 workers, almost one in every six of New York labourers, earned their livelihoods in the clothing trades. Although the clothing trades' economic importance was remarkable, other manufactures were also significant. But New York businesses were small in the age of conglomerate industries such as Standard Oil, American Tobacco and United States Steel. Small firms with minimal capital investments carrying on limited production characterized New York's industrial structure.[22]

However, even in New York there were large industries. In New York City and the Borough of Brooklyn, 39 279 workers were employed in shipbuilding yards. Some were large establishments, but it was not just a matter of establishment size; all yards employed carpenters, and those who were in the AFL-affiliated carpenters' union had city-wide contact with those involved in construction. New York's docks and harbours also provided large-scale employment.[23]

By 1920 those 'gainfully employed' in Greater New York totalled 2 531 412, of which 27 per cent were women, 14 per cent of whom were in trade unions. The majority worked in the clothing and textile trades.[24] The number of trade unionists in New York City was at least 639 330 by 1920; thus over 25 per cent of the total work force was in unions. New York had a union membership well above the national average. The majority of AFL trade unionists were American-born, or of Irish, German and English origin. Italians, and Jews from Eastern Europe, predominated in the clothing trade unions outside the AFL (the Amalgamated Clothing Workers (ACW) and other needle-trade unions). But the majority of unskilled labourers, apart from those in the needle trades, belonged to no union at all.[25] New York City had more strikes than any other city, with 484 in 1917 and 1918, and 360 in 1919. Of course New York had more establishments than any other city, but nonetheless many of the strikes involved large numbers of workers, and many occurred in sectors outside of clothing. This aspect of New York labour militancy is detailed further in Chapter 2.[26]

Unions in New York, as was the case in most urban centres, were affiliated to city- and state-wide bodies. In 1918 there were two active central labour bodies in New York City affiliated with the American Federation of Labor. They were the Central Federated Union of New York (CFU) and the Central Labor Union (CLU) of Brooklyn. Central bodies formally existed in the Bronx and in Richmond, but these were defunct. Two other central bodies existed, the United Hebrew Trades and the Women's Trade Union League. Though not official AFL bodies they consisted of unions affiliated to it. The CFU and the CLU were the most important labour bodies in New York. They included the majority of the AFL workers in the city. Of the two the CFU was by far the larger and the more important.[27]

Unlike Chicago or Seattle the trade-union movement was divided, with half of the unions affiliated to the AFL, and the majority of the needle-trade unions unaffiliated. To complicate matters further the city AFL unions were often at loggerheads with the unions affiliated to the State Federation. New York City had far more unionists than the rest of New York State. However, upstate New York had a greater number of locals reducing the city central bodies to a minority within the more conservative Federation.[28] For the most part, Gompers supported the State Federation, and they him. However the State Federation leadership was not a consistent ally, for it had another agenda, namely its alliance with Tammany (a faction of the Democratic Party machine in New York that had strong links with sections of the Unions and the Irish). Gompers would discover, to his cost, that the Federation feared losing the patronage of Tammany more than the support of the AFL president.

In Seattle and Chicago the AFL city central labour bodies had no serious competitors for the leadership of the local movement. In

Chicago, even unions outside of the AFL, such as the ACW, had a good relationship with the CFL. This was not the case in New York City; the central bodies were mainly related to craft-organized AFL unions and hardly related to the separately organized Socialist progressive unions (these mainly existed in the clothing trades). Indeed, the largest union in New York was the Amalgamated Clothing Workers (ACW), which was outside of the AFL and worked closely with the Socialists.

After the war the leadership of the New York central bodies became dominated by the progressives. The war had radicalized some of the city's AFL leadership, and some of its craft unions, causing them to break with non-partisan politics. However, this radicalization could not immediately overcome the divisions that existed in the working-class and union movement. Nor were the central bodies, as recent converts to progressive politics, able to overcome old suspicions and hostilities. These weaknesses, dealt with in later chapters, created difficulties for a leadership recently converted to independent political action.

Chicago

Chicago was a city with production on a far larger scale than New York or Seattle. It was a major centre of industrial production and, due to its geographical position at the juncture of water and rail transport, a market-place for agricultural and primary goods. The largest national manufacturer of agricultural machinery, International Harvester, had its Deering and McCormick plants based there. Between 1909 and 1919 the packinghouse workforce more than doubled, growing from 22 064 to 46 474.[29] The industry's need for refrigerated rail cars and extensive rail links explains the demand for the large-scale production of steam railroad cars.[30] Chicago was a major steel manufacturing area, with plants in South Chicago, Chicago Heights and neighbouring Indiana. Hence the importance and centrality of Chicago in the meatpacking, steel, coal and rail strikes of the immediate postwar period.[31] Chicago had a far more concentrated manufacturing industry than New York, confined to a smaller geographical space and with far larger workforces per establishment. However, some sectors were similar to New York's: for example, the men's clothing industry employed 31 287 workers and women's clothing 9147, mostly in small establishments.[32]

Two-thirds of the population of Chicago was either foreign-born or of foreign-born parents. Of the remainder Charles Merriam believed that 'perhaps 200 000 are colored. The number of persons actually born in Chicago is of course very small . . .' As many as 40 different nationalities worked in the stockyards, of which 20 per cent were black by December 1918. This, as we will see later, had consequences for the political and trade-union situation in Chicago.[33]

By September 1903 there were 243 000 trade union members in Chicago, and according to David Montgomery:

> The city could challenge London for the title, trade union capital of the world. Possibly one-third of those members worked in the packing houses, where militant shop committees united the activists of dozens of craft unions . . . The CFL of Labor defiantly used sympathy strikes as the touchstone of its success.[34]

By 1918 the CFL had 300 000 affiliated members. The CFL did all it could to encourage the foreign-born and blacks to join the unions. Organizing drives in steel and the stockyards attempted to recruit the unskilled irrespective of nationality or colour. Though in the stockyards 90 per cent of Northern-born blacks were members of the unions, very few of the three-quarters of the blacks who had recently arrived from the South joined the unions.[35]

The CFL also did all it could within the confines of the AFL to encourage women's trade unionism. Margaret Dreier Robins, a leading member of the WTUL was elected to the executive board of the CFL.[36] When it came to recruiting the unskilled, blacks, women and foreigners, Chicago was in advance of the policies of the AFL and was in the vanguard of American trade-union struggles. But its vanguard position was not translated into dominance inside the AFL or the local State Federation.

The CFL, like the New York central body, never dominated its State Federation. Its 300 000 union membership never produced more than a third of the delegates at Illinois State Federation Conventions. However, unlike New York, the relationship between the CFL and the State Federation was friendly, and for the most part each gave the other support.[37] Chicago was also a centre of strike activity. Two of the nine most important disputes of 1919 took place there. Sixty-five thousand stockyard employees struck in the August, and 115 000 building trades workers were locked out in July. In surrounding Illinois, steelworkers and miners took part in mass disputes.[38]

Chicago's large-scale manufacturing may well have made it easier to establish 'federated unionism'. Unlike New York, the CFL was the only trade-union centre of any significance. Also, John Fitzpatrick, a major figure in Chicago progressive and trade-union politics, was much respected and commanded the loyalty of a wide grouping of trade-union activists. He was on good terms with Sidney Hillman, President of the ACW, and with leading members of the WTUL, and was involved with progressive, Irish and Catholic organizations. No leader with such a wide variety of contacts and support existed in New York. Thus the CFL had widespread influence in the locality and did not have the problem of a rival power base. Not having a majority inside the State Federation was not a problem when the two organizations had a good relationship. However there were problems, as we shall see later, in particular the failure to organize black workers into the unions and the ethnic rivalry encouraged by the existence of Republican and Democratic party machines.

Seattle

Seattle did not initially have a large manufacturing base: it was war-time production that created a large workforce there. Though syndicalism was widespread in Washington State, in Seattle it was the AFL-organized Seattle Central Labor Council (SCLC) which dominated the labour movement. In spite of the presence of radicals at its meetings it remained firmly under the control of local AFL leaders. However, the defeat of the General Strike in February 1919 weakened Seattle labour. The Farmer Labor Party (FLP) came about, partly, as a consequence of this defeat. Labour was also weakened by what proved to be a temporary economic boom. The city lacked the economic diversity and strength of New York and Chicago and suffered greatly from the ending of wartime production.[39]

Seattle was a smaller city than either New York or Chicago. In 1920 its population was only 315 312. Its population was far more homogenous than New York or Chicago; blacks, for instance, were less than one per cent of the total population. Over 73 per cent of the population were described as 'native white'. Of the 23 per cent 'foreign-born white', 48 per cent were naturalized. The remaining 3.5 per cent of the population were of Indian, Chinese or Japanese origin. Thirty-three per cent of the foreign-born came from Canada and the United Kingdom. The rest came from a variety of mainly Western European States, and a smaller number from Eastern and Southern Europe.[40]

The main industry before the war was lumber and timber production. However the war created dramatic changes, especially in shipbuilding. More than 35 000 persons worked in the metal and wooden shipyards and allied trades. The shipyards became the largest employer in Seattle. In 1919 there were 110 AFL local craft unions in Seattle, and though the unions could not enforce a closed shop, unionization in the shipyards was almost 100 per cent. The largest of the shipyard unions was Local 104 of the Boilermakers and Iron Shipbuilders, whose membership peaked at 20 000. Next in size were the Machinists Hope Lodge 79 and the Shipyard Laborers with about 4000 each, and then a score of crafts, many with more than a thousand members each. These came together in the Metal Trades Council, which met weekly to consider major strategy and became the most progressive wing of the local labour movement. These locals and those from other branches of the movement were represented in the SCLC, the main voice of Seattle unionism.[41]

The Pacific North West had a strong syndicalist tradition. The belief in 'One Big Union' was quite common, and the IWW claimed that their membership had increased in the Seattle shipyards during the war. Nevertheless syndicalists had no option but to operate inside the AFL. One reason for this is that, unlike areas of more primary industry outside Seattle, the AFL unions in the City represented workers in negotiations with the employers. Established skilled workers in the shipyards were especially loyal to the AFL, though not necessarily to its national leadership and policies. Even among these skilled workers there was a feeling that industrial unionism would be preferable to craft organization. Although James Duncan, Secretary of the SCLC, opposed Gompers frequently, relations between the SCLC and AFL headquarters, though often strained, remained intact. Seattle's labour leaders, for all their differences with the AFL leadership, refused to be isolated from the mainstream of American labour. Although defiant speeches were made at the SCLC, they were rarely acted upon.[42]

Though the SCLC supported industrial unionism it never managed to establish it as a formal structure. Duncan was pragmatic and encouraged informal cooperation to avoid punitive measures from the AFL. When, in 1920, the SCLC tried to modify its constitution to create a form of industrial unionism, Gompers forced it to rescind the changes. The failure to achieve these aims inside the AFL led to increasing tension between those who supported diluted industrial unionism and those who wanted 'pure' industrial unionism. However it was the SCLC that spoke for all AFL unions and labour took its final decisions at the weekly meetings.[43] Friedham in his book on the Seattle General Strike observed that:

Seattle labor was not formally organized in a distinctive manner, but rather than feeling primarily responsible to national unions Seattle locals gave their loyalty primarily to their local coordinating bodies – the trade councils and the Central Labor Council. No matter what union a worker belonged to, he was conscious of being a member of a Seattle labor organization. The Seattle labor movement supported everything Samuel Gompers rejected – the Farmer Labor Party, industrial unionism, and nationalization of key industries.[44]

However, informally the SCLC did organize in a distinctly different manner. 'Duncanism', named after the SCLC secretary James Duncan, substituted for industrial unionism. In practice 'Duncanism' meant strong central control of all unions in the area by the SCLC, close cooperation of all allied trades and trades councils, and an attempt to synchronize wage claims and disputes within a single industry. It is worth noting the similarity of 'Duncanism' to the 'federated unionism' practised by the CFL in Chicago.[45]

The SCLC was sympathetic to women's suffrage and the unioniza-tion of women, and its newspaper, the *Union Record* (*Record*), gave prominence to women's activities. In July 1917 the SCLC appointed a women's organizer after the State Federation claimed it could not afford to do so. New unions of women workers and new women's sections in male craft locals were formed in Seattle as a result.[46]

Across the nation as a whole there were nine strikes or lockouts in 1919 involving 60 000 workers or more; the Seattle General Strike of February 1919 was one of these major disputes. But overall Seattle's workers took part in fewer disputes than those in New York and Chicago. Thus in 1919 there were 18 strikes and lockouts compared to New York's 360 and Chicago's 124. This partly reflects the devas-tating blow to the movement caused by the failure of Seattle's general strike and the following repression. The strike was in sympathy with striking shipbuilding workers. The vote in favour of solidarity action was overwhelming, not just in the metal trades but even among prin-ters, carpenters, teamsters and cooks. The strike was in solidarity with the shipbuilding workers and some believed that it could lead to revolution. Nonetheless the SCLC controlled and directed the strike, and revolution was not its aim;[47] it assumed the employers would back down. In spite of impressive organization, which included food kitch-ens, emergency supplies and workers' stewards to keep the peace, the strike collapsed. It collapsed in the face of the intransigence of the employers, and the fear on the part of the SCLC leadership that the strike might get out of hand in an increasingly repressive situation. It ended quietly, leaving the shipbuilding workers to strike on their own.[48] The defeat strengthened the hands of the conservatives in the SCLC. For progressives feared that if the radicals continued to get their own way the Seattle labour movement would be destroyed. They did not completely disown the radicals but subordinated them to their own policies; this meant allying with the conservatives against them. Of course this exacerbated the tension between the radicals and progressives, and strengthened the moderates. This led to a series of bitter rows and factional fights which seriously weakened the progressives.[49]

The weakness of the Seattle economy also added to labour's problems. With the war's end, employment in the shipyards declined rapidly. In a situation of growing unemployment, thousands of shipyard workers lost their jobs; those remaining suffered wage reductions. The closure of the shipyards devastated the metal-trade unions. The membership of Boilermakers' Local 104 fell by two-thirds. The Shipbuilding Laborers' Local, formerly a thousand strong, became reduced to 15 diehards with $7 in their treasury by the spring of 1920.[50]

Defeat weakened the Seattle labour movement in advance of New York or Chicago, but the SCLC remained under the control of the progressives, and kept its leadership position within the local movement. But its ability to challenge the AFL nationally and at state level was weakened by the defeat of the general strike. Like New York and Chicago, it was a minority inside the State Federation. At the 1919 annual convention of the Washington State Federation, Seattle had over 250 delegates out of 700. Even more important was the control conservatives had of the convention's machinery. Of 73 committee positions, only five unimportant ones went to either progressives or radicals. In spite of being hit harder and earlier than the other two cities by the employers' offensives against union organization, the SCLC remained capable of further initiatives due to its dominance of the local movement.[51]

So far this chapter has outlined the state of the economies and the labour movements of the three cities; now it will turn to the political background of each movement and the actual formation of labour parties. The following section describes the political situation faced by those advocating labour parties, including the obstacles posed by the Democratic and Republican party machines, and the opposition from inside the labour movement, whether from Socialists or the AFL nationally.

PARTY TIME

New York

To sum up the political affiliations of New York labour is a difficult task, for alliances constantly changed. To complicate matters further, the leadership of the movement suffered frequent division. Thus in 1905, large numbers of workers deserted the Democrats and voted for William Randolph Hearst, the newspaper magnate. The CFU supported him while the State Federation opposed him. James Holland, a leader of the CFU and later president of the State Federation, was friendly with Tammany, but Tammany opposed attempts to legislate for workmen's compensation. Holland and the State Federation switched to opposing Tammany. But the breach with Tammany was temporary, for in 1920 Holland again became known as a strong Tammany man.[52]

Only one factor remained constant in this world of ever-changing political alliances: whatever the issue, the CFU and the State Federation were most likely to be on opposite sides. However, the CFU was more consistent and fought for comprehensive reform legislation, wanting politicians to serve the needs of labour. The State Federation preferred horse-trading and rejected independent political action. The constant conflict and rivalry meant that even the AFL unions did not speak with a single voice. Unlike Seattle and Chicago, the CFU did not have its own newspaper, although in 1915 it did endorse the Socialist Party daily the *New York Call*. This it did to ensure the publication of official labour news and reports. Inevitably a request by the CFU that the State Federation give financial support to the *Call* was refused.[53]

A sizeable minority of the New York population consistently voted for the Socialist Party. Central to winning the Socialist vote were the activities and support of the progressive trade unions, especially the ACW. The electoral success of the SPA and its roots in the progressive unions in New York would prove to be a barrier to those building a labour party. It was not until the SPA had seriously declined that the New York Socialists became centrally involved in building a labour party.[54]

In late 1918 the central labour bodies formed reconstruction committees. The reconstruction committee's chairman, Thomas J. Curtis, President of the International Tunnel and Subway Constructors Union and Deputy Commissioner of the New York State Workingmen's Compensation Commission, issued the call on 29 November for the organization of an independent labour party in New York City. The CFU endorsed the proposal on 6 December 1918, stating that a reconstruction programme favourable to labour could not be achieved without a 'political medium' in full sympathy with its provisions. They needed to educate workers by 'hand and brain' in the need to secure for their own benefit a greater share of the wealth they produced. This meant building a 'political movement' as well as the 'industrial movement'. The only effective means of securing the democratic reforms and rights wanted by workers was for them to form their own party. All affiliated organizations were requested to attend a conference in early January 1919 to create the American Labor Party (ALP).[55]

Gompers responded by meeting the ringleaders on 10 December 1918, lecturing them against independent political action, but the insurgents continued with their plans. The conference went ahead, and it adopted a platform similar to the 14 points proposed by the CFL. These included: the right of free speech and assembly; public works to prevent unemployment; public ownership of all public utilities; the democratic control of industry, commerce and education; equal rights for men and women; and representation of labour in all governmental departments and commissions. A demand for progressive taxation of income was followed by a call for world peace and for a league of workers.[56]

Eight hundred and eighty-six delegates, of which 360 were affiliated to the CFU and 180 to the CLU, attended the founding convention. Another 50 were affiliated to the WTUL, while 288 came from local unions. The United Hebrew Trades and the United Board of Business Agents of the Building Trades were each represented by two delegates.[57] At first sight the amount of support appears impressive, but the number of union locals and local unions represented adds up to only 146, a fraction of New York labour's organizations. Significantly there is no trace of the ACW at the conference. The ACW complained that its locals had not received invitations. Unaffiliated organizations like the ACW were only offered two delegates. The ACW believed there was great enthusiasm and support in labour bodies for a labour party. It stated that 58 of its locals had supported the Cook County Labor Party. The mistreatment of the ACW proved to be a serious mistake for the New York Party, one that strengthened the hands of those Socialists who opposed the project.[58]

Many of the smaller progressive unions had attended, but they were represented by Socialists. The most active progressive organizations in the city, the Women's Trade Union League and the Hebrew Trades, supported the new party. Whatever the founding conference represented, very few of those attending became active supporters.[59] The attitude of the SPA proved to be problem for a weak organization trying to establish itself. The Socialists had a traditional base of support at the polls and received financial assistance from many progressive unions. This meant less funds were available to the new party and created an electoral barrier that was difficult to surmount.

The new party faced many difficulties from the outset, including the barrier of an influential Socialist Party and fierce opposition from the national and state AFL leaderships. Though founded on a wave of enthusiasm, it was the weakest of the three parties compared here.

Chicago

Mainstream Chicago politics were a highly confusing affair: the Democrats dominated the city council, and the Republicans the mayoralty. To complicate matters further, both parties were split into factions. The incumbent Republican Mayor, William Thompson, was in the habit of backing Democratic candidates in ward elections. Thompson liked to appear as a progressive. Although his platform was not particularly radical he tried to appeal to Germans by taking a neutral stance on the war, to the Irish by attacking England, to progressives by calling for municipal ownership of transit lines and cheap fares. To impress workers he emphasized the opposition he faced from the Loop newspapers (Chicago city press) to demonstrate his independence from business interests.[60]

Thompson had the support of a small section of organized labour and enjoyed substantial black support. Thompson offered blacks in Chicago more than rhetoric; he had opened city jobs to them in unprecedented numbers. On the city council, the two black aldermen from the second ward became the Mayor's floor leaders. The Democratic machine looked elsewhere for its support. Rivalry between the parties and the bases of ethnic support was a source of constant tension and was a contributory factor to the racial rioting of July 1919.[61] The Democratic Party was in the early stages of constructing the ethnic-based machine which came to dominance in the 1930s, but in 1919 that development was in the future and by no means assured. However, the Democrats did have some areas of ethnic support. The Polish community, concentrated in the factory districts in the North-West and South-West areas of the city, was a notable backer. Another example of patronage was the Irish gangs involved in the race riots of 1919, which were linked to Ragen's Colts, an 'athletics club' sponsored by Democrat Alderman Frank Ragen.[62]

The Socialists claimed that they had increased their vote in the elections of November 1918, but in April 1919 the Chicago vote stagnated. The Socialist candidate for Mayor gathered 24 079 votes in 1919; in 1915 they had received 24 452. Also more Socialists in Illinois and Chicago switched allegiance to the Labor Party than in New York. For example Duncan McDonald, a veteran of the Socialist movement in Illinois, endorsed the Labor Party of Cook County and spoke on behalf of its candidates. Adolph Germer, Secretary of the Socialist Party, appeared before the ACW Executive Board in Chicago to urge them to endorse the Labor Party 'because the left-wingers are rapidly getting control of the Socialist Party'. Local Socialists, for the most part, ignored Germer's appeal.[63]

At the CFL meeting of 17 November 1918 a discussion took place on the forthcoming mayoral elections. Delegates were dissatisfied with both parties; the Democrats represented 'the vested interests' while Republican aldermen on the city council had prevented labour nominees from sitting on the school board. The CFL was so enraged at this denial of fair representation that it decided to recommend the formation of an 'Independent Labor Party' in Cook County and Illinois and endorsed 'Labor's Fourteen Points' (see Appendix I). The 14 points, based on the British Labour Party's programme, were drafted by Basil M. Manly, well-known progressive and Frank Walsh's successor as chairman at the War Labor Board. The 14 points also demanded representation of labour, in proportion to its voting strength, in all departments of government. In other words, it believed that the election of labour party officials into the existing structure of government would achieve labour's aims. On 29 December, the CFL, not waiting for the State Federation to act, formed the Labor Party of Cook County (CCLP). It also decided that the new party should have a weekly newspaper, *The New Majority*.[64]

Nearly 1000 delegates representing 165 local unions attended the founding convention. Some 170 local affiliates of the CFL, with an estimated membership of 150 000, unanimously voted to join and send delegates to the Party's next convention by January 1919. Among the endorsers was the largest of the building crafts, the Chicago District Council of the Carpenters, representing 24 000 workers in 36 local unions. Edward Nockels reported that 50 000 people received the first issue of *The New Majority* and that it had 2000 subscribers.[65] Nockels, secretary to the CFL, was highly regarded by its activists. He headed a group of mainstream activists that included Margaret Haley of the Teachers' Union and socialist carpenter Anton Johannsen. Fitzpatrick depended heavily on Nockels for the administration of the CFL and its policies.[66]

Support also came from beyond the labour movement. Fitzpatrick was of Irish descent, and had good relations with Catholic and Irish organizations including Sinn Fein. Perhaps more important was his close relationship with Frank Walsh, who liaised between Fitzpatrick and the Catholic establishment. In March 1919 Fitzpatrick agreed to sign his name to an article endorsing the reconstruction programme of the Catholic Church. In some respects Walsh believed the programme went beyond Labor's 14 Points. The article appeared in *America*, 'the big highbrow Catholic publication'. Every Catholic priest and religious institution in Chicago received a copy.[67]

The CFL also enjoyed the support of the Chicago Women's Trade Union League. Its February bulletin urged its readers to attend a public meeting on the Labor Party, to be addressed by Fitzpatrick, candidate for mayor on the Labor Party ticket. The subsequent bulletin advertised subscriptions to the *New Majority*.[68]

In the chapters on Chicago the electoral experience will be analysed, but at this stage it is important to note that trade-union support for the new party was far more solid in Chicago than in New York. It also had the added strength of support from the Illinois State Federation. The New York Labor Party never gained State Federation support, and the Seattle Party had to wait a year.[69]

It is clear from the above that Chicago had the best organized labour movement. The local economy was large scale and diverse, providing possibilities for workers to exercise powerful industrial muscle. A dynamic and imaginative union movement did not waste the opportunities presented to it. With its concept of 'federated unionism', it suffered little opposition from the Socialists and syndicalists. It enjoyed cooperation with the progressive unions inside and outside of the AFL. It is not surprising that the CFL took the lead in launching the Labor Party, nationally and locally, in 1919. However, it proved easier to initiate the Party than successfully build it. The two chapters on Chicago will consider the reasons for this.

Seattle

Washington State was strongly Republican with a very weak Democratic tradition. Farmers received little support from the Democrats so they and their organization, the Grange, often allied with labour. Though, for the most part, the Washington State Federation of Labor (WSFL) opposed prohibition, the Seattle Central Labor Council (SCLC) and the Grange supported it. James A. Duncan, leader of the SCLC, was an ardent prohibitionist. This was an unusual position for an AFL leader, since the Federation bitterly opposed it. Prohibition became a major election issue in most states, with referendums taking place. It was an issue that labour and many ethnic groupings strongly opposed; however, there was strong pro-temperance sentiment in Seattle.[70]

In 1914 the Republicans swept the board in Washington State. However, in the senatorial race the combined vote for progressives and Democrats was 40 000 over that of the Republican total. However, the Republicans believed progressivism was dead and proceeded to try to roll back reforms, including the removal of the right to picket. This had the effect of uniting the opposition in the 1916 election, which was a major victory for the Washington farmer-labour forces, the Democrats and their urban middle-class allies. Wilson swept the state by an average of 15 000 votes over his Republican opponents, although one Republican returned to the Senate with a majority of 65 000 votes. But in 1917 the issues raised by the war created divisions between labour and its middle-class allies. The *Seattle Union Record* declared that labour opposed it, but the State Federation and the SCLC declared full support for the war effort. The *Record* believed that 'anti-war sentiment was strong in Seattle labour circles, especially among the metal trades workers'. This difference of opinion over the war strained the progressive alliance.[71]

Progressivism did not die out completely. The coalition broke up, but farmer-labour leaders, though believing that the war should be won, felt that to make the world safe for democracy, 'autocratic methods should not be adopted at home'. But even this approach was not enough to stop former allies becoming enemies. Though middle-class allies were lost, the unity of farmers and workers was intensified. The cost of living doubled by 1919; both farmers and workingmen had cause for grievance. In June 1918, the Grange and the State Federation of Labor decided to enter the 1918 elections on a non-partisan basis. In the past many farmer-labour leaders had supported Wilson as they believed him to favour labour. The *Record* considered many Democratic county organizations pro-labour because they advocated democracy, government ownership of the railroads and 'labor measures'. However, Seattle was not typical of Washington State

politics, and contrary to the rest of the alliance the SCLC decided to
back the Republicans as they had a better chance of winning. Nevertheless it was the farmer-labour nominees among the Democrats that
had more success. This success had an important effect on the politics
of the SCLC.[72]

The strength of the Republican Party had pushed the SCLC to try to
make progress within it. However, the failure of this strategy, combined with the weakness of progressives and Democrats, made the
Council amenable to the idea of a new party. When the SCLC finally
turned to a labour party, the existence of the *Record* and of a whole
layer of discontented farmers and other Democrat supporters gave it
an ability to succeed at the polls. In some districts entire Democratic
party organizations defected to the Farmer Labor Party (FLP). Unlike
New York or Chicago the Labor Party inherited a ready-made electoral machine. The major parties did not directly dominate the administration of elections in Seattle. Thus it was easier for the new party to
place its candidates on the ballot than it was in New York or Chicago.

The Seattle Labor Party did not come into being until June 1919,
and by this time the Socialists had already disintegrated. Relations
were friendly with the few remaining members. No doubt the weakness
of the Socialists explains why they cooperated with, or even joined, the
new party. Hulet Wells, a well-known Socialist Party member, joined
the party as soon as the SCLC endorsed it.[73] The SCLC had the
advantage of owning a daily newspaper, the *Union Record*, which had
a circulation of some 80 000 in 1919.[74]

There were three main groupings inside the Seattle labour movement: conservatives, radicals and progressives. The strongest grouping
was the progressives, led by James A. Duncan, the Council's secretary,
and Harry Ault, the *Union Record*'s editor. The radicals, who advocated industrial unionism and the general strike, were the smallest
group but they and the progressives often found common ground.[75]
The radicals were important because the progressives depended on
them for support against the conservatives. After the defeat of the
general strike, the AFL executive council declared that only national
unions could call strikes, not city bodies. With the radicals isolated and
the economy in recession, local employers did not miss the opportunity
to start a drive against the unions, ending union recognition and
driving down wages. Increasing disagreement between the progressives
and the radicals pushed the former group closer to the conservatives
and weakened the SCLC's support for the FLP. The Conservatives of
the SCLC opposed the new party, and the radicals disagreed on the

issue, but at first there was no effective opposition to it. William Short, President of the State Federation and a close supporter of Gompers, did oppose the new party, but this did not deter the SCLC progressives who went ahead to form it, although the Party did not campaign openly under its own name until 1920.[76]

The SCLC had come late to the idea of independent political action. The failure of the general strike had a sobering effect upon them. By the spring of 1919, 'Ballots, not bullets and heroic stances, seemed safer.'[77] As was the case in Chicago, the SCLC had the support of the bulk of the unions in Seattle, but unlike Chicago it did not have the support of the State Federation. They were also in a weaker position due to the defeats outlined above. In spite of this, they were more successful at the polls than the other parties detailed in this book.

CONCLUSION

This chapter has dealt with the formation of labour parties in New York, Chicago and Seattle. The following chapters will deal with the attempts to consolidate these parties, their electoral interventions and progress towards a national party. In establishing strengths and weaknesses we can already see, as outlined above, that New York had the weakest labour party movement. Chicago's party had far stronger roots, but existed in an unfavourable political situation, especially in regard to machine politics and the black voter. Both New York and Chicago were unable to obtain a ready-made party machine in the way that the Seattle labour movement did.

Seattle's experience was closer to Chicago's than New York's. It had a labour movement united under the leadership of one central body without a powerful rival outside of it. It had a successful labour press, and leaders such as Duncan commanded respect and support. Though the Seattle labour movement was weaker by early 1919, it was still a major influence for progressives. The loyalty of workers, the ownership of the *Record* and the collapse of the Washington Democratic Party combined to give the new party a ready-made machine to intervene at the polls in 1920.

Finally it is useful to reflect on the opposition from the AFL nationally in the period covered by this chapter. The AFL leadership had made its opposition to the new parties clear. However, in this early period of enthusiasm it was unable to stop their formation. In Seattle and New York it was able to restrict them, for a time, to a city-wide basis. Nor was it the case, for the most part, that the new parties suffered from state repression. However, the opposition of the AFL was important; this and other barriers to the development of the new parties are investigated in the chapters that follow.

2 False Dawn: Labour Politics in New York 1919–20

The years 1919–20 proved to be key for the labour party movement, containing its highest and lowest tidemarks. New York's labour party was the weakest of the three labour parties compared in this study. However, though it did not achieve very much, its failure can help illuminate the strengths and weaknesses of a movement as ably as successes which can obscure mistakes and failings. Such an analysis provides a basis for comparison with Chicago and Seattle, revealing which factors contributed to success and failure in all three cases. However, before doing that it is necessary to detail the specific situation in New York.

As outlined in the previous chapter the New York-based Central Federated Union (CFU) was the main motivating force behind the New York City American Labor Party (ALP). The majority of AFL unions affiliated to the CFU supported the Labor Party initiative, as did those of the Brooklyn-based Central Labor Union, the Women's Trade Union League (WTUL) and the United Hebrew Trades. At first sight support for the new party seemed solid enough, but within a few months the leaders of the Brooklyn central labor body turned against the party it had co-founded. Only the progressives of the CFU and the WTUL remained loyal to the party in the two years covered by this chapter.

The fact that the new party suffered from founders who eventually deserted or turned against it undermined its ability to make headway in the tough world of New York politics. The two main initiators of the ALP were the central labour bodies of New York and Brooklyn. The fact that many of the officials were former supporters of Tammany caused great rejoicing amongst the Socialists who believed the defections proved that massive radicalization had taken place among workers.[1]

This was true, and it was quite clear that there was great dissatisfaction with the old non-partisan politics of the AFL and considerable sentiment for the new party. However, the motives of the initiators were not in all cases free of self-interest. Whether consciously or not, some were just going with the swell of sentiment until it was possible to reverse the new policy and return to the fold. Others felt discontented with the recent lack of patronage from Tammany. Thus the Socialist rejoicing failed to take into account that some of these leaders would become a destructive fifth column. Some ex-Tammany supporters remained faithful to the new party, but later they were marginalized by an alliance of defectors to Tammany, the State Federation and the AFL nationally.[2] During this period the AFL effectively opposed the Labor Party initiative in New York but failed to undermine it in Chicago and Seattle. One reason for this was that the New York labour progressives faced a hostile State Federation. This was not the case in Chicago and Seattle where the central bodies' support proved more solid, with a network of supporters throughout the local craft and progressive unions. The progressive labourites in New York had no such base.

One reason for this lack of base was that the past actions of New York labour officials had ramifications for the new epoch, including their turn to independent political action. Their past relationship with Tammany and their isolation from the progressive unions meant there was deep suspicion of their motives, especially by the Amalgamated Clothing Workers (ACW) and the Hebrew Trades. The past experience of some of these officials may also explain why they were so poor at involving the rank and file in their campaign. They had more experience of the politics of wheeling and dealing in the corridors of Tammany and City Hall than of mass campaigning.

However, not all the problems that confronted the new party were of an internal or organizational nature. Even when the party did get enough signatures for Thomas J. Curtis's candidacy for Chairman of the Board of Aldermen, the commissioner for elections ruled the nomination ineligible – no doubt at the behest of Tammany. Curtis had to resort to a write-in campaign, and his actual votes remained unknown. The incident demonstrated that the lack of democracy in New York made it very hard for a new party to enter a field traditionally dominated by Republicans and Democrats. Indeed the corruption of the New York City electoral system was notorious. Perhaps Edward Hannah, President of the CFU, had this in mind when he had opposed standing in elections at the founding convention of the ALP until the party became established. He had argued that they should first organize the districts. Events proved that his assessment was more sober than that of those who opposed him.[3]

It is claimed that the craft orientated and non-militant nature of the American labour movement led to the domination of Samuel Gompers' brand of voluntarist trade unionism. Put obversely the lack of industrial unionism made the development of a labour party impossible. The previous chapter described the proto-industrial-style unionism (federated unionism) of Chicago and Seattle; the fact that a similar tradition existed in New York is often ignored. The New York movement is often characterized as one in which AFL members adhered rigorously to the craft ethic and that progressive unionism of any importance existed only outside of the Federation. However, the reality of New York in 1919–20 was different. For though many New York unions were based on small workplaces, they organized on a city-wide basis. Thus city-wide strikes often took place in this period. Also there were large concentrations of workers in the port and railway areas. These organized themselves into joint negotiating bodies in the same way that trade unionists did in Chicago and Seattle. A closer look at the reality provides a different picture than would be expected from the industrial structure of New York. Therefore it is necessary to look at this reality in greater detail.[4]

NEW YORK UNIONS 1919–20

During 1919 to 1920 New York saw more strikes than any other city; some of these strikes involved large numbers of workers. In 1919 11 346 653 days were lost due to strike action in New York State as a whole, and in 1920 a further 10 608 483 days were lost. These strikes did not just involve small numbers; even workers employed in small units organized across their industry. These unions, made up of small branches, involved large numbers and gave strikes an industrial character. For example, the five separate unions involved in the city's printing industry that formed the International Allied Printing Trades Council organized a strike involving thousands for eight weeks in the face of opposition from national officials. There was an aftermath of great bitterness resulting in the removal of local militant leaders. As the above example illustrates, strikes took place not just across industry, but against the wishes of craft officials. Other workers took action beyond the single workplace. The United Brotherhood of Carpenters and Joiners, representing 300 000 men, declared war on all New York builders in retaliation for the lockout of 5500 men. Their action, which spread to other cities, forced the New York

Employers Association to confer with the General President of the Carpenters.[5]

In early 1919 the most impressive of these movements was the Marine Workers Affiliation composed of the six craft unions of New York City Harbour. The organization coordinated demands for pay and conditions, forming a strike committee to represent the unions as a combined force. Twenty thousand skilled workers organized and acted like industrial unionists, striking across craft boundaries. On one occasion nothing moved on the harbour for 24 hours as a result of the walkout of the boatmen, a demonstration of the power wielded by only one section of the powerful Marine Workers Affiliation. This was not the only example: striking railroad workers in New York State and immediate surrounds representing 150 000 men organized as the United Railroad Workers of America. These examples of 'federated unionism' were little different from those among Chicago or Seattle trade unionists.[6]

The examples above demonstrate that the New York labour movement of this period went beyond pure and simple 'craft unionism'. Strikes generalized into national or statewide movements, often critical of their own officials. Different groups of workers united across industries; for example, the Marine Workers Affiliation had supported the rail strikers. In concluding this section it is important to note that the above examples demonstrate that federated unionism was not unique to Chicago and Seattle. The difference between New York's central labour bodies and those in Chicago and Seattle was that the former did not control or initiate federated unionism. It was this, rather than the absence of a militant industrial tradition, that made the New York labour progressives weaker than their Seattle or Chicago counterparts.[7]

IMPULSE FOR THE NEW PARTY

In early 1920, the 100 unions that attended the ALP's City Convention confirmed the durability of the impulse that had created the new party. This was in spite of a year's campaign against the Labor Party by the AFL. The organizers expressed gratification at the turnout, after the determined effort made by 'powerful men in the AFL to wean unions away from the political organization that has been flourishing here for over a year'. Among those who attended were the delegates of 200 000 city employees who had become fed up with niggardly treatment by both Republican and Democrat administrations. Even by late April 1920 the response to a call for a state-wide Labor Party Convention elicited an impressive response, demonstrating that the party still carried high regard among union activists. Delegates representing 350 000 workers from the Central Federated Union, the United Hebrew Trades and the Women's Trade Union League had promised to attend. The delegations included 16 painters' locals; 58 Longshoremen's locals; the Railway Clerks of New York Harbor; the Marine Engineers, Masters, Mates and Pilots; several locals of the needle trades; upholsterers, waiters, plumbers, stenographers, electrical workers and carpenters. The Plumb Plan League with 14 branches and 40 affiliated local unions agreed to send a delegation. The Protestant Friends of Irish Freedom and groups of suffragists also nominated delegates. Considering the substantial opposition to the CFU's new party, it was an impressive rollcall. Clearly, there was still considerable sentiment for change in the spring of 1920.[8]

By late summer the mood remained buoyant at a nominating convention for the Fall elections. Thomas L. Delahunty, President of the Marine Workers Affiliation of the Port of New York, declined candidacy for Sheriff of Kings County but nonetheless delivered a keynote speech. The above examples show that broad-based sentiment existed for the party. Yet when the progressives had their leadership of the central bodies removed they got little effective support from trade unions that had supported the Labor Party project. Why did the union progressives, who supported independent political action, fail to turn the impulse into solid support?[9]

There was considerable sentiment in favour of the ALP, not just from local officials or the affiliated unions, but also from the rank and file. For example, 800 women upholstery workers voted to support it. However, the problem was turning sentiment into active support. The Secretary of the New York Women's Trade Union League (NYW-TUL) illustrated this point when she complained that the ALP left it to the women to 'accomplish everything and make ourselves unpopular'. The work took up a good deal of the women activists' time. But when it came to the Fall election campaign, many NYWTUL activists were not available due to attendance at the International Congress of Working Women in Washington.[10] However, some did help, and Hilda Svenson reported that she had been very active in the last week of the Party's campaign: 'a great deal of sentiment had been accursed [*sic*] among the workers'. She urged all to help and give some time to build up the party, so that 'in the next campaign we could be strong enough to win something'.[11]

Even after the CFU withdrew its support from the Party, the NYW-TUL remained loyal. It rallied its forces for the 1920 upstate election campaign and once again granted leave to its officials for party activities. However, the fact that affiliated organizations such as the NYW-TUL provided so much help in terms of administration and organizers covered up the underlying weakness of the Party. Maud Swartz noted that she and Frank Voght were the only members in the 5th Assembly district. The president of the NYWTUL pondered whether 'they would ever get the party across to the trade union rank and file'.[12]

The party lacked experience and active workers, and local organization was weak. Enthusiasm for state activities diverted attention from the reality of grass-roots weakness. Its organizers depended not on rank-and-file activity, but on that of affiliated organizations. Of course this could be a strength, as trade-union bodies could provide money, members and resources. At this stage it is important to evaluate how much strength the New York FLP derived from its union affiliates.

TRADE UNIONS AND THE LABOR PARTY

Though only a minority of all unions in NYC supported the new party, for a time the majority of those affiliated to the CFU and Hebrew Trades formally did so. Yet many of these affiliates were either sympathetic to, or members of, the Socialist Party. The new party was to the left of the AFL leadership, but to the right of the Socialists. It was careful not to identify itself with the more radical ideas of the Socialists or syndicalists. This approach did not flatter the Socialists, but many were impatient for success and saw the new party as a step in the right direction. Others saw the new party as nothing more than a bourgeois progressive party. The contradictions and ambivalence that resulted from the attitude of the two organizations to each other created a barrier to cooperation.

A large delegation of Socialist trade unionists attended the ALP's founding convention, but due to the non-committal attitude of their party took no active part in the new movement. Many of the unions in the clothing and furrier trades were Socialist dominated. Indeed, most of the unions affiliated to the Hebrew Trades were loyal to the Socialists. This situation made it very difficult for the founders of the new party to turn union affiliations into active support.[13] The attitude of the progressive International Ladies Garment Workers Union (ILGWU) illustrates this point. Though sympathetic to the new party, the ILGWU did not commit itself to anything; its attitude was one of wait and see. It also believed there was much suspicion of the CFU by radical unions. It was only the year before, after all, that the CFU had planned annihilation of the United Hebrew Trades. The ILGWU also expressed disappointment that the new party had failed to attract the Amalgamated Clothing Workers (ACW) into its ranks. The ACW, strong supporters of the Socialist Party, remained completely aloof from the new party convinced it was not welcome. Though the ILGWU had a 'wait and see' policy, it believed that there were reasons to expect the new party to do well. The last election results had been 'an humiliating setback' for the Socialist Party, and some workers were enthusiastic because they believed a new party could make a fresh start. Edward Hannah of the CFU had stated that they would work with radicals and socialists in the new party. That an old Tammany man should issue such a statement was encouraging. Even James Boyle (of the Brooklyn CLU) had agreed to include every amendment suggested by the Socialist delegates in labour's political programme. The ILGWU believed this was proof that the air was 'replete with change and revolution'.[14]

The ILGWU's optimism was not fulfilled; only a few workers shifted their voting loyalties to the new party. Even those that normally supported the Socialists failed to vote for the ALP, remaining loyal to their own party even if disappointed at its stagnant electoral performance. The continuing electoral strength of the SP remained a problem for the ALP. Nor were all Socialists as friendly towards the new party as the ILGWU. The national executive of the Socialist Party had warned against hasty action, either for or against the new party. This attitude of wait and see did not prevent friction between it and ALP supporters. James J. Bagley, president of Franklin Union No. 23, made it clear that the attitude of the Socialist Party to the ALP was resented by the CFU, CLU and WTUL. If necessary they would fight the Socialists in every electoral district.[15]

Some supporters of the Socialists were friendly. J. M. Budish, editor of the *Headgear Worker*, the union magazine of the United Cloth Hat and Cap Makers of North America, welcomed the setting up of a 'National Labor Party'. He called on the Labor Party and Socialist Party to cooperate. However, when it came to the election campaigns of the Fall of 1919 and 1920, the ALP received little support from the Socialist unions, nor was there any joint campaign. Not only did the

Call ignore it, but so did the union newspapers. Some made it clear that Eugene Debs, the Socialist Party presidential nominee, was the only candidate for them.[16]

In July 1920 the National Labor Party movement met in Chicago. Parties from several states, including New York, amalgamated with the Illinois Labor Party to form the Farmer Labor Party (FLP). There had been talk of standing La Follette, the progressive Republican senator from Wisconsin, as the FLP presidential candidate. However, La Follette refused the nomination. Parley P. Christensen, a little-known lawyer and Labor Party activist from Utah, served in his place.[17]

The ACW, which was sympathetic in 1919, became hostile in late 1920. Its journal called for support for the Socialist Party candidates in the 1920 General Election. It labelled the new Party as liberal, employing the policies of the newly formed Farmer Labor Party against it in the run-up to the elections. It also misrepresented the national Labor Party conference to berate the new party. The ACW claimed that the Party feared going out on its own. This was untrue, as the FLP had nominated candidates for the 1920 presidential election.[18]

This did not stop the ACW from claiming the FLP could be no more than a party of protest at the forthcoming election. However, if the Labor Party would have the courage to endorse Debs, it would be a stimulus 'for the building up of an INDEPENDENT political power of the American working class!' The party was also criticized for demanding nationalization, as strikes would be forbidden in industry under government control. The irony that this was also Gompers' argument against nationalization had escaped the writer of the editorial. Workers would not benefit from such plans; who owned the government was the key. The Plumb Plan was also criticized, and 'besides that he [Glen Plumb, the plan's author] is closely connected with the Railway Brotherhoods.' The FLP stood condemned for refusing to nominate the presidential choice of ACW members, Eugene V. Debs. The ACW attack on the FLP was not an isolated outburst restricted to the pages of a union newspaper. The *Call* also published the article for the benefit of all. Thus 'wait and see' had turned into open hostility in the New York socialist press. Abraham Lefkowitz, a leading member of the ALP, replied stating that the article had misrepresented it. The FLP stood for workers' control and not for state capitalism. He rejected the accusation that the FLP would sacrifice its platform to get La Follette to stand; it stood by the principle of building the party before personality. Joseph Schlossberg, General Secretary of the ACW, declined to reply, but stated he had written the article to make positions clear, not to be antagonistic. But the factual basis of the article would not bear scrutiny. The FLP had not given up its programme to get La Follette on board, and it quite clearly was standing as an independent party. After the dispute between Schlossberg and Lefkowitz, the ACW ignored the FLP for the rest of the election campaign.[19] This antipathy of the Socialists created real problems for the ALP for the Socialists were stronger in New York than just about anywhere else in the country. As outlined above, the Socialists dominated the progressive unions. New York was also the centre of a mass circulation socialist press which included the *Advance*, *Call* and the *Jewish Daily Forward*. Even if they had not opposed the FLP, they remained a barrier to advancement.[20]

The division of the New York labour movement into three major factions that had little in common – Socialists, Tammany and the progressives – explains why the AFL executive was able to move against the central labour body in New York City far earlier than it did in Seattle or Chicago. The progressives who temporarily controlled the New York central body lacked a solid base. The Socialists and the progressive unions were a sizeable block who owed them no particular loyalty. In Chicago the ACW was friendly towards the FLP supporters; in New York they were hostile. However it was not to the Socialists that Gompers turned to begin his assault on the ALP men (at least not openly), but to the Tammany 'old guard' of Brooklyn and the State Federation.

THE ROLE OF THE TAMMANY UNIONISTS

The lack of unity inside the CFU and the weak roots of the progressive leadership led Gompers to move first against the supporters of the ALP. To ensure outright victory it was necessary to strengthen the hands of the Tammany old guard. Gompers proposed amalgamating the two central bodies on the grounds that it would strengthen the New York labour movement. It would coincidentally strengthen the Tammany old guard. The old guard was stronger in the Brooklyn CLU, and bringing them into the CFU would outflank the progressives. Participants at the amalgamation meeting reported that Gompers had avoided controversial matters such as support for striking pressmen, the Labor Party and the radical spirit of the functioning central bodies that were 'obnoxious to a number of old-time labor leaders'. Gompers had given the impression that no attack would follow on the present leadership of the Central bodies, or on any particular policy. But less than three weeks later the gloves came off when the CLU announced it had quit the ALP for the AFL's 'Non-Partisan' Plan. John P. Coughlin, president of the CLU, announced that it was pulling out of the committee to organize the joint New York Party, and that it would be supporting Gompers' non-partisan policy. This proved the *Call*'s suspicions correct, that consolidation was a shrewd manoeuvre by the old guard to undermine the American Labor Party. Coughlin claimed that the ALP was only a paper organization and that it would be irresponsible to waste time trying to develop a new organization in such short time. It would also be foolish to fight the Socialist Party in working-class districts where it was strong.[21]

The CLU's defection was a serious blow to the new Party, but its supporters tried to make light of it. William Kohn, business agent of the Upholsterers Union and a prominent member of the FLP, believed that the movement's progress would remain unhampered. He described the defectors as weaklings and political scabs who had done nothing for the Party. Nor did he fear Gompers' attempts to persuade national union chiefs to put pressure on locals to undermine the party. Kohn believed that the party's growth would be unaffected, and that the sincere men and women of the Brooklyn unions would continue to work for it. He found encouragement in recent examples of changed attitudes of formerly conservative trade-union members, who at recent meetings had supported the party. Confidently he declared: 'The Labor Party is here and making progress. Let them stop it if they can.'[22]

Kohn stated that the Party was strong in Brooklyn and would survive there. This was either false optimism or the putting on of a brave face in response to events. However, he failed to foresee that it was not just a matter of losing 'official' support in Brooklyn but that support for the Party would be undermined in New York as a whole. It was the first step in driving the progressives out of all positions of influence in the central labour bodies. By the end of the year Gompers had rid himself of all those who opposed his non-partisan policy in New York, and replaced them with men loyal to himself and Tammany, though later he would discover that, for some, loyalty to Tammany was more important than loyalty to the AFL.

Pressure against those supporting the ALP increased. James P. Holland announced that the New York State Federation would support the AFL's non-partisan plan, and would not favour any Socialist or Labor Party candidates because to support either would 'divide the forces of labor and defeat labor's objects'. The rest of 1920 saw an increasing offensive against the progressives, including the use of violence and thugs. Ernest Bohm, Secretary of the CFU and Labor Party activist, suffered humiliation when refused entrance, on the grounds that he was not employed in his trade, to the State Federation Convention.[23]

The progressives were also hampered by their relationship to the AFL nationally. At times they criticized the leadership, yet they could not afford to make a complete break with it. The threat of losing the AFL charter could not be taken lightly. A consequence of this was that they often muted their opposition, pulling their punches. They shrank from trying to raise national support from the AFL for the new party. At the AFL convention in Canada Lefkowitz argued with delegates not to raise the FLP on the floor of the convention, claiming he would fight to the finish to prevent it. He asserted that the party existed, was making progress and was worthy of labour's support. Nor did Lefkowitz try and raise the party at the New York State Federation Convention that year, even though Gompers had unleashed an attack on its supporters at the convention.[24]

No doubt Lefkowitz's fears were well founded, as the analysis of AFL conventions by the progressive journalist Heber Blankenhorn demonstrates. Blankenhorn emphasized the bureaucratic nature of the AFL convention when he compared the 1919 United Mine Workers Convention with its AFL counterpart. He described the delegates as men from the pitheads, rudely dressed:

> Their names are mostly English, Scotch, [sic] Irish or Welsh and they are notorious readers...This Convention is no more like the A. F. of L. Convention at Atlantic City than a regiment in the field is like the Stock exchange. 'These delegates,' said a British labor leader... 'seem all to come from jobs where they dispose of their own time.' That an A.F. of L. Convention is made up almost altogether of paid union officials, astounded the British delegate whose own Trade Union Congress is half composed of rank and file.[25]

Blankenhorn's observation of the AFL convention's domination by full-time officials was confirmed in the negative. The miners passed a resolution calling for the founding of a labour party. No such decision could or would occur at an AFL national convention.

Lefkowitz preferred not to fight for the official endorsement of the AFL, as the most likely outcome, official condemnation, would do great damage to the infant party. This may have been tactically correct, but it meant leaving arguments against the party unopposed. However,

from the safety of their New York fiefdom the progressives did sometimes launch attacks on the non-partisan policy of the AFL. Using the
Reconstruction Committee they issued a communication stating that
labour had no friends in either the Democratic or Republican Parties
and should support an Independent Labor Party. They ignored a
request by Gompers that they should organize a non-partisan rally,
and instead requested that the AFL donate $10 000 to the Labor Party
campaign state- and city-wide. They told Gompers they agreed with his
characterization of Republicans and Democrats as bankrupt and
would therefore be supporting independent labour. They noted that
years of rewarding friends and punishing enemies had achieved nothing for workers in New York apart from higher rents. This provocative
letter was signed by William Kohn in his capacity as Chairman of the
Reconstruction Committee. Compared to the normally timid
approach of the CFU leadership, this was an act of bravado that
probably only served to irritate Gompers further. Only a month earlier
they avoided taking Gompers head-on over non-partisan policy, passing a resolution timidly querying if the policy was behind the times.[26]

At no time did the progressives take effective action to block the
amalgamation of the central labour bodies. Gompers had the advantage of clear strategy and policy, using the joint strength of the Brooklyn and New York conservatives to defeat the New York progressives.
Yet, as outlined above, the progressives had no clear strategy in reply.
They did not seem concerned that right-wing officials were denouncing
and deserting them. There was no preparation for what was quite
obviously a coming onslaught. Unlike the Socialists or the supporters
of Tammany, they had no clearly defined power base and they made
no attempt to build one. Their ideological position was also weak.
They did not campaign boldly for the labour party idea inside the
AFL, but restricted themselves to cleverly worded resolutions. For the
most part they trod carefully with regard to the AFL leadership, but
even this was inconsistent, and they occasionally issued provocative
statements. This lack of ideological clarity and strategy made it difficult to rally support. Whatever their motives, the failure to build an
effective defence against the AFL conservatives cost them dearly.

DEFEAT OF THE PROGRESSIVES

Such was the animosity between the main factions that it took nearly
ten months to complete the amalgamation of the CFU and the CLU.

But in early December 1920 the newly amalgamated Central Trades and Labor Council (CTLC) finally met to elect a new executive committee. This proved to be a conclusive defeat for the progressives. Gompers and AFL aides were elated as John Sullivan, executive member of the International Union of the United Brewery, Flour, Cereal, and Soft Drink Workers Union of America and Treasurer of the old CFU, defeated Edward I. Hannah, the previous president, for the presidency of the new organization. John P. Coughlin, President of the Brooklyn Central Labor Union, defeated William Kohn. William F. Kehoe, Secretary of the District Council of New York Teamsters, defeated Ernest Bohm. Only two progressives won elections to the executive committee: Thomas J. Curtis, President of the Tunnel and Subway Contractors Union, and M. Feinstone of the United Hebrew Trades. However, Feinstone had the support of both factions. The winners were conservatives from unions such as the Teamsters, Sheetmetal, Bartending and Electrical Workers. On average progressives received between 40 and 45 per cent of the vote. Lefkowitz got 282 votes, but a vote in the high three hundreds was required for victory. It was not the case that the progressives were massively outvoted – the margin at times was narrow – but it was enough to completely remove them from any influence in the council.[27]

The next day the *Call* noted that the old guard had a far more effective machine than the progressives. The longshoremen had provided a block vote of 20, rushed in on the last day. Fifty radical unions had not bothered to send delegates. The Socialist view was that the progressives' lack of programme had failed to persuade the independents present to vote. This explanation as to why there had been such a poor response by the radical or progressive unions, most of which the Socialists influenced, seems rather weak. For in the build-up to the assault by the conservatives, the *Call* had warned how serious the issues were. Here was a major attack by the old guard on the progressives in the union movement; yet the Socialists did little or nothing to mobilize radicals to defend the CFU leadership against the attack of the right. The analysis is that of a handwringer standing on the sidelines. However it is possible that the socialists were guilty of more than just handwringing.[28]

For, surprisingly, a United Hebrew Trades representative had won a place on the new committee. However, it was the Hebrew Trades who were responsible for the 50 missing radical unions. The Hebrew Trades, as was widely known, supported the Socialists and the Labor Party initiative. Indeed, if its delegates had turned up to support the progressives, their vote would have made an important difference. The Hebrew Trades organized unions mainly formed by the Socialists during the early part of the twentieth century, and consisted of needle-trade workers, bakers, butchers and grocery clerks, with some Jewish painters and carpenters. They were the backbone of the socialist movement in New York, supporting Socialist Party candidates at elections both with resolutions and money. Although not itself affiliated with the AFL, the unions composing the Hebrew Trades were.[29]

Lawrence Rogin noted that these unions rarely sent delegates to meetings of the CTLC. Thus, the progressives got on with more or less passive support from the Jewish unions, though Hebrew Trades delegates did normally attend for elections. However, on the occasion of the elections for the newly amalgamated central body they had not been present, even though the importance of the meeting was well known. It was the opinion of progressives present that even those who had attended had not solidly supported the progressive ticket. Lefkowitz believed that the Jewish unions had sold out to the conservatives. The only proof he had of this was that the Socialist Morris Feinstone, President of the United Hebrew Trades, gained election to the executive committee almost unanimously. Lefkowitz believed that if the Jewish unions had supported the progressives they could have won. He had a strong case, as there were only 56 votes between victory and defeat. But Lefkowitz had no evidence for his suspicion, and he was unaware of a letter sent a month earlier by H. Lang, labour editor of the New York *Jewish Daily Forward*.[30]

Lang congratulated Gompers on the reorganization of the central bodies. He also stated that he accepted Gompers' argument that the reason for the rough nature of the central labour body meetings was the long-term division of the two bodies. This led to different lines on the same issues, and vilification of each other. Thus when they finally met the tension naturally exploded.[31] It is unlikely that the writer was unaware that the real cause of the 'explosions' was the violence of pro-Gompers and Tammany thugs at amalgamated meetings. For back in May the *Forward*'s sister English-language newspaper, the *Call*, reported that the Gompers machine, loaded with the city's reactionary elements in the trade-union movement, had flattened out the progressive element in the Central Federated Union. A block of 60 teamsters, longshoremen and 'black element' (reactionaries) among the printing trades had physically threatened delegates, including Edward I. Hannah; Lefkowitz had a gun held at his back, and another progressive was informed he would be thrown out of the window. Officials of the Central Federated Union became so disgusted at the organization's action that they tendered their resignations. The progressives were outvoted 110 to 40 and the ALP's endorsement was removed. It was announced that the delegates to the AFL convention would support the Non-Partisan Policy.[32]

H. Lang, labour editor of the *Forward*, made no mention of this violence in his letter nor of the ALP's loss of support. But he did claim that the Jewish labour press was behind Gompers on the issue, and that the forming of one New York body was a dream come true. Lang's friendly letter suggests that Lefkowitz's suspicions were well founded. Whatever the motives of the Hebrew Trades and the Socialists, the outcome was to isolate the progressives and end Central Trades and Labor Council (CTLC) support for the new party. This was a deadly blow from which the Party would never recover. The Hebrew Trades on its own had not sunk the progressives – the initiators were those loyal to Tammany and Gompers – but its abstention had fatal consequences for the ALP supporters.[33]

The progressives had lost all positions of influence in the CTLC, and the Labor Party had lost its official recognition. The progressives were isolated; the Socialist Party had not mobilized its forces to defend them. All of this weakened the new party, and later we shall see that this caused further losses of support. The Party had not got off to a good start with much of its trade-union support removed even before it entered a major election campaign.

OUT ON THE STUMP

In 1919 the Party had been unable to get its candidates on to the New York ballot papers. In early 1920 it launched a statewide Labor Party even though it had achieved little in New York City. In the 1920 election it did manage to get its candidates on the statewide list, but four candidates for municipal justiceships were barred from the ballot. Required to obtain 3000 signatures, they had gathered 4000 for each candidate, but were disqualified because the signatures had not appeared 'on the last registration list'. John R. Voorhis, Chairman of the Board of Elections, claimed that the petitions were fraudulent, that some were written in the same hand and that some appeared to be copied from registration lists. However, apart from this one setback, the Party did manage to field candidates for the Senate, the House of

Representatives and Governor. The elections of 1920 were the first real test of how successfully the Party had built support beyond union affiliations. The most prominent candidate was Dudley Field Malone, a former collector of the port of New York, standing for Governor.[34]

Meanwhile O'Connor of the Longshoremen called for support for Harding. However, the bulk of the New York old guard supported the Democrat candidate for governor, Al Smith, and Gompers' non-partisan policy. Thus the Party was opposed not just by Tammany and Republicans, but by union officials on a national and local basis. The election results proved to be very disappointing apart from Malone's New York City vote and the congressional vote of Jeremiah O'Leary (see below).[35] The presidential vote was particularly poor. Parley P. Christensen, the Farmer Labor national candidate, got 18 413, a mere 0.6 per cent of the presidential vote cast in New York. In comparison the Socialist candidate Debs received 203 201, 7 per cent, of the votes cast. Dudley Field Malone's vote ran 50 000 ahead of Parley P. Christensen's at 69 908, with less than 9000 coming from outside NYC. Rose Schneiderman also ran ahead of Christensen, but she polled only 27 934 votes. The Socialists took many liberal and discontented votes, but in spite of this Malone got 52 000 votes in the City of New York. Schneiderman, it was believed, had done well among women garment workers and in the East Side. Why did Malone get a vote far in excess of his comrades?[36]

It could have been due to the fact that he was a well-known local politician. However, it could equally be due to the fact that he had an effective campaign machine, one that came about almost by accident. The Women's Independent Campaign Committee, formed to oppose Senator Wadsworth, got behind Schneiderman's campaign. It also supported Malone because he had resigned from the Democrat administration over Wilson's failure to keep his word on suffrage. A WTUL activist, Geneva M. Marsh, described the enthusiastic campaign organized by these women.

> Women speakers visited the piers in New York, the Brooklyn Navy Yard, factories in all parts of the city and the most promising street corners. Meetings took place at noon as well as in the evening. Large quantities of literature were distributed, including some excellent leaflets outlining the program of the Farmer Labor Party–towards the end of the campaign Malone and Schneiderman buttons were also distributed.

The Women's Committee consisted of women interested in politics from the liberal viewpoint. It included writers, teachers, settlement workers and a group who had come over from the old militant suffragists. These willing supporters gave every assistance they could toward helping the Party. Having long experience in campaigning for suffrage they were well qualified to do this work. Also women new to politics, not members of any organization and some with no experience of campaigning at all, had also made 'fine agitators'.[37]

It is hard to gauge how much their intervention achieved, but it is probable that this joint effort of militant women and progressives won extra votes. Another example showing that a well-known political figure backed by effective organization could do well was the result in the 18th Congressional District (see Table 2.1). Here Jeremiah O'Leary got 25 per cent of the poll. This was perhaps the most successful result for the ALP. The Democrats won the district with only 12 169 votes; O'Leary's vote was 9998 and the Socialists 5668. If the Socialists had stood aside for O'Leary, it is possible there would have been an FLP congressman in the 18th District.

Table 2.1 Election result 18th Congressional District

Democrat	Republican	FLP	Socialist
12 169 (31.2%)	11 148 (28.6%)	9998 (25.7%)	5668 (14.5%)

O'Leary's vote contradicts the assumption that the FLP returns in New York were laughable. The key to Malone's success was his stand on women's suffrage; with O'Leary it was his stand on Irish freedom. Well-known throughout New York for his campaigning on the issue, he was discontented with Democrat policies for not opposing the British over the issue and this spurred O'Leary to stand on an FLP platform. The district had a large Irish population, and O'Leary had the advantage of being both well-known in Irish circles and well connected with many of the community's organizations. It almost certainly provided him with an effective electoral machine.[38]

Though the overall vote was disappointing, the above experience does demonstrate that a well-organized campaign with well-known candidates could improve the Party's performance at the polls. It also demonstrated that women, the Irish and progressives in general could be won to the politics of independent labour.

CONCLUSION

Considering that the New York Party suffered from a lack of official union support and a weak electoral machine, it is arguable that it did surprisingly well. It had also suffered from a city hall that had kept them out of the local elections, and a Socialist Party that was still a substantial third-party force. The problem for the new party was how to stop being the fourth party, rather than becoming the second or even first.

Although the New York vote was not entirely disastrous and perhaps could have been used to build the beginnings of a new party, contemporaries did not feel that way. To face up to these disappointments and to sustain the Party required some form of a stable base, either of individual membership or union support. However, as we have already seen, the Party had already lost its central official union support and had not built an active membership. The inability to maintain union support at a local level was a factor that further undermined the Party's attempts to build an effective membership.[39]

The new party also failed to establish its own newspaper; this meant that for the most part even its successes failed to gain publicity. It had to depend on the AFL union machine and other affiliates to spread its organization. When it lost the support of these organizations, it became isolated with no way of extending its support beyond the layer of minor labour movement officials. It was one of the Party's central activists, Lefkowitz, who described it as a party of minor union officials. He believed that, given a little more time, it could have gone back from the 'central body into the local unions and gotten the support of the rank and file'. The problem with this strategy was its reliance on official union administration. The starting-point was the central body, and even when Lefkowitz and his comrades were in control of the central body there were many barriers, with some local union officials blocking progress.[40]

Perhaps activists such as Lefkowitz were prisoners of their own past experience, used to passing resolutions inside the unions and passing on the results to members. Having gained control of the central body, they overestimated the power it gave them to involve the rank and file. Using minor union officials and the women of the WTUL for administration and electioneering the progressives became blinded to their shortcomings. When the struggle was on the up and up, as it was in 1919, this did not matter. The conservatives had their hands full dealing with insurgent workers; it might even have suited them to let militancy find an outlet on the political field. This situation gave the progressives the upper hand; however, once the struggle subsided the conservatives were able to use the weight of a long-established union machine against the progressives. They had powerful allies: the AFL national leadership, leaders of the international unions and the political strength of Tammany.

In a situation such as this, the progressives needed a power base from which to defend themselves. They had tried to use the central body as one, but it proved to be an unreliable weapon. The Socialist unions offered little support and, having failed to build any independent foundation, the progressives were easily defeated. The progressives had failed to sink any lasting roots into the insurgent spirit of 1919. They had failed to bridge the gap between the impulse for a new party and actually establishing one.

Tammany was quick to learn the lesson of this episode. For a brief while officials loyal to Tammany had switched to the new party. It could not take union officials' loyalty for granted; it had to be more sensitive to the aspirations of these officials. Those who had organized the defeat of the progressives at the CTLC were rewarded. Holland gained a $5000 a year post on the Board of Standards and Appeals, and Costello and Coughlin accepted minor positions. A number of officials who had supported the ALP ended up in the Tammany fold.[41]

3 One Step Forward: the Birth of the Labor Party, Chicago 1919–20

Chicago labour was the first of the three movements to form a labour party and take part in a major election. Although the Chicago Federation of Labor (CFL) had a long tradition of progressive activity and strong trade union support, the party did not fare as well as its Seattle counterpart. In the 1920 general election the new party performed badly at the polls, a blow from which it never recovered.

Considering that the CFL leadership had a far stronger base for its initiative than labour in the other two cities, why did it not achieve more? This chapter investigates why the CFL leadership was unable to turn union support for the labour party into electoral support from Chicago workers. Of course, the failure of the CFL's initiative was not just a matter of a lack of will. When it launched the party in 1919 the unions were growing. By the time of the 1920 election the union movement was in decline. Chicago politics were tougher than the Seattle variety, and city bosses did not shrink from exploiting ethnic and 'racial' divisions to block their rivals. Nonetheless in 1919 the new party's mayoralty campaign was the most successful ever in Chicago for independent working-class politics.

In assessing the strength of the new party it should be kept in mind that electoral results are not the only indicator of a party's influence. Large numbers of workers, immigrants and women did not vote in Chicago elections. However, the fact that electoral success was not immediate may have disillusioned many of the party's most optimistic supporters. Moreover it is not realistic to judge a party only three months old purely by the number of votes obtained. Nonetheless the question why did union membership outnumber the votes cast for the labour party is relevant. Also why did the largest working-class vote for Mayor not prove to be the beginning of greater things? To answer these questions it will be necessary to assess the strength of union support for the Cook County Labor Party (CCLP) and the key features in its development.[1]

UNION STRENGTH

Formally the majority of Chicago locals supported the new party. Though the CFL claimed to represent over 300 000 workers it could not communicate with them all. The main link was between local officials and delegates to the central labour body. Edward Nockels admitted that the Federation had never reached more than 5000 union members on any proposition because it did not have the machinery. He wanted the *New Majority* (*Majority*) to become that machinery. Unfortunately the *Majority* never achieved a consistent mass circulation. Thus, for the most part, the message never extended beyond the 5000 activists. The *Majority* lacked the tradition and roots of New York and Seattle's Socialist and progressive newspapers. It was the result of transforming the CFL's news-sheet into a newspaper at the launching of the CCLP. Without a broader political tradition to build on its distribution depended mainly on union branches; this proved to be a fundamental weakness.[2]

The radicalization of the period spurred unions into supporting the CFL's political initiatives; however, it was a matter of block affiliation, not of converting individuals. Those wishing to oppose the new party may not have blocked it at CFL meetings, but there were other means of obstruction. The party's newspaper depended on local union branches for distribution and some did their best to promote it, but others did their best to block it. In this they were aided by the AFL constitution, which prohibited payments to outside or political organizations. Opponents used delaying tactics, such as the holding of referendums or raising the problems of cost.

The CFL encouraged individual subscriptions but overall the circulation was never substantial. In an attempt to increase circulation, and to overcome the reticence of some union locals, Robert Buck replaced W. Z. Foster as business manager. However, the organizational change made little difference and circulation failed to increase. The *Majority*'s circulation did rise at times of major strikes, such as those in the stockyards, steel and rail. Circulation rose and fell with union activity; however, such spontaneous expansion did not provide a wider base of committed political support. Unfortunately strikes did not always occur at the same time as elections. As the party's strategy depended on winning elections, this was a serious handicap.[3]

The *Majority* gave extensive coverage to strikes, raising money for strikes and trade-union news. It emphasized that only in its pages could readers find the 'truth' about strikes, corruption, Russia and the two parties. Yet the CFL and CCLP failed to overcome the divide that existed between workers' union activities and their political loyalties. Workplace allegiances to the CFL were not transformed into political ones in the community. Conversely issues concerning production were raised only in a general sense in party policy. The party did not raise the issue of workers' control. It was a reformist party; however, to assert that the party was reformist does not, on its own, explain the cause of failure.[4]

The Labor Party in Seattle had far more electoral success, but related even less to workers' economic struggle, and was also a reformist party. Secondly, labour parties by definition are 'reformist' – that is they operate inside the parameters set by existing political institutions. They also operate within the geographical constraints of electoral democracy. The contradiction posed by the separation of the workplace and the electoral arena is a problem that all labour parties confront. In spite of this divide many have succeeded, and it is not necessary to look outside the USA to find examples of such success. The successes of the Minnesota Farmer Labor Party, and to a lesser extent those of the Washington FLP, prove the case. None of these examples succeeded by forsaking reformist politics.[5]

This has a direct bearing on understanding the Chicago situation for even though the CCLP often rejected the language of class it remained a working-class party. The actual politics of the party did not rest on a revolutionary understanding of class, or directly on struggle. However, it is not the case that the Party did not relate to class or workers' struggles; rather, the Party mirrored the division between politics and the workplace. At election time it raised municipal issues at workers' meetings and stood candidates linked to the unions. Thus meetings took place to raise support for striking rail workers and the *Majority* gave the steel strike massive coverage. However, the *Majority* did not always make it clear if it was the voice of the Party or the CFL. Nonetheless, it was clear that the *Majority* supported both. The newspaper's coverage inspired letters of gratitude from those involved in strikes.[6]

However, the firmest link between the new party and workers was the fact that most of its leading activists were also local union officials. As in New York, it was, for the most part, a party of the lower layer of trade-union officials. The new party also had the added strength that the Illinois State Federation and the majority of Illinois United Mine Workers (UMW) locals endorsed it. Thus it had an organic link to the locally organized working class. There is no doubt that the divide between workplace and community in Chicago was an important factor. Nonetheless, Seattle, using an almost identical strategy, had a degree of electoral success, so why not Chicago? To answer that it is necessary to cover the same ground detailed earlier on New York. That is how the party operated, how it sought electoral support, the role of women and progressives, the effect of the main party machines and ethnic division. The attitudes and actions of the Socialists and the AFL are also detailed.

Chicago was no different to New York or Seattle when it came to women's and progressive support. The Women's Trade Union League (WTUL) supported the new party and used its monthly bulletin to advertise the activities of the Labor Party. Also its leading organizers played a prominent role in helping the party. However, the CCLP was not as dependent on the WTUL as was the case for the New York's ALP. The personal interest of Nockels and Fitzpatrick ensured that CFL activists were central to party administration. Additionally the CFL had a far better relationship with the Amalgamated Clothing Workers (ACW) than their New York counterparts; Hillman spoke on CCLP platforms and donated money to the party's funds.[7]

PROGRESSIVE AND LIBERAL SUPPORT

There was a mixed response from Chicago's liberals and progressives. Some prominent individuals did support the new party and were active in supporting the mayoralty campaign, though neither the CFL nor the Labor Party nationally ever managed to get the majority of organized progressive support. The CFL did not play the leading role in progressive political activity that the Seattle Central Labor Council (SCLC) did. At times it received limited support from some of the progressive magazines and Frank Walsh gave financial support, but he never joined the party. A number of minor progressive figures and organizations supported the CCLP. The University of Chicago's Political Science department supported Fitzpatrick's mayoral campaign, as did Margaret Dreier Robins, leader of the WTUL, and Mary McDowell, the Director of the University of Chicago Settlement House. The Municipal Voters League endorsed six labour candidates and the *Daily News* endorsed three, but this was not as extensive as the wholesale progressive support given to the Seattle movement in this period.[8]

Though some in the Chicago Socialist Party wanted a good relationship with the new party, on the whole relations between the two parties remained bitter and hostile. Socialists often made attacks on the new party, and Fitzpatrick replied with equal vehemence. Some local Socialists had already left for the Labor Party; others split to the left joining the new communist organizations. The remaining rump could not afford to drop their electoral intervention for fear of criticism from the left. During this period splits and state repression bedevilled the Socialist Party. With many of its members either in prison or facing trial for anti-war activity, there is little evidence of coherent thought given to responding to the new labour parties.

The Socialist Party in Chicago was far weaker than the party in New York, but far stronger than the Seattle party. Those that remained loyal to the Socialist Party continued with their electoral activity, and relations between them and the CFL became increasingly acrimonious. The CCLP was only months old when the CFL leadership felt the need to pour scorn on the Socialists. James Duncan of Seattle, addressing the CFL, 'suggested that the Socialist Party swallow its pride and go along with the Labor Party'. A delegate from the Machinists Union Local 478 replied that he had associated with the Socialist Party for 25 years. It had made some mistakes but it would continue its work and would not step aside for anyone else. Fitzpatrick replied that he had offered to speak on Socialist Party platforms in the past but was prohibited 'from speaking for their candidates'. Nockels took a further swipe, stating the Labor Party had difficulty getting on ballot papers, but it would succeed in spite of the fact:

> That for one time at least the Socialists, Samuel Gompers and the Executive Council of the AFL were in agreement in opposition to organized labor entering the political arena to speak for labor.[9]

The acrimony did not diminish and by mid-1921 relations were so bad that Robert Buck claimed he had found Socialists trying to wreck his efforts from within.[10] Electorally in the first year the Socialists trailed behind the CCLP in Chicago; later in 1920 they improved their position, but at this stage the Socialists were not a barrier to the Labor Party. Nor was there a block of Socialist unions that could or wanted to deprive the CFL of money and resources, but in the 1920 election campaign the Socialists displaced the CCLP as Chicago's leading worker's party.

ORGANIZING THE PARTY

The organizers of the new party declared that 'The Labor Party is a young giant, or it is nothing.' The men who had won the war could win the city with a party barely two months old. This raising of the stakes did nothing to prepare supporters for defeat. Although some did argue the need for a long-term approach, it was the more upbeat declarations that dominated the *Majority*. Perhaps carried away by the heady atmosphere of early 1919, supporters believed that a party that had existed for only a few months could win Chicago at its first attempt. Yet party leaders were well aware that there were 3000 voting precincts in the city, and that unlike the other parties they could not afford to pay poll watchers.[11]

However, CFL activists believed they could cover the precincts by organizing a 'political picket line' on the election day. The CFL called on all organized workers to take election day off to ensure the honest casting and counting of votes. Though the call was blazoned on the front page of the *Majority* no more than a minority of workers responded. The party, only months old, had not established itself sufficiently in time for the election. Indeed by 26 March 1919 the party had only received per capita payments for 59 482 members, not for the 300 000 claimed at its founding. As the per capita fee was a block payment by unions active membership was probably less than the smaller figure. Another indicator of involvement was the sales of the *Majority*. The Stockyards Labor Council (SLC) bought half of the first run, while the teachers purchased 5000 copies and milk-wagon drivers and truckers another 5000. Yet by 12 April 1919 the paper had only 4336 subscribers. [12]

However, not all plans were as wishful as the picket line of the ballot and, in spite of the heady rhetoric, the Party did methodically build ward organizations, establishing 27 ward branches by 22 February. At the election the Party was able to stand candidates in all but two of Chicago's 35 wards. However, when the municipal election took place many of the wards were only weeks old. This rapid growth raises the question as to how it was possible for such an infant, and untried, party to do as well as it did. Describing the CCLP's mayoral election campaign and an analysis of the election results will answer this question.[13]

THE CAMPAIGN

The Cook County Labor Party did not enter the primary elections; instead it entered directly the city election of 1 April 1919. It is likely that the abstention of the CCLP from the primaries was a disadvantage, but it was a decision born of necessity as the party had not completed building its ward organization.[14] By late February the *Majority*'s campaign was in full flow for the April election. Although the CCLP's programme was a narrow one based on progressive municipal reforms, the actual campaign was broader. Chicago labour leaders, and their supporters, used class terms at many of the big campaign rallies held in Chicago. There was a massive gap between the militant rhetoric offered by the campaigners and the solutions actually proposed. However, as we shall see below, it was not irrelevant to the experience of Chicago workers. It was also a rhetoric far to the left of that used in the 1920 James Duncan mayoralty campaign in Seattle.[15]

Fitzpatrick used his platform to highlight the poverty of workers and the brutality of the police against strikers. During 1917–19 the CFL organized mass recruiting drives in meatpacking and steel, and Fitzpatrick did not fail to draw the links between the political and industrial. He attacked the excessive profits of the 'Meat Kings' made at the expense of packinghouse workers. This was a prelude to the intensification of recruiting drives in the stockyards in June 1919. He also attacked the anti-labour record of his opponents. If the Labor Party obtained power, it had a programme that would rapidly relieve 'oppressed' workers. He singled out Thompson, the Republican incumbent, for bullying striking streetcar men into submission and especially for his use of the police against striking women garment workers. W. Z. Foster also played a prominent role in the campaign, and the *Majority* gave the campaign to organize steel extensive coverage.[16]

The *Majority* stressed that the election battle was between big business and labour: 'United Capital would meet United Labor' at the ballot box. Here was a rhetoric far more class-conscious than the progressive or 'Americanist' tones of the *Seattle Union Record*. Neither Lincoln nor Marx were invoked, and though the language was closer to Marx's than Lincoln's it would be the state legislature that would carry out immediate reforms, not a workers' revolution. Frank Walsh spoke on Fitzpatrick's behalf during the campaign calling for 'Hands Off Russia', an end to all kings and a free Ireland. He attacked high profits, low wages, poverty and inhumane conditions. The situation was resolvable only by workers' control and industrial democracy. Industrial democracy, for Walsh, meant cooperation between employer and employees. Workers would have a voice equal to the employers, not overall control. The *Majority* appealed, just before election day, for voters to help prevent revolution. This could only be done by allowing labour to implement its constructive programme. Those who opposed the Labor Party were stoking the fires of revolution.[17]

NOT ALL ICE CREAM AND BARN DANCES: WOMEN AND THE CAMPAIGN

The campaign did not restrict itself to issues that concerned those involved in industrial conflict. It also specifically set out to win the support of women. The Fourteen Points of Labor adopted by the CFL demanded complete equality of men and women in government and industry. It called for the full enfranchisement of women (women already had the vote in Illinois by 1913), and equal pay for men and women doing similar work. An appeal was made to every trade-union woman, and to the wives, mothers and sisters of male trade unionists. They could help elect the ticket that would protect every home by ensuring fathers had a sufficient wage to make child and wife labour unnecessary. The party believed its municipal platform, with its demands for better street lighting, buildings, plumbing and recreation facilities, was a platform for women. Margaret Dreier Robins specific-ally endorsed Fitzpatrick for Mayor. Long before it had been the order of the day he had supported women's enfranchisement and had helped women to industrial, economic and political equality. He had organized the provision of food for 50 000 people during the 16-week-long garment workers strike. Women's trade unions, and additionally women's auxiliaries of unions, including those of the Milk Wagon Drivers', Post Office Clerks' and Switchmen's Unions, received the appeal.[18]

For the most part the *Majority* addressed women as mothers and as consumers who were sometimes workers. Women that ignored plain political argument could be cajoled into agreement by the 'hilarities' of barn dances and card parties. Clare Masilotti enticed support by giving away free ice cream in her store. However, it was not all ice creams and barn dances. The women's campaign committee raised a number of serious issues and did a substantial share of the canvassing. Agnes Nestor and Margaret Haley were among those on the executive com-mittee. Elizabeth Maloney of Waitresses Union 484 was appointed Chairman (*sic*) of the Women's Campaign Committee. Ida Fursman was one of the most prominent aldermanic candidates of the whole campaign. In particular she raised the issue of wages for teachers; she believed that wages were so low that 'better women' could not be induced to become teachers.[19] The two female candidates were very prominent, and a number of prominent women activists supported the Party. Women were responsible for collecting a third of signatures on candidates' petitions, and in the 26th ward distributed 20 000 election leaflets. However, it was far easier to get women activists involved in canvassing than it was to get working-class women to register for the vote.[20]

Unions are strongest where they can relate to workers in a collective situation, the workplace. In 1920 women were a smaller percentage of the workforce than they are today. Of the 1 231 468 persons gainfully employed in Chicago only 311 615 were women, that is 25 per cent of total workforce. Thus women were a minority of the workforce and unions; the link between women and the unions was weaker than was the case for men. This was not just a matter of labour's attitudes but of women's position in society overall. This explains why the approach to women voters was mainly a community-based one, and why the response of women was weaker in spite of some very good reasons as to why they should have supported the new party.[21]

UNIONS, WARDS AND VOTERS

The decision to stand for the city municipal elections on 1 April created a focus for building ward organization. For the city-wide contest the Party had chosen an ethnically balanced slate of Fitzpatrick for mayor (Irish), John Kikulski (Polish) for city clerk and Knute Torkelson (Swedish) for city treasurer. Kikulski was president of Local Union 546 of the Amalgamated Meat Cutters and Butcher Workmen of North America, and a leading union organizer in the Union Stock Yards for the Stock Yards Labor Council (SLC). Torkelson was a member of the left-wing Carpenters and Joiners Local Union No. 181. However, the slate extended beyond union officials with Morris N. Friedland's nomination for municipal court judge. Friedland was an attorney in the City Hall Square, and though well known in legal circles, was not a union activist. William E. Rodriguez, an ex-Socialist Party member, stood for judge of the Superior Court. Well-known politically, he had served three years as alderman for the 15th ward and had a reputation of supporting labour.[22]

The majority of aldermanic candidates were prominent local union officials. The 26th ward chose as their aldermanic candidate T. F. Neary, a member of the Teamsters for 20 years. The 29th ward stood

Martin P. Murphy, President of the Stockyards Council, for alderman. Ida M. Fursman, President of the Chicago Teachers Federation, stood in the 27th Ward. Clare Masilotti was nominated for the 19th Ward; though the owner of a florist's shop, she had played a leading role in the 1910 garment workers' strike among male and female Italians. The ward had a substantial Italian population.

Nonetheless not all the candidates were trade union militants. In the 17th Ward Henry Anielewski, a Polish journalist and socialist, was the candidate. In the 11th ward, a carpet and rug contractor, who still considered himself a union man, was the candidate. However, the majority of candidates were trade-union activists and it is this direct link to organized workers that explains why the new party won a respectable vote on its first outing. In other words, where the unions provided a strong organic link between the Party and the local population it proved possible to win workers away from the old parties. This also proved to be a weakness, for it meant that those responsible for running union locals on a day-to-day basis had to wear two hats. At times when there was no union activity this was not a major problem, but during intense union activity it was not possible to wear both hats at once. Usually the political hat was discarded, but in the run-up to the election of April 1919 this was not the case. Up to 1 April 1919 ward organization was all important but the following campaign for the Constitutional Convention ('Con Con') required district organization. The party changed its organization accordingly, amalgamating wards into districts. This interruption of routine contributed to a weakening of ward organization by the time of the municipal elections of 1920. By 14 February 1920 the number of aldermanic candidates definitely standing was reduced to 16, and when a candidate died of pneumonia it fell to 15. The reduced number of candidates, and the inability to defend them against disqualification, is evidence that the wards were far weaker after a year of activity. What caused this decline in Party strength after its first year of activity? [23]

The answer, partly, lies in the activity that followed the mayoral election of 1919 when the CCLP shifted to campaigning for Con Con. The Party provided a special programme for a new state constitution. The measure most directed at workers was that of Democracy in Industry. This proposed the reorganization of mining, manufacturing and mercantile industries, putting such industries upon a cooperative basis, including the right of employees to elect representatives to boards of directors. The importance of Con Con was explained to workers, with a stress on the need to curb the power of big business and the judiciary. Though the Constitutional Convention was the main campaign of the CCLP, the *Majority* did cover other issues, including the urging of open trade with Soviet Russia as a means of reducing unemployment. Also the national steel strike and the recruiting campaign in the stockyards made the front page.[24]

The campaign for Con Con failed, with no labour candidates elected. However, the defeat received scant analysis and attention and the *Majority* immediately switched its attention to the founding of the National Labor Party. It argued that workers had suffered at the hands of a Democratic administration; little better could be expected from the Republicans. Thus it was imperative that workers now had their own national party. The rhetoric now moved to the left as it declared labour was starting an 'Open Drive On Plutes'. Workers were preparing to take over the industries of the nation peacefully and run them in the interest of those who produce its wealth. Rather disingenuously, the *Majority* attempted to boost the campaign by claiming that Samuel Gompers supported the Labor Party. This claim resulted from a loose interpretation of Gompers' speech outlining the AFL's non-partisan policy. Two weeks later it admitted that although the logic of Gompers' doctrine led to advocating a labour party, in fact he was against it. The ensuing row between Gompers and the CFL became the main concern of the *Majority* for the whole of March. It completely eclipsed the campaign of the two labour candidates standing for alderman. Apart from reproducing the municipal platform with added emphasis on public ownership of all utilities, propaganda for the party became almost non-existent.[25]

The pending Fall elections, which included congressional and local county positions, saw the *Majority* return to more outward-going matters. Candidates campaigned not just on the municipal platform, but on National and State Labor Party programmes. Once again Frank Walsh gave his services, stating that he believed the Labor Party could win. The old parties were hopeless and a party of the workers was inevitable. The *Majority* launched its campaign with the slogan 'All Power to the People'. It emphasized that the Party was the workers' own party, financed by workers, and in the interest of 'workers of factory, farm and office'. [26]

At its national convention the Labor Party became the Farmer Labor Party (FLP) and nominated Parley P. Christensen for President, with Max Hayes as his running mate. The *Majority* became the organ of the national party. With the General Election approaching it concentrated on national issues at the expense of local ones. It reproduced the platform of the FLP, combining an emphasis on 'Americanism' with a call for an end to Imperialism at home and abroad. It also advocated the democratic control of industry and a bill of rights for labour. For the rest of the campaign the *Majority* carried reports on the progress of Christensen but few arguments as to why workers should vote FLP. Indeed the paper seemed to find the most persuasive arguments for voting labour in the pages of the *Nation*. It reproduced an article that half-heartedly recommended a vote for Christensen or even Debs, not because either could win, but because it might create a political realignment in the future. In the final days before the election the *Majority* concentrated on Parley P. Christensen's campaign; meanwhile the campaign for Cook County posts received scant attention.[29] In the transition from being the newspaper of the CFL and the CCLP to the national organ of the FLP, the *Majority* had lost its way. Local issues were hardly visible among the national news. Lacking any consistent ideology, the *Majority*'s content veered from class rhetoric to municipal reform and, at times, it declared it was not a party based on any one class. The paper had lost its 'local feel' and relevance.

GAUGING PARTY SUPPORT

The three major election campaigns, the founding of the FLP, and the actions of the CFL, party activists and the *Majority* are detailed above. The question is now raised: to what extent did this activity influence the rank-and-file members of the union and beyond?

The CCLP was capable of holding large meetings, rallies and picnics. Six thousand attended a ratification meeting for Fitzpatrick, addressed by Governor Lyn Frazier of North Dakota and the Non-Partisan League, raising $3600. A few weeks later 8000 heard Walsh speak at a Labor Party meeting, with $4800 raised. Moreover, not only the big-name speakers addressed large meetings. John Kikulski spoke to large numbers in English and Polish, especially in the areas adjacent to the stockyards and in the Polish Northside. In the 29th ward Martin P. Murphy, President of the SLC and candidate for alderman, spoke to a Labor Party meeting of 250. Stanley Borzinski, of Local 658 of the Butcher Workmen, addressed the meeting in Polish. Even though the Party was weaker after the spring 1919 defeat, it was still capable of holding large meetings. Thus in the September thousands attended a Labor Party picnic to hear Glen Plumb outline his plans for the railways. In District Four, a district that contained 50 000 workers, 2000 attended a Labor Party meeting. Although Christensen won few Chicago votes in the 1920 presidential election he did attract large crowds. Thousands, including women and children, attended the 'monster picnic' that opened the FLP general election campaign.[28]

ACTIVE UNION SUPPORT

Neither the large meetings addressed by the big names nor the support of prominent local progressives can explain the depth of support that the Party gained. The key to that support was the trade-union movement of Chicago and beyond. It is clear, as detailed above, that there was a discrepancy between the support offered by the local unions and actual delivery. There was some opposition: some local officials supported the Socialists, some the Democrats; and one publication, the *Unionist*, attacked the CCLP and supported Gompers' non-partisan policy. However, the opposition was not substantial enough to block the CFL's determination to build a party. The supporters of the *Unionist* produced 400 000 copies of their newspaper for the election. It meant the CFL had to spend time and energy refuting the paper and trying to stop its production. The CFL withdrew union status from the *Unionist*; however, its pro-Gompers propaganda probably boosted those trade unionists who supported the official AFL position.[29]

The *Unionist* could not block Fitzpatrick or the CCLP, for both had Illinois miners' endorsement. Delegates representing 95 000 organized mine-workers voted to endorse the FLP. The miners debated as to whether dues should be compulsory or not, finally agreeing that they should be voluntary. The miners' decision demonstrated enthusiasm for the FLP, coupled with fear of upsetting the AFL establishment. Miners' locals provided much-needed electoral success. Though these electoral successes were outside of Chicago they encouraged the activists of the CCLP. At least they could point to FLP councils and mayors in these outer districts.[30]

Overall the level of official union support was more impressive than in New York and even Seattle. For Chicago could bring out the 'big guns' on its campaign platforms – Sidney Hillman, Duncan McDonald and John Walker all spoke on Fitzpatrick's behalf. Union support did not just remain on an official or formal level; many of those who officially endorsed the party gave practical help, while other trade unionists gave unofficial support. Thus the Carmen allowed the Party to use their labour temple. At a national level, an unofficial gathering of rank-and-file railroad craft workers meeting in Chicago, representing 400 lodges and objecting to a wage settlement, also endorsed the party.[31]

The unions also provided the bulk of financial support, although it was never enough for the Party's needs. Only half of the money required for the 1919 Mayoral election was raised by 5 April 1919. At one CFL meeting $6951 was pledged for the mayoral campaign, including substantial donations from the Teamsters Joint Council, the Brick and Clay Workers Council and Stockyards locals. The fact that the Teamsters alone had given $3000 speaks volumes about the depth of union support: in New York the Teamsters had led the assault against the Labor Party. Nor was it just during election campaigns that donations were received. The ACW donated $3000 to fund the *Majority* outside of any electoral activity. However, while the solid trade-union base of the CCLP could not guarantee success at the polls or provide unlimited funds, it did provide the Party with a stability and longevity that its comrades in New York could not achieve.[32]

THE PARTY AND BLACK CHICAGO

Though the party had the black AFL organizer John Riley on its executive and stood a black candidate, propaganda aimed at the sizeable black population of Chicago was, for the most part, conspicuous by its absence. William Robert Wilson ran in the mainly black second ward. Black butchers set up a Colored Club of the Cook County Labor Party in the spring of 1919. Fitzpatrick sat on the Negro Workers Advisory Board, and his supporters in the packinghouses successfully recruited many black workers. But the political work put into winning blacks to the Labor Party bore little comparison to the effort put into the trade unions generally. At election time, for example, the CFL systematically worked at winning trade-union support for its political ambitions. A resolution called on every delegate to get the 'Committee of 21' to visit their local to promote the *Majority*.[33]

In Chicago the majority of blacks had allied themselves to the Republican machine. However, this was not unconditional loyalty for in 1923 over half of the black vote deserted the Republican mayoral candidate. Black voting strength in the North had increased tremendously before the First World War. Although by 1920 blacks were only 4 per cent of Chicago's population their alliance with the Republican

Party in the 1920s did at times prove to be crucial, as was the case in the 1919 mayoral election.[34]

At a national level there was no substantial counter-argument by black organizations to the political position of Chicago's African-American community. In 1912 W. E. B. Du Bois had at first supported Theodore Roosevelt's third-party movement, but Roosevelt defeated a resolution demanding equal rights for Negroes. This had disaffected many blacks from third-party politics. It was not until the La Follette campaign of 1924 that Du Bois and his circle supported a third-party campaign. However, the majority of blacks in Chicago remained allied to the Republican machine. It was not easy to break this voting tradition in the Chicago of 1919–20, and the Cook County Labor Party was ill-equipped to do so.[35]

The problem was not that the CFL and the *Majority* opposed unity with blacks, but a failure to understand how to relate to Chicago's black working class. The belief that there was 'no Negro problem' was held for the best of motives. United union action could solve all problems, but not all African-Americans accepted the invitation to join. A large proportion of Northern-born blacks did join the union, but thousands of Southern migrants working in the stockyards were less receptive. Who was to blame for this recruiting difficulty? At best the CFL believed it was due to the naivety of blacks misled by employers and their own community 'misleaders'. The CFL did not consider the problems of discrimination that blacks faced on a daily basis from employers, landlords and some sections of the AFL. For the most part there was no consistent propaganda on the issue; except during the July race riot and the packinghouse crisis, articles directed at the black community were rare in the *Majority*.[36]

The black community had its own press, although only two of these newspapers were consistently anti-union. One of these was the *Negro Advocate*, whose virulent denunciations of the stockyard unions attracted little black interest. A more significant newspaper the *Broad Ax*, also ignored labour activity. The less influential *Chicago Whip* took an interest in CFL activity and carried a regular column by black AFL organizer John Riley. However, by the 1921–22 packinghouse strike it began ignoring union campaigns, even by black organizers. The most influential newspaper in black Chicago was the *Defender*. It had far more influence in the black community than the *Majority* or any rival black newspaper. During Fitzpatrick's election campaign the *Defender* supported Bill Thompson, and a majority of blacks voted for him. At Thompson's re-election the *Defender* trumpeted that they were the only major newspaper to support him. It reproduced the *Chicago Daily Journal* headline 'NEGROES ELECT BIG BILL'. Thompson thanked the *Defender* for its support, but denied that he had 'given undue recognition to the Colored people'. Although a majority of blacks voted Republican in the 1919 Mayoral election, 40 per cent voted for other parties; of these 24 per cent voted official Democrat.[37]

By the general election of 1920 the *Defender* had not lost any of its loyalty to the Republicans. There was much jubilation over Harding's victory and no mention of the FLP in its election analysis. However, it would be wrong to assume that the *Defender* was anti-labour. Though it often criticized organized labour it occasionally reported labour's activities with much enthusiasm. In 1918 it proclaimed 'LABOR DAY PARADE LARGEST IN HISTORY', claiming that 'Members of the Race were represented in many of the unions'.[38] The *Defender*'s opinion changed after the hot summer of 1919 exploded with race riots and steel and stockyard strikes, and it became more cautious and circumspect in its attitude to labour and class.[39]

In June 1919 the Stockyards Labor Council (SLC) intensified its recruiting campaign. On Sunday, 6 July thousands of black and white workers attended an outdoor rally. The *Majority* proclaimed: 'If the colored packinghouse worker doesn't come into the union, it isn't the fault of the Stock-Yard Labor Council.' J. W. Johnstone, Secretary of the SLC, welcomed the 'checkerboard' crowd. Kikulski also addressed the meeting, in Polish, emphasizing the need for cooperation between blacks and whites if the union was to achieve 100 per cent membership. After a speaker from the Urban League several black trade-union speakers outlined the benefits of trade unionism to the crowd. C. Ford, a black organizer for meat cutters in St Louis, claimed that there was no special colour problem, it was no different to the Irish or Russian problem. The SLC had opened the door of union membership to black workers, but if they 'didn't stampede through it then they only had themselves to blame'. The problem that some of the AFL unions practised exclusion in the stockyards did not merit a mention. The SLC made numerous attempts to recruit African-Americans, but most who enrolled in the unions were Northerners. The task proved harder than that envisaged by the *Majority*'s enthusiastic reporting.[40]

It was not until the race riot of late July that the issue of 'Race' made the front page of the *Majority*. It blamed the meatpackers (the employers) for the riots; they had discriminated against union men, sacked them and replaced them with non-union black workers. They had subsidized black politicians and religious leaders to propagandize against the unions. Notwithstanding all this, it claimed that the unions had managed to recruit large numbers of black workers. The *Majority* complained of police interference in the SLC's attempt to organize a joint demonstration of black and white workers on 6 July. The *Majority* believed that the bosses had told the police that the blacks were armed and would attack the whites. The police forced the unions to form two separate demonstrations, one black, one white, though the final rally became integrated. The *Majority* argued that union leaders tried to prevent the race riot, claiming that 'neither black nor white union men participated in the rioting, despite the lying accounts published daily by the kept press'. Locals of several black unions passed resolutions calling for unity and an end to strife. The WTUL called on black workers to join the union and offered every possible assistance in their organization.[41]

As soon as the crisis passed so did the *Majority*'s coverage of the race issue. The crisis also explains why the *Defender* became more moderate. Only a few weeks previously it had suggested labour might rule; now it stated that capital had rights that labour must respect. Workers should seek improvement in a dignified and lawful manner. Though striking iron and steel workers were mostly lawful, their actions could encourage lawlessness. Blacks were not strike-breakers, but if the AFL did not recognize their increasing importance to the economy they could feel impelled to form their own separate unions. A week later the *Defender* became even more conservative urging union men, black and white, to remember they were employees not employers, to take orders not give them, and to give a fair day's work for a fair day's pay. For a brief while in 1919 the *Defender* moved ideologically closer to labour's progressives. Now it moved closer to labour's conservatives, its trajectory caused by objective conditions, the failure of the steel strike and the Chicago race riot. Whether the progressives could have halted the *Defender*'s shift to the right is a matter of conjecture. It is possible that a different approach to the 'colour problem', might have split some of the *Defender*'s readership away from its conservative leadership.[42]

This was not an impossible task, for several thousand black workers did join the unions and a small number the CCLP. The tragedy was that the CFL approached African-American workers on the supposition that 'there is no colour problem'. Though an economistic approach that stressed class interest was, to an extent, progress for trade unionists, the *Majority* was not just a trade-union newspaper, it represented a political party. It was the political approach to black workers that was sadly lacking. Thus little effort went into breaking black Chicagoans from their commitment to the Republican Party.

LABOUR AT THE POLLS

The election of 1 April 1919 gave 55 990 votes to Fitzpatrick, or just over 8 per cent of the votes cast. Compared to the victors' vote of 37.6 per cent or the main Democrat vote of 34.5 per cent, it was not that impressive. However, Thompson's plurality was very small, a mere 21 622; he only won because the Democrats had split. Therefore the black vote was an important factor in Thompson's victory. If the CCLP had taken just 12 000 black votes then the Democrats would have won, and labour could have claimed to hold the balance of power.[43] However a more appropriate measure of labour's effectiveness is to compare the result with previous working-class party interventions in the mayoral election. In Chicago that meant the Socialist Party, whose highest vote ever had been 25 883 in 1911. In 1919 the Socialist vote remained static at 24 079. Thus the combined working-class vote in 1919 of 81 557 was the highest ever. *The intervention of the CCLP had increased the working-class vote by over three times.* Considering that the CCLP was only months old and had not taken part in the primaries, it was a creditable result.[44]

Analysis of the vote shows that the key to the vote was the working-class nature of the wards and their proximity to workplaces. Fitzpatrick's vote averaged 8 per cent, but it was higher in working-class wards. Thus he got 16 per cent in the 29th ward (adjacent to the stockyards), but only 2 per cent in the 2nd. In 16 out of 35 wards he received more than 8 per cent. These included the traditionally Democratic working-class 5th, 29th and 30th wards, all located in the areas of the stockyards where many new immigrants lived. As some workers in these wards did not have the franchise or register to vote, the result may have underestimated labour's support. The most successful aldermanic candidate was Ida Fursman, the only Labor Party woman to remain on the ballot, who polled 5212 votes, far more than any other CCLP aldermanic candidate. Only in ten wards did the party get less than 7 per cent; this occurred for the most part where there was no aldermanic candidate, or where ward organization was weak. The party did well in wards that were mainly working class, with substantial immigrant populations and Democrat majorities. These were also areas where the party had held large rallies and effective campaigns.[45]

THE AFTERMATH

The mayoral election of 1919 proved to be the high point of labour party voting in Chicago. It was not just voting numbers that declined, so did union support and finance. With one or two exceptions the party's general trajectory was downwards. As outlined above, the Constitutional Convention campaign, which failed dismally, undermined ward organization. Fitzpatrick and Walsh had good reasons for emphasizing the importance of Con Con. They feared the introduction to Illinois of legislation similar to the Kansas Industrial Bill, which made striking to all intents and purposes illegal. The poor result probably reflected the fact that most of Chicago's workers did not take such a threat that seriously.[46]

The ability to stand in the yearly municipal elections declined, as did ward organization and union support. This was paralleled by serious defeats in the stockyards and steel. No doubt Gompers' stand against independent politics and his advocacy of a militant non-partisan campaign in early 1920 deterred many union activists from maintaining their commitment to the new party. It is also probable that the resources and exertion required for day-to-day trade-union survival reduced active support to passive loyalty. Many union constitutions forbade the use of funds for political purposes. This explains the difference in number between those who supported the Party officially and those who actually gave money: the former number was far larger. By the election of 1920, in spite of the launching of a national party, the Party had made little progress.

Parley P. Christensen, the FLP presidential candidate, was hardly known in Chicago. Eugene Debs, the Socialist Party candidate had a far wider reputation. This added up to humiliation at the polls, with only 4381 voting for the FLP presidential candidate. Only a year earlier the FLP had outstripped the Socialists at the polls in Chicago; now the tables had turned. However, there was little for the Socialists to celebrate either, for Debs had won 13.2 per cent of the vote in 1912. In the 1919 mayoral election the joint CCLP and Socialist vote had been 11.6 per cent: now it was only 6.6 per cent of the presidential vote. For the FLP the situation was worse, for its share was only 0.6 per cent of the vote.[47]

ETHNIC AND CATHOLIC VOTING

Some historians maintain that the Catholic Church has had a conservative influence on sections of the working class. In particular workers of Irish, Polish and Italian descent are cited as a barrier to independent political activity. In Chicago Americans of 'native origin' were in the minority, and the Catholic Church accounted for over half of regular churchgoers. The Irish also had substantial influence in the Democratic Party of Chicago, and to a lesser extent so did the Poles and Italians. However, it is not the case that between 1919 and 1920 these groups were straightforwardly pro-Democratic, anti-Republican and anti-FLP. Moreover, before 1919 it was even less the case and ethnic attitudes towards the main parties and the trade unions were not always that different from the rest of the population nationally.[48]

In national elections, ethnic voting patterns in Chicago did not differ from national trends to the same extent as they did in local elections. In other words, local party loyalties did not automatically transfer to national candidates. Although many Poles came from a peasant background and were unskilled, unions in the stockyards did recruit the newcomers. At times between 10 to 15 per cent of Chicago's Poles voted Socialist. Though the Socialist Party never built a mass base in 'Polonia' this was not particularly unique to Polish areas of Chicago.[49]

A substantial number of Poles consistently supported the Democrats. The Democrats' opposition to prohibition became interpreted as support for Catholicism. Church leaders also preferred the Democrats because of the growing anti-Catholicism of Republicans. However, the Poles, like most Americans, took more interest in national elections than local ones and, to a lesser extent, were affected by national trends at general elections. Thus many Poles voted for Roosevelt and Debs in 1912. The bitterness felt at the strife between worker and employer affected them just as much as any other worker. This is demonstrated by the number of Poles who voted for the Socialists at the general election of 1912. Edward Kantowicz noted:

The Socialists, despite the usual opposition from the Catholic church and the Polish nationalist leaders, gained almost 11 per cent of the Polish vote, comparable to Debs' 12.5 percent city wide. In some Polish precincts around the steel mills of South Chicago, the Democratic vote dipped to 30 percent and the Debs' tally rose to nearly 20 percent.

There was no automatic Polish allegiance to the Democrats, for in 1912 Poles had been suspicious of Wilson. In 1916 war conditions swung them behind him, but in 1920 the tide of 'normalcy' saw Harding receive almost as much Polish support as Cox.[50]

Nor was it just at a national level that a substantial number of Poles voted Republican. In the 1915 Mayoral election the 45.9 per cent who voted for Thompson played their part in electing a Republican. However, Thompson so alienated his Polish supporters with his views on the League of Nations that in 1919 his share of their vote dropped below 14 per cent. Fitzpatrick got 16 per cent of the Polish city-wide vote, double the percentage of the electorate taken as a whole. Fitzpatrick did particularly well in two wards near the stockyards, with 27.5 per cent of the Polish vote in the 4th and 18.7 per cent in the 29th. In the 17th ward only 8.8 per cent of Poles voted for Fitzpatrick, yet it was here that the CCLP stood the Polish journalist Anielewski. This suggests that Poles did not vote purely on ethnic lines, as Fitzpatrick had performed better in wards without Polish candidates. In other words, for many Poles class was a more important factor in voting behaviour than national origin. Of course the majority of Poles had voted Democrat, but in 1919 this was not inevitable. Indeed, in some instances Poles gave more support to working-class organizations than the population around them.[51]

THE IRISH

The Irish had strong associations with the Democratic Party in Chicago, and in wards where the Irish predominated they usually made up the majority of its committeemen. However, the Republicans had their share of Irish activists too on the City Committee. It was a close race between the Irish and native Protestants as to who dominated with the Irish having the narrow edge. In the Democratic Party the Irish drew strength from alliances with other Catholics, such as Poles and Italians. This alliance should have made the Party invincible; if it had not split in the 1919 mayoral election the total of united Democrat votes would have been 50.5 per cent, far in excess of Thompson's 37.6 per cent.[52]

However, it would be a mistake to assume that Chicago voting patterns were solidly Democratic by 1919. Catholic voters were not a monolith, nor were they voting fodder for any particular party. Indeed, only four years earlier Thompson had got a majority that had included many Catholic voters. Between 1915 and 1919 many Polish voters swung away from the Republican Party, or at least from Thompson in particular. For some Irish the pendulum briefly swung the other way as they became disillusioned with Wilson's foreign policy. In Chicago, Irish-American meetings drew crowds of between 40 000 and 70 000, ready to attack Wilson's administration if it failed to grant self-determination to Ireland. Fitzpatrick and his supporters, aware of growing Irish discontent, campaigned vigorously around the issue of self-determination. In the stockyards a meeting of 8000 voted unanimously to demand recognition of the Irish Republic. A black butcher workmen's local passed a similar resolution. Walsh also procured Irish support, placing an article in favour of Fitzpatrick's mayoral campaign in *America*, a weekly Catholic review. The *Irish Press* of Philadelphia also had an article on the campaign, accompanied by a picture of Fitzpatrick.[53]

Relations between the CCLP and various Irish groupings were friendly. Fitzpatrick was prominent on the platforms of the Friends of Irish Freedom. The Chicago Local Council of Friends of Irish Freedom endorsed the action of the Farmer Labor Party for having included in its platform a demand for recognition of the Republic of Ireland. De Valera also endorsed the Labor Party. There is no evidence of widespread hostility from Irish Nationalists or the Catholic Church. Indeed, if there was any hostility it was often reserved for Wilson. However, friendliness towards the FLP did not necessarily transform into votes. Those Irish concerned with the Nationalist cause were seeking great-power intervention on Ireland's behalf. The Democrats were refusing to provide it, and the fledgling FLP, though willing, lacked the wherewithal to do so. The logic of this for the Friends of Irish Freedom was that the Republicans were the best party for Irish Independence.[54]

The *Majority* claimed that the Nationalist Irish voted Republican in the 1920 Presidential election to revenge themselves on Wilson. Less than a quarter of Chicago's population voted Democrat in that year's presidential election. The Polish did vote disproportionately Democrat (50.4 per cent in all), but this was a major drop from the 70.5 per cent who voted Democrat in 1916. Thus the Polish figures prove that many of Chicago's Catholic voters switched allegiance in 1920. The switch may have been greater among the Irish as they were far more dissatisfied with the Democrats' foreign policy than the Poles. Nonetheless national issues affected Poles to almost the same degree as most Americans. It is clear, from the above, that immigrant or Catholic workers were no more hostile to the FLP than workers of different origin or religion. Indeed, in some areas the opposite was the case. Thus the failure of the party had more to do with its general inability to win workers as a whole than with its appeal to specific religious or ethnic groupings. However, this was not the case with black workers where the failure had far deeper and more specific roots.[55]

CONCLUSIONS

Though labour's vote in Chicago was not as impressive as that in Seattle the mayoral result was still a reasonably good start. Electoral support was more substantial in areas where the unions were strongest. But to enthusiastic supporters with high expectations the vote received was less than satisfactory. The vote could possibly have been higher, but many factors militated against it. Fitzpatrick dominated the CFL, but at the local level this did not always turn into real commitment. For even the pro-Labor Party Illinois miners were reluctant to break union rules and pay official dues to the party. The pro-Gompers' newspaper, the *Unionist*, had more resources than the *Majority* and was able to issue vast numbers at election time. The *Majority* did not have a large circulation and never became a daily newspaper. Thus the CFL's influence never spread much further than its immediate activists. The political machines that the CCLP faced were, to an extent, as powerful as Tammany. The CCLP did not face one powerful party machine but two. Unlike the Seattle experience, none of the major parties disintegrated. The Seattle FLP had only faced a well-organized Republican party, having won over much of the Democrats' membership and resources. If the CCLP had been capable of more input across the whole of Chicago, it might have been able to get even more votes. Nonetheless in areas where the unions had influence the party did reasonably well. This raises the question as to why the CCLP was unable to relate to these areas of strength and build on them?

Instead, after the mayoral election, the Party went into decline; several factors explain this and one was the Party's organic link to organized workers. In concrete terms that link meant local union officials who were loyal to the party. It was they who turned trade-union loyalty of the workers they represented into political support. However, the loyalty of these officials was first and foremost to the union. When the time required to build the party conflicted with union demands it was the latter that came first. This was not always a political decision. For many it was a pragmatic decision forced on them by the need to defend union organization. In particular for W. Z. Foster and his allies, industrial unionism was far more important than building the CCLP; whatever the motive, syndicalist and progressive trade unionists behaved alike for different reasons. The obligations of party officials to union duties reinforced the sectionalist aspect of trade unionism at the expense of the political.

At the same time Chicago's 'federated unionism' was unable to include most of the unskilled. The CFL did try to compensate for this by having organizing campaigns in steel and meatpacking. This diverted resources and personnel away from building the Party. This over-dependence on the workplace and the lack of any community-based machine meant that at times of struggle the Party took second place. The *Majority* did not ignore workplace struggles; it regularly covered strikes. When it came to African-Americans, the CCLP did not ignore them as workers. It was in the field of community politics and civil rights that the party failed. This was a sort of unconscious syndicalism by those who believed in political action.

Fitzpatrick challenged such syndicalism in its more open form, for instance forcing Foster to put Labor Party propaganda in the Steel Bulletin. However, for the most part, trade union activity and politics remained separate. The progressives were aware that a stronger union movement would help overcome divisions in the working class and help build the FLP. In practice this was proved by the CCLP's better results in wards where unions and community coincided. Unfortunately the unions' campaigns to extend and generalize membership were defeated. Of course the defeats were partly the result of the narrow craft unionism of the national leaders of the AFL, but that does not change the fact that these defeats weakened Chicago labour. Enormous effort and expense went into industrial campaigns that affected far more workers than the April electoral campaign. Industrial defeat followed the electoral failures of 1919. Having failed to make electoral capital out of the 1919 election, industrial defeat undermined the confidence of Chicago workers to pursue independent political activity even further. One defeat had reinforced another.

In Seattle the electoral road opened in the wake of the industrial defeat. Bitterness at defeat channelled into the desire to win justice at the polls. As the following chapter on Seattle will demonstrate, local conditions there combined to make a belated electoral intervention very successful. In Chicago, labour was aware of its electoral weakness but failed to win an industrial battle that could have strengthened it politically. In 1912 and 1919, working-class parties had won significant minority ethnic support, with the vote concentrated in areas where organized workplaces predominated. In wards next to the packing-houses and steel mills, community and workplace had merged to give labour a stronger political impact. By the end of 1920 unionization had suffered a serious setback in these areas, and labour's vote dropped. With Chicago's labour weakened by industrial and electoral defeats, its ability to appear as a credible alternative also weakened. Neither was it the case, as shown above, that Chicago's Catholics were hostile to the CFL and the CCLP. But with prospects for change diminishing in 1920 for some Irish and Poles, overseas national aspirations became the imperative. Therefore industrial defeat became a serious blow, not only to trade-union organization, but also to the possibility of spreading workers' independent politics. Perhaps at a more fortuitous time Fitzpatrick's vote could have been the beginning of a growing movement, but events conspired to see a 'good start' stall and lead nowhere.

4 A Long and Winding Road: Seattle 1918–20

Seattle labour was the last of the three movements to form a labour party, yet electorally it was the most successful. In the Fall of 1920 the party averaged 31 per cent of the vote in King County, the electoral area for Seattle, pushing the Democrats into third place. For one historian of the Seattle Farmer Labor Party (FLP) its failure to transform itself into a party capable of winning a majority is central to his analysis. Splits in the trade-union leadership and the problem of the alienation of Catholic and anti-prohibition voters are cited as major reasons for electoral failure. Unemployment and the open-shop campaign, as explanations, receive less attention. This approach will not be dealt with in specific detail at this point; rather this chapter will commence with a different line of enquiry: why did the FLP in Seattle do so well?[1]

The answer to this crucial question will also add to a deeper understanding of the successes and failures of the Chicago and New York labour movements. This chapter will also evaluate how it was possible for a party, only a few months old, to do so well at the polls, and why it did not do even better. To do that it will also be necessary to consider factors beyond the control of labour.

Though the Seattle Central Labor Council (SCLC) was the last of the three city central bodies to form a labour party, it was no stranger to independent political action. It had a tradition of supporting union men for local council and municipal elections. Even before the first FLP candidate stood, Seattle had labour councillors. Part of the reason for this success was the specific nature of Seattle municipal elections. Since 1911 elections took place on a non-partisan basis; this meant that candidates stood as individuals rather than as party nominees. Parties could not campaign for, or finance, candidates for mayoral or council elections. However, it was no secret who organized labour or who big business supported. Also the procedure for nomination was far easier than that of New York or Chicago; thousands of signatures were not required to get on the ballot. This meant that Seattle labour candidates did not suffer the kind of obstruction faced by New York and Chicago candidates.[2]

From 1918 onwards labour candidates also had the support of a daily newspaper, the *Seattle Union Record*. However, it was not until the general election of 1920 that labour stood its first truly independent candidates. Before then the FLP supporters utilized the King County Triple Alliance (KCTA) – an alliance of farmer, railroad brotherhoods and SCLC organizations. The FLP supporters dominated the KCTA but did not operate independently of it, preferring to wait for the Washington State Federation of Labor's (WSFL) endorsement of the FLP.[3]

Thus the most successful central labour body in electoral terms was the last to form its own party. It was not until the Fall of 1920 that the Seattle party became truly independent. The State Federation's rejection, in 1919, of plans to form a statewide party caused the SCLC to delay the launching of the new party. Instead they contented themselves with working inside the KCTA. Though they failed to win any positions in the school board or port elections, the results encouraged them to enter the mayoral and council elections in early 1920. The main thrust of the campaign was SCLC Secretary James Duncan's candidacy for mayor. The SCLC and the KCTA supported Duncan and other labour candidates. However, there was not complete unity. Robert Hesketh, a conservative council incumbent, refused the KCTA endorsement. The Associated Industries, the major employers' organization in Seattle and advocate of the open shop, praised Hesketh and offered their support. Hesketh wanted to distance himself from Duncan and his more radical supporters, objecting to their militant ideas and their commitment to prohibition. Whatever the differences between Duncan and Hesketh, the *Record* treated all labour candidates equally. It campaigned for all of them as labour and people's candidates.[4]

The centrepiece of the campaign for the SCLC and *Record* was Duncan's campaign for mayor, though not under a labour party banner. However, Duncan was clearly identified as a political labour candidate, unlike previous union candidates. He suffered unprecedented attacks from the Seattle press which accused him of not having supported the US war effort. Other articles linked Duncan with the Industrial Workers of the World (IWW), and predicted that Duncan's election would lead to the 'Bolshevization' of Seattle with repeated general strikes, class war and the 'nationalization of women'. In spite of all this Duncan polled 34 053 votes – the largest total that any defeated candidate for mayor had ever received. The victor, Hugh Caldwell, received 50 850 votes, the largest vote ever for a winning candidate. The more conservative Hesketh got over 38 000 votes and a place on the council. Why had Duncan garnered a substantial vote, but finished behind the two winning labour council candidates?[5]

Duncan complained that the trade unionists around Hesketh had deliberately not pulled their weight. If this was the case then they had influenced 4000 votes at the most. Even if the votes had gone to Duncan he would still have gone down to defeat, albeit with a larger vote. However, before analysing the reasons for defeat, it is necessary to consider how Duncan and his allies mobilized their vote. For though it was less than Hesketh's, it was in percentage terms more substantial than Fitzpatrick's vote for mayor in Chicago, or Dudley Field Malone's total for governor in New York. Duncan had defeated the Associated Industries (AI) candidate for mayor, Fitzgerald, in the three-horse primary. But against a single candidate, in the final round, he suffered defeat. However, the question remains as to how he did so well? To answer this it is necessary to detail the campaign organization.

THE CAMPAIGN

The response to Duncan's candidacy by the mainstream press and the AI was a massive wave of red-baiting. A vote for Duncan was an anti-American vote. The AI warned 'loyal Americans' not to be misled by reds, and urged them to register to vote and, if necessary, become naturalized. The *Record* responded by also urging voter registration.[6]

On 27 October 1919 the *Record* reported labour's response to this propaganda. The SCLC had formed a 'TRUE AMERICANISM CLUB'. The club challenged the idea of 'autocratic capital' or that any section of the public had a monopoly on patriotism. The 'True Americanism' campaign looked to the Declaration of Independence and the ideals of Jefferson and Lincoln. Members would pledge themselves to take part in the 'government of our country and insist on honesty in its political affairs'. They would campaign for just compensation for the efficiency gained in shops, schools and factories, defending themselves against industrial autocracy. They would fight for an industrial system under which all would have equal opportunity and none special privilege. However, loyalty to the USA did not mean they would approve and defend industrial autocracy or any other evils that existed 'within our country'.[7]

The *Record* reported that 300 officers of Seattle unions endorsed the Club. The Club urged workers to unite in political action, filling offices with people who understood the real meaning of 'True Americanism'.

Thus the response of the SCLC to the AI's offensive was not based on class terms but on a 'true' definition of 'Americanism'. This was not a call for workers' control and was not equatable with Bolshevism, and was less radical than the programme of the FLP. Indeed it was ambivalent enough for the Republican Governor of Washington, Louis F. Hart, to add his name to the membership roll as he prepared to use troops against striking miners. This campaign was the centre-piece of the SCLC efforts right up to the elections. District 10 of the United Mine Workers of America (UMWA) enthusiastically sup-ported the Americanism campaign, placing large advertisements in the *Record* and holding rallies on the issue. The *Record* reported that 4000 attended one rally, with a thousand of those present joining the club. Ten thousand buttons were produced to encourage support for 'True Americanism'.[8]

In the middle of the campaign the Centralia tragedy occurred. A union hall in the Washington town of Centralia was fired on as an American Legion parade marched by. IWW members returned fire killing four marchers. This led to the arrest of several Wobblies (IWW members) and the lynching of the IWW war veteran Wesley Everest. The effect throughout Washington was electrifying, with many con-vinced that bloody revolution was about to start. The *Record* tried to present what it believed to be the truth about the Centralia incident. This was too much for the federal government, which moved in and seized its press. The *Record* survived by moving to a friendly local printer, but its circulation, the number of editions per day and actual size of the paper were cut losing advertising revenue.[9]

Centralia was a turning point with much middle-class progressive support becoming frightened by hitherto working-class allies. Work-ing-class progressives, who had already shifted to the right due to the defeat of the general strike, feared losing these allies. The *Record* wooed them even harder, waving the Stars and Stripes on its editorial page, declaring it was the flag of their country which was the best on the face of the globe. It was their ambition to have the best and most honest officials serve such a great country: 'That is why the Triple Alliance was formed.' No gang of profiteering anarchists would take the flag away from labour's progressives.[10]

The *Record* hardly had time to catch its breath between the Centralia crisis and labour's intervention in the school board and port elections. John A. McCorkle, Triple Alliance candidate for port commissioner, told a packed Grand Theatre that he accepted that 'True Patriotism' was a platform issue. He defined 'True Americanism' as free speech, free assemblage and a free press. He attacked the bankrupt condition of the two old parties, referring to the need for a new party, but considering he was a founder member of the Seattle FLP its profile remained low. The *Record*, urging support for labour's school board candidates, boasted 'ALLIANCE NOMINEES ARE AMERICAN BORN'. However, the next day it struck a more class-conscious note with a special Sunday edition appealing directly to teachers. Though the Alliance did not win any positions on the School Board, its candidates averaged over 18 000 votes with the winners averaging over 27 000. Since it was the Triple Alliance's (TA) first major election campaign, and considering the atmosphere of anti-labour hysteria and the shutting down of the *Record*'s plant, it was a reasonable result. A few days later the *Record* reported that the TA had made further advances. McCorkle had narrowed the gap between the TA and the victor with 17 773 votes compared to the business-backed candidate's 22 345.[11]

On 13 January 1920 the *Record* announced that Duncan had filed for mayor. He stood on a non-partisan platform pledged to defend publicly owned utilities. The next day the paper praised the introduction of Prohibition and men like Duncan who had worked for it. Duncan told a 200-strong meeting of members of the Cooperative of Food Producers that the Seattle general strike would not have been necessary if he had been mayor. They rewarded him with a unanimous endorsement. In response to allegations that he had opposed America's war effort, Duncan replied that once the USA had entered the War he had argued that workers must unite behind the President. It was true that Seattle labour had tried to prevent war, but once it had started it had forgotten such differences. Short also defended Duncan, claiming he would be a 'good business Mayor for all the people', unlike other candidates who would be good business mayors for businessmen only.[12]

The next day the *Record* reproduced wartime articles from the *Times* praising the SCLC on raising the Stars and Stripes on its flagpole and Duncan for urging workers to get behind the President. Proof that he had purchased Liberty Bonds and War Savings Stamps was provided. Meanwhile the 'True Americanism' campaign continued. The *Record* greeted Primary day with the banner headline 'Vote as Lincoln Would' and a list of labour candidates. Duncan defeated the AI favourite, but was beaten into second place by Caldwell, who received 28 518 votes to Duncan's 26 040 and Fitzgerald's 21 419. In the council elections Hesketh polled highest among the labour candidates with 33 454. Duncan was in the final round, and the campaigning started again.[13]

With Fitzgerald out of the race it was not enough to keep repeating the same 'True American' message. More importantly, the business vote which had split in the primary had united behind Caldwell. New tunes were needed and attempts to woo Fitzgerald's former supporters began. Siren noises were made at business; the *Record* proclaimed, 'Businessman Is For Duncan'. It noted that M. A. Griffin, Manager of the Mutual Laundry, was voting for Duncan. The article did not mention labour politics, nor that the Mutual Laundry was a labour-run cooperative. The *Record* presented Duncan as the respectable candidate, reporting that the police at Headquarters had given him sustained applause. Smaller articles noted union and women's organizations' support, but the *Record* put the main emphasis on Duncan's appeal to business and the need to clean up municipal government. This was not radical labour politics. The issue of race did not play a prominent part in the campaign. But Duncan's final campaign meeting took place at the Afro-American Hall 'where leading colored citizens assured him of a virtually solid vote from the people of their race'. African-Americans were less than one per cent of Seattle's population, and whether their leaders could deliver this vote is questionable.[14]

ORGANIZING THE CAMPAIGN

Though the campaign made little mention of class struggle and no mention of the Labor Party, the votes won came, mainly, from the organized working class and those who lived in the working-class districts of Seattle. If Duncan and his followers had not made the election a matter of extreme class polarization, their opponents certainly had. Duncan's claims of moderation had cut no ice with them, and they had treated him as a dangerous anti-war radical. It was quite clear where the divide between the candidates lay; it was not a matter of ideology or rhetoric, it was in their support. Only the *Record* supported Duncan; the rest of Seattle's press supported Caldwell. One was the candidate of business, the other of labour. It is unlikely that the *Record*'s attempt at respectability won many voters. So how was it that, in spite of such vilification, Duncan was able to do far better than labour candidates in Chicago and New York? After all, they had not run class-based campaigns either. The answer is not located in the ideological nature of the campaigns but in the local leadership's ability to build an effective campaigning machine and in the strengths and weaknesses of the opposition. In Chicago the two main party machines remained solid. With blacks supporting Thompson and some immigrants either supporting or forced to support the Democrats, the Cook County FLP found it difficult to appeal beyond a minority of class-conscious workers. In New York the American Labor Party (ALP) encountered the barrier of union leaders committed to Tammany. In the end it was the Tammany forces, with Gompers' help, that came out on top.[15]

In comparison winning electoral support was easier for Duncan and the SCLC. Firstly, the Democrats were a spent force; and secondly, the Republicans had moved so far to the right that some progressives in their ranks became friendly to labour. Duncan and other labour candidates did not face a Socialist opposition. The Seattle Socialist Party (SP) was too weak to stand candidates. The electoral process in Seattle, with its non-partisan organization system, was also more open. In addition the official labour movement of Washington State and Seattle had supported Duncan's campaign with even the conservative William Short in support. Thus conditions were more favourable; nonetheless the vote had to be won. Electorally the Seattle labour movement had better organization than its counterparts in New York or Chicago. The *Seattle Union Record* provided a ready-made propaganda machine, committed 100 per cent to the Labor Party. Of course, on its own the *Record* would not have been enough, but there is no doubt that it was central to the whole campaign. It did not simply print propaganda; it provided information on how and where to vote, the location of meetings and identified precinct organizations needing help. It was a practical aid to raising votes. However, without organization on the ground it is unlikely that the *Record* would have been so successful in its urging of a labour vote. For the bulk of the *Record*'s funding came from union donations. The unions and the *Record* were an essential partnership and were an important contribution to the success of the Duncan election campaign. Grass-roots organization was also central to the gathering of the vote at the district and precinct levels.

As stated earlier, the SCLC delayed the practical building of the FLP until they could obtain WSFL endorsement. Although the FLP did not at first operate as a clearly defined and separate body, it did form a King County FLP Committee that included the Pomona Grange, the SCLC and the railwaymen. The party consisted of labour, unions, granges and precinct parties. Affiliated with the King County Triple Alliance it operated as a division of the county organization. Individuals who pledged themselves to the aims of the Labor Party were allowed to join. Originally only AFL unions could affiliate, but later the rail brotherhoods and all other unaffiliated unions became eligible to join. Thus the Labor Party did not operate openly as an electoral machine, but under the cover of the KCTA.[16]

The KCTA had first built its electoral machine to intervene in the school board elections, organizing 65 precincts by late September 1919. Though the schools and port campaigns failed to elect any labour candidates, the FLP and the *Record* gained valuable experience and credibility. In particular labour was able to identify with first-generation Americans kept from registering to vote by demands that they produce their parents' naturalization papers. Rectified in late 1920, the change came too late to benefit the TA or FLP. However, immediate success on the issue of opening hours for registration meant that more people voted as a result. These earlier efforts of labour paid off, feeding into enthusiasm for the Duncan campaign.[17]

The alliance also organized Duncan's campaign for mayor. His own Hope Lodge of the Machinists Union endorsed him overwhelmingly. Late January and February saw a number of local unions pledge support to Duncan. These included the 3000-strong Carpenters Local 131 and the influential Boilermakers Local No. 104, as well as a broad range of union locals such as the Teamsters and Locomotive Firemen and Engineers. The Building Trades Council also endorsed Duncan. Women of the Seattle Card and Label League formed a Women's Duncan Campaign Committee; many were wives of leading Seattle trade unionists.[18]

Duncan beat Fitzgerald in the primary and a campaign ensued for the run-off. The task now became far harder as he faced the united opposition behind Caldwell. The SCLC and the KCTA after four months of electioneering had only two weeks to prepare for the final mayoral election. However, the SCLC recommenced its campaign with enthusiasm, picking up further support from the unions. The Laundry and Dye Workers Union endorsed Duncan, supplying him with the use of a bus for the campaign. All paid officials of the Mill Carpenters Local No. 338 were put at Duncan's disposal. Duncan, like Dudley Field Malone in New York, attracted the support of progressive women. However, the reasons were somewhat different. Malone won support because of his stand on Women's Suffrage, Duncan for his support of Prohibition. Mrs Mary Walker, Chairman of the Women's Duncan Campaign Committee, explained they were supporting Duncan partly in recognition of his pioneer work for Prohibition. Though the FLP did not electioneer openly most of the activists involved were from unions that supported the FLP. Women had separate organization, with the hard core supplied by the 100 or so activists of the Women's Trade Union Card and Label League. William Short of the State Federation spoke in support of Duncan; however, the ideological thrust was not of labourism but of Americanism. The emphasis was on voting for James Duncan rather than supporting a party, but nonetheless the campaign's strength was the Seattle unions. [19]

It is quite clear that by the spring of 1920 the Seattle Labor Party had not defined membership of a labour party, either in ideological or practical terms. Its strategy was to work inside the existing union machine and to hope to capture it for labour party activity. This meant that the more conservative unionists, who emphasized 'True Americanism', spearheaded the Duncan Campaign rather than those who believed in the ideology of labourism. Of course grass-roots activists were committed to independent labour politics. Nor did the 'respectable' Duncan campaign assuage conservatives like Hesketh who did their best to distance themselves from, or even undermine, it. Duncan's mayoral campaign also failed to create any permanent independent political culture of substance. It was not until the 1920 general election that the FLP campaigned under its own name. The reason for the delay was that Duncan and his allies were unable to capture the Washington State Federation of Labor. When they finally got state-wide official support it was through the state Triple Alliance. It became, almost by sleight of hand, the Farmer Labor Party. Thus the FLP did not result from the mass political conversion of workers, but by the capturing of the union organizations. Though the 1920 WSFL convention rejected Gompers' Non-Partisan Policy, it did not endorse the FLP. Not feeling strong enough to take a decision on how to intervene in the 1920 general election, the issue was put to the Triple Alliance. Though not a clear cut victory for the FLP it kept alive the hopes of those who wanted a State Federation backed labour party. The fight for a labour party had moved to another arena.[20]

To decide which candidates labour and progressives would support, four conventions assembled in Yakima in mid-July: the Triple Alliance, the Railwaymen's Welfare League, the Non-Partisan League (NPL) and the Committee of 48. The TA was the biggest of these with 250 delegates. In spite of a brilliant speech against by Short, it endorsed the third party by 149 to 57. The Committee of 48 also backed the third party, but the Railwaymen decided to enter the Republican primaries. The TA agreed that the question of affiliation to the FLP be put to a referendum. The secretary of the WSFL, L. W. Buck, boosted the FLP publicly, urging independent political action and non-involvement with the other parties. The mood swung in favour of the FLP when the NPL reversed its original decision to only enter Republican primaries. Local organizations could support the FLP if they wanted to, or where they had already failed in Republican primaries.[21]

The decision of the NPL gave the new party added momentum. Short gave up his opposition and called for its support at the Washington State Miners' convention. State Chairman David C. Coates claimed that months of hard work had paid off and that interest in the FLP had mushroomed state-wide. The new party had got the break it wanted, but by a circuitous route. Nonetheless it demonstrated that there was strong antipathy to the AFL's old non-partisan road. However it was not the WSFL that had endorsed the FLP, but the Triple Alliance. This proved to be a major weakness.

FORMING THE PARTY

A union referendum decided by 6862 to 174 to end the TA in favour of the FLP. Coates, Chairman of the TA, claimed that the FLP had 20 000 members state-wide. This was achieved by transforming TA membership into party membership. Short was worried by the speed of events and of losing control, but he could do nothing to stop the parties' growing support. Coates announced a state FLP convention and asked the old TA locals to rename themselves FLPs. However the Committee of 48 and the NPL kept their own identity but acted in concert for the elections. It would appear that the TA had captured itself, but it did mean that in urban areas it could begin to build independent party organizations. Though it was not the WSFL that was endorsing the new party, the capturing of the TA and the alliance of the farmer and progressive organizations gave the state FLP strength and credibility. The coalition was invaluable. It made it very difficult for Short to openly oppose the party. Indeed Short even agreed to go on a speaking tour for the FLP.[22]

Now for the first time there was open organization of the King County Labor Party. Phil J. Pearl, a former Socialist Party activist, became the elected chairman of the new organization and Stuart A. Rice its secretary. From its new position of strength the SCLC felt able to campaign more rigorously, rebuking any union organization endorsing candidates of the old parties. It urged all its affiliates to endorse the new party and to work for FLP candidates. During the general election campaign it sent speakers to every local union meeting that took place.

The ideology of the campaign was also different in tone and content to that of the Duncan mayoral fight. 'True Americanism' took a back seat as more orthodox FLP policies, based on Labor's Fourteen Points, came to the fore. The victory at Yakima had given the progressives the confidence to relegate the policies of the SCLC conservatives to the background. The progressives had emerged reasonably unscathed from the effects of the red scare following the general strike and Centralia, and they regained control of the SCLC's political orientation. Having survived the onslaught there was no longer any need to make concessions to 'Americanism'.[23]

As the 1920 General Election approached, the FLP state convention nominated Robert Bridges, a progressive well known and respected for his work on the Seattle port commission, for governor. C. J. France, less well known and also involved in the port commission, received the Senate nomination. James Duncan, the only trade unionist, well known but perhaps not for reasons to his advantage, stood for the sixth congressional district. The FLP presidential candidate Parley P. Christensen, nominated nationally, was hardly known at all in Washington. Though the campaign was clearly a labour party one, emphasis was placed on the personality of Bridges and his reputation as a commissioner for the port of Seattle. Nonetheless the unions were the bedrock of the campaign machine.[24]

THE FARMER LABOR PARTY CAMPAIGN

Short called for support for 'Bridges and the ticket', and for unity up to the election. Short demonstrated more enthusiasm for Bridges than for the FLP, but he could not admit this openly, and formally he supported the whole ticket. However, the *Record* made no mention of any division inside the campaign. The grass roots were more enthusiastic than Short, and Carpenters' Local 131 suggested that a trophy be awarded to the local that most successfully recruited to the FLP. Later 131 announced the formation of an FLP club, with open meetings every Thursday evening, excellent entertainment and the best political speakers. A 'Railwaymen's Branch' of the FLP was created; however, for the most part activities and fund raising were directly under local union auspices. Union involvement in the campaign was diverse, and the three winners of 131's competition were the Auto-Mechanics, the Locomotive Engineers and Firemen and the Stage Employe's (*sic*).[25]

Volunteers were sought for the campaign, and Green Lake district claimed it had 100 activists. District organization for the King County FLP campaign was formed with a separate women's organizing committee. Seattle was divided into 25 districts, each with a manager. Managers appointed precinct captains, and each district was responsible for distributing literature, raising money, holding meetings and canvassing. A mass meeting of streetcar men endorsed 'All FLP candidates' and pledged themselves to work for the campaign. University students formed an FLP club; 50 members elected officers and covered the University district with literature in the run-up to the election. The SCLC gave permission to business agent Charles Doyle to organize automobiles, decked with pro-FLP banners made out of $100-worth of muslin donated by working men, for election day. Two days before the election the *Record* led with a massive front-page headline urging 'Vote Bridges and the Third Party Ticket'. Like Short, the *Record* believed that Bridges was the party's main asset. Just in case the headlines had created over-confidence, the next day's editorial warned readers not to be complacent; they needed to turn out at the polls.[26]

CAMPAIGN ISSUES

The FLP campaign platform was not a radical one, and was not dissimilar to progressive demands of the previous decade. It reflected labour's specific concerns, with calls for free speech, the right of free assembly and all other rights guaranteed under the constitution. It also called for the repeal of the Criminal Syndicalist Act and the release of all those imprisoned under it. It demanded the right to collective bargaining and to strike unhampered by injunction. It also asked that labour be given a 'just share in the management of industry'. A State Labor Department was advocated, 'for the purpose of efficiency and economy, and extending and strengthening of laws enacted for the protection of the workers.' These demands were specific to labour, but certainly were not couched in terms of workers' control. The rest of the platform dealt with a variety of issues that would appeal to progressives. These included: public ownership of public utilities and natural resources under democratic management; election reforms and home rule for cities; proportional representation; and support for the Bone Dry Law, a traditional progressive demand in Washington State. Better support for schools, especially in rural areas, with more democratic control and management was advocated. The most radical plank in the whole platform was opposition to compulsory military training. However, the platform was less defensive than that for the mayoral campaign, with the emphasis on a programme of moderate reform that appealed to workers and beyond. It reflected a political shift leftwards, not because of a higher level of workers' struggle, but due to Duncan and his allies temporarily gaining the upper hand in directing State Federation political policy.[27]

Short, the WSFL President, did not mention the FLP platform as he addressed its mass rallies. Instead he concentrated on defeating his enemies and electing Bridges. Thus he directed all his fire at the Republican Governor, Louis F. Hart, attacking him as an enemy of labour and a friend of the employer. Short gave two reasons for voting for Bridges: the first that he would make the best governor; the second that if he was not elected, the worst possible governor would win office. Bridges, Duncan and France made wider-ranging speeches than Short. They attacked excess profits in industry while one-third of all families did not earn basic subsistence. Bridges offered his support to rail-workers, and attacked the Esch-Cummins Bill which had returned the railroads to private ownership.[28]

Bridges attracted far more votes than Duncan or France. However, he had an advantage. His opponent Hart had made many enemies, and John C. Lawrence, a prominent Republican, publicly called on Republicans and Democrats to unite behind Bridges. This was a well-needed boost for Bridges, for it was a period when some of Seattle's middle class ran a vehemently anti-Japanese campaign. The Anti-Japanese League had successfully persuaded the Seattle city administration to refuse licences to many Japanese businesses. The main criticism directed at Bridges was not the platform of the FLP or his support of railworkers, but that he leased land to Japanese farmers. A below-the-belt campaign labelled the FLP the 'Japanese Labor Party'. The propaganda the FLP had to counteract was not an attack on the platform it so proudly reproduced in the *Record* every day, but the accusation that Bridges and the FLP supported Japanese immigration.[29]

This was embarrassing for the Seattle labour movement. After all, Duncan on many occasions had opposed Japanese immigration on the grounds that docile labour was deliberately introduced to cut wages. However, Duncan was in favour of better relations with the Japanese, and organized labour gave little assistance to the Anti-Japanese League. Some unions accepted Japanese members. Bridges held a more complex position, believing that there should be free movement of peoples between countries. However, he qualified this by adding that this should be of economically independent people. He opposed large corporations importing people wholesale into the country for the purposes of reducing wages. He also opposed arousing racist feeling by denunciation and discrimination. Bridges was 'not a hater of any race', and did not believe 'that natives of any country, irrespective of race, color or religion should be discriminated against'. Bridges therefore stood by his leasing of land to the Japanese. This put the FLP in a difficult position; it did not want to offend Bridges, but many unions favoured exclusion of the Japanese. The *Record* tried to square the circle, claiming that Bridges was only complying with the law as it stood. The Japanese had a legal right to carry out business and hire land. Since many other businessmen leased land and had commercial dealings with the Japanese, why single out Bridges? The *Record* believed that Bridges was such an effective candidate that the only way his opponents could defeat him was to raise the red herring of his leasing arrangements. Therefore if the issue was really about the Japanese leasing land, those raising the issue should campaign to change the law. The *Record* did not say how it would react to such a proposal.[30]

The issue did not go away and when Parley P. Christensen arrived in Seattle, the press relentlessly pressed him on the Japanese question. Afterwards at a rally of 2500 with thousands more locked out, Christensen ignored the Japanese issue and delivered a speech more radical than that given by the local candidates. This was due to the fact that his was a national platform more in keeping with the national programme of the FLP. The Seattle party's platform came out of Yakima and the alliance with progressives and more moderate union officials. Christensen had no such restraints. As the campaign drew to a close, the *Record* increasingly concentrated on Bridges and not the FLP. Though committed to the FLP, the *Record* was campaigning similarly to Short – concentrating on electing an individual at the expense of the party.[31]

WOMEN AND THE CAMPAIGN

The King County FLP took the winning of the women's vote very seriously forming a women's committee and standing five women candidates. It was so proud of this fact that it claimed it had become known as a 'woman's campaign'. The women's page of the *Record* contained election news for women daily, and women trade-union speakers addressed every major FLP rally. Ritza Freeman led the women's division of King County and conducted special propaganda for women. Born in America of Russian parentage and connected with the University of Chicago settlement, she had served George Creel in the Food Administration. She insisted she was not a 'direct actionist', but believed in political democracy.[32]

May Frazee stood for Superintendent of King County Schools; a former 'political independent', she had studied at both Chicago and Washington Universities, having spent the previous five years in King County. She demanded better resourced education, better pay for men and women teachers, and taxation to provide full state funding for every child's education. May Duffy stood in the 43rd District for the State Legislature; she demanded a living minimum wage for women of the state. Gladys Small, business agent for the Lady Barbers Union and another campaigner for a higher minimum wage for women stood in the 45th District. Minnie K. Ault, wife of E. B. Ault, editor of the *Record*, a business agent for the Book Binders Union and President of the Women's Card and Label League, stood for the 46th District. She demanded political and industrial equality for men and women. As the campaign drew to a close, the main reasons why a woman should vote FLP were given as a living wage, 'justice for our boys' and 'a Bone Dry State'.[33]

THE ELECTION RESULTS

The FLP stood candidates for state wide, county-wide and district elections. In King County Robert Bridges collected 39 034 votes for governor, the highest vote for any FLP candidate in King County, but due to a high poll this represented only 36 per cent of the vote (see Tables 4.1 and 4.2).[34]

Bridges' popularity does not fully explain the reason for his success in King County, since his state wide average was less at 30.4 per cent. Thus Bridges had won more support in King County. Indeed it was one

Table 4.1 Vote for Governor

	Republican	Democratic	FLP
King County	53 081	15 292	39 034 (36%)
State Vote	210 662	66 079	121 371 (30.4%)

Table 4.2 Duncan's vote in King County (1st congressional district)

Republican	Democratic	FLP
46 528	10 386	23 950 (29.6%)

of the rare posts where the Republicans had not got the majority of the vote. In contrast James Duncan got a congressional vote of 29.6 per cent. This was slightly lower than the average FLP vote in King County, but by less than one per cent. Duncan's percentage of votes cast was higher than Christensen's average of nearly 25 per cent in King County.[35]

King County FLP had concentrated on electoral districts in the Seattle area. Here the vote varied from a high of 43.64 per cent in the 41st District to a low of 18 per cent in the 47th (see Table 4.3).[36] Though the FLP did not carry any district in King County, the result in the 41st took them closest to it: here the Republicans won the 41st with 45.7 per cent. An extra 2 per cent of the vote would have given the FLP the seat. This was not the case elsewhere, where an extra 10 or 15 per cent would still have denied the FLP victory. Nonetheless they had replaced the Democrats as the second party, city and state-wide, though the Republicans had outvoted the FLP and Democrats combined.

One approach to analysing the FLP's vote is to ask why it was not substantial enough to gain victory. It is unrealistic to expect a new party to win in its first major election. However, having said that, is it the case that certain polices of the FLP cost it votes? It has been argued that the FLP's, and Duncan's in particular, support of Prohibition and Protestantism alienated the Catholic and Irish vote. There is no doubt that an Irish worker, or any worker who liked a drink, may well have disliked   Duncan's   missionary   zeal.   However,   the   Irish

Table 4.3 FLP's state legislature vote in 41st and 47th districts (two candidates per party)

District	Republican	Democratic	FLP
41st	9 667	2 297	9 196
	9 553	2 170	9 152
47th	12 731	2 504	3 410
	12 772	2 473	3 364

population in Seattle was relatively small, and Prohibition had not featured as a major issue in either Duncan's mayoral campaign or the general election of 1920. Prohibition was simply not a major issue in Seattle in 1920. This is not to say there were no opponents of Prohibition; those who worked in the brewing trade were outspoken in their opposition, though opponents of prohibition faced a political conundrum for all three parties in Washington State supported it. Progressives in the Republican Party, and even the Democratic Party urged their leaders to strengthen Prohibition measures. Thus Duncan and the FLP's view that alcohol was an evil was not a monopoly and it left the voter with little choice. Therefore it is unlikely that the FLP's policy, or Duncan's views on Prohibition, was a major factor preventing them from winning the election.[37]

If Duncan had alienated those who liked to drink, he most certainly alienated those who did not like strikes. Duncan was identified with the SCLC and the General Strike far more than any other candidate. Duncan had lost the mayoral election by 50 873 to 34 053. The conservative Robert Hesketh had achieved 4000 votes more than Duncan in his aldermanic campaign. The difference in votes won between the two men was not enough to have changed the outcome of the mayoral election, but it may have reflected Duncan's closer identification with trade-union militancy. The fact that Duncan was not in Seattle at the time of the General Strike made little difference to those who accused him of syndicalism and Bolshevism. When compared with other leading union or FLP candidates, his background is radically different. Unlike Hesketh, Duncan did not have a reputation for involvement in municipal politics. His reputation, warranted or not, rested on his leadership of the SCLC and its role in the General Strike. Therefore Duncan may have represented a hard-core labour vote in a way that the rest did not. Bridges' higher vote was an exception. Duncan's was the rule in that he received a vote close to the FLP average. The fact that his vote was slightly lower may have been due as much to his high profile on strikes as to his views on Prohibition. It was Duncan's connection to the general strike that the press had emphasized.

It has been argued, on the basis that the unions had 35 000 members in Seattle, that labour should have dominated city elections.[38] However, this figure is erroneous. Organized gas workers, printers, tailors, cleaning and dye workers, carpet workers, bookbinders and workers throughout the building trades industry lost the closed shop. Workers in the shipyards had already suffered major defeats and wage cuts.

The Chamber of Commerce estimated that 85 per cent of firms belonging to the Associated Industries had closed shops in April 1919; in October 1920, the Associated Industries claimed the numbers nearly reversed: 75 per cent had liberated themselves from unions. A tiny 9 per cent of Seattle labored in union shops. The giant of the Seattle AFL had been brought to its knees.

Mass unemployment, wage cuts and de-unionization had cost the unions members and income.[39] That trade-union organization with only 9 per cent of the workforce gathered 30 per cent of the vote suggests that the labour vote was higher than could be expected, not lower. Unrealistic assessments of the unions' strength leads to over-exaggeration of the possibilities for success, and then to the extent of failure in this period.

Rather than analyse labour's weakness others have blamed defeat in the mayoralty campaign on 'the failure of the conservative unionists', many of them Catholic, to support Duncan. However, as demonstrated above, the difference between support given to conservative trade unionists and to Duncan was not a decisive factor in the mayoral election. Nor can we be certain that Duncan's vote was lower due to his militancy and prohibitionism. Hesketh was a regular contestant in council election – this fact could explain his higher vote – but his extra votes would not have given Duncan victory. So even if Duncan had not alienated Irish and Catholic conservative trade unionists he would still have lost the election. The key factor in labour's failure to get an even higher vote in 1919–20 is more likely to be the weakened condition of the Seattle union movement than the opposition of conservative unionists or Catholics.[40]

Well-organized workers, such as the Streetcar Men of Seattle, gave Duncan's a larger share of the vote compared to the rest of the population. Over 76 per cent of streetcar men voted for Duncan, compared to 39.9 per cent of the population at large. It is true that streetcar men gave Duncan a slightly lower vote than they did to La Follette in 1924, or even non-labour candidates for mayor. However, they still gave him substantial support. [41]

What is the explanation for this lower vote? Union officials during the 1920 election campaign held mass meetings to endorse the FLP. Union officials claimed they played a major role in swaying the voting intentions of their members. Only a small number were regularly involved in union activities, but 'before an election, they act as leaven for the general body of car men.' Car men also had a commitment to municipal ownership as their industry belonged to the Seattle public. The SCLC and the car men's union had united in a campaign to achieve this. Though only a minority, including union officials, read the *Record*, its progressive beliefs, especially its support for municipal ownership, were in keeping with the views of much of the membership. Therefore the progressive ideas of the *Record*, Duncan, the SCLC and the FLP fitted the experience and views of the politically active minority of the car men. This being the case, why did Duncan fare least well among the candidates solidly supported by the car men (though the majority of car men supported him)?[42]

The answer lies in the relationship of the streetcar union to the SCLC and the general strike. The car men had joined the strike, but after two days, a national official ordered them back to work. Although local officials promised they would rejoin the strike, they never did. This probably created tension between the car men's officials and the SCLC. Thus the smaller vote for Duncan may have reflected an embarrassment felt by some car men officials over the general strike. Nonetheless the union gave Duncan substantial support and was active on behalf of the FLP in 1920. In conclusion, it is worth noting that the experience of the car men demonstrates that well-organized and politically motivated unionists can affect working-class voting behaviour.[43] Unfortunately we lack similar information on workers' voting behaviour in other unions. However, it is likely that in other well-organized areas union activists exercised an important influence.

Seattle was a far more homogeneous society than New York or Chicago, with 73 per cent of its population described as native white. For the most part the city's 'old immigrants' did not cluster in clearly defined ethnic neighbourhoods. However, due to housing discrimination, the tiny black population resided in two 'racially mixed' neighbourhoods. Nonetheless, in electoral terms ethnic groupings had no major influence in Seattle politics. That is not to say that race and ethnicity did not become an issue at election time, as the example of Bridges and the Japanese affair clearly demonstrates. The Japanese issue, and labour's embarrassment with it, may well have cost the FLP votes, but then the SCLC and the WSFL were well-known for their advocacy of Japanese exclusion. Ironically it was Bridges, the most principled candidate on the issue, who received the highest FLP vote. It is possible that the issue cost Bridges votes, but if he was perceived as a firm supporter of the Japanese, it did not prevent his becoming the most successful FLP candidate. The Seattle Labor Party did not aim special propaganda at different ethnic groupings but advocated political equality for black and white while opposing unrestricted immigration. On one or two occasions it received support from elements within the black and Japanese communities. It is unlikely that this policy, in Seattle in 1920, was a tremendous electoral handicap.[44]

It is difficult to evaluate the effect of gender on the outcome of labour's vote, as election results are not available categorized into male and female. However, the Seattle FLP, as outlined above, made greater efforts to win women's votes than even the progressive SCLC had done. Most of this propaganda dealt with women as housewives or mothers, though the issues of women's and children's wages and working conditions also took place. Though we cannot tell how women actually voted, we know how many FLP supporters voted for women. Voting figures show that whether a candidate was male or female made absolutely no difference to FLP supporters. In district 45, for example, where the FLP stood male and female candidates, each received exactly 1125 votes. In every district with mixed candidates, there was no significant difference in the vote. A woman standing for a county-wide post received 30 019 votes compared to 30 359 votes for a male candidate.

CONCLUSION

The Seattle SCLC created a Labor Party far later than its counterparts in New York and Chicago. Before 1920 industrial action had taken priority over the political. Only the defeat of the general strike pushed the progressives into taking political action. However, the delay was partly of the labour progressives' own choosing as they did not want to launch the party without State Federation backing. At first campaigning was carried out under the auspices of the Triple Alliance with the ideology of 'True Americanism'.

In this early period labour's conservatives had got the upper hand due to the open-shop onslaught on the unions. Their method of fighting back was not militant action, but a defensive effort to conserve union resources. Progressives' plans for industrial reorganization of the unions, 'The Duncan Plan', were shelved, as Seattle unions resorted to the time-honoured tactics of sectionalism and boycott. The failure of the General Strike had undermined progressive and radical confidence. Yet as labour's powers diminished the progressives in the SCLC were able to take the initiative away from the conservatives. The victory of the progressives in the Triple Alliance enabled them to take the political initiative away from the more conservative local union officials.[45] This progressive victory was not due to a sudden flowering of militancy, but to an increasing disillusionment of many union activists with the two-party system. The growing weakness of the unions focused attention on the need for political reform. If the threat of injunction could be removed and the right to collective bargaining guaranteed by government, then the unions could defend workers' conditions. But, by mid-1920, it was clear that neither of the main parties would endorse such a platform.

There was a progressive tradition in Washington State and Seattle that overlapped both Democrats and Republicans. This sentiment was not unique to Seattle, but a similar strength of progressivism combined with the weakness of the Democrats did not exist in New York or Chicago. In these cities the Democrats did not crumble in 1920. It is true they suffered from the Republican backlash of that year but they remained intact. In Seattle the Democrats collapsed even before the election took place. This was the background that made it possible for the SCLC to put its new party at the head of a progressive and labour movement in 1920. Rather than question why labour did so poorly, this chapter has asked how it was possible for such a weakened movement to do so well. Was the key its prestige as leader of the General Strike?

It is difficult to answer with certainty. Of course, the strike was a failure, and the FLP and Duncan did not campaign on its tradition. He and many FLP supporters made it clear that they advocated political action, not direct action. Many of the keenest supporters of the strike took no interest in political action, going as far as denouncing it and Duncan. Others tried to set up an alternative central labour body because of the SCLC's commitment to political action. They received little support from the mainstream of the SCLC itself and were easily defeated. In terms of the SCLC it was Duncan's view of labourism that prevailed.[46] Therefore it is hard to judge to what extent the strike affected political consciousness in Seattle. It is likely that the backlash against labour after the general strike and the Centralia incident won the movement just as many friends as it lost. Even those who objected to militancy were no doubt surprised at the level of reaction, especially with the attacks on conservative and moderate sections of the trade unions. Thus the need for political solutions to labour's problems arose for both moderate and progressive unionists; independent action at the ballot box became preferable to further strike action. That some conservative trade unionists would support the labour party was proven by the progressives' winning of the Triple Alliance. Others may have had a less defensive agenda, seeing labour as a necessary counter-balance to the 'interests', but for a brief while, for whatever motives, moderates and progressives could agree on political tactics. The SCLC was able to utilize this mood. It had a long tradition of working with progressives and moderates. It had a well-respected newspaper, experience of electioneering, organization and resources. The decision to form a labour party had coincided with the mass discontent of progressives in the two major parties, some of whom defected to the FLP.

With the bulk of the unions in the TA agreeing to back the party conservative trade unionist opposition bordered on futility. Short, against his own inclinations, was forced to campaign for the party. Thus the advantage enjoyed by the Seattle FLP in 1920 was that it had the genuine support of the SCLC and the indirect support of the WSFL. At a grass-roots level many of the local unions, such as the Carpenters Local 131, District 10 of the UMW, the Streetcar Men and many more, gave imaginative and enthusiastic support. Here was a broad coalition with a well-organized core of union activists at its centre. The campaign message reflected the coalition but even in FLP terms it was not particularly radical. The more radical, but less well-known, Parley P. Christensen polled far below the other FLP candidates. That he was less well-known is probably the key factor in his poor performance. In the better organized King County his vote was 7 per cent higher. Nonetheless, the press did everything it could to present the FLP as pro-IWW and Bolshevik. A large majority of those who voted for the FLP must have rejected this propaganda as nonsense; some might have voted for it because of it. However, it is important to keep in mind that, however mild labour's platform and however extreme the propaganda against it, those who voted for the FLP were well aware of at least one reality: union organization was the party's bedrock. So though the party's platform was politically in keeping with progressivism and not based on clear class interest, none-theless its vote came from the working class.

However, there was a weakness in the FLP's activists' strategy; it had, for the most part, concentrated on winning the official union machine. Electoral success was not due to the widespread ideological conversion of workers but to winning control of WSFL political policy. Conversion to the Party's creed was made from above, not below. *The winning of official union support gave the FLP leadership a ready-made coalition and electoral machine. The problem was that what could be won by resolution could be taken away by the same method.* The new party was vulnerable to the actions of the conservatives who still controlled the WSFL. Those who wanted to build the party had understood the need to get official trade-union support, but in doing so they had sacrificed any independent party-building activity. The failure to build the labour party at grass-roots level, combined with the absence of total election success in 1920, undermined the future of the party. There was no solid foundation of a political party culture.

If the party had won major posts in 1920 then the conservatives and the WSFL might not have turned against it. It had reduced the Democrats to third place, but even if it had won every Democrat vote it would have remained in almost every case second to the Republicans. To win, it needed Republican voters, but the Grand Old Party in Washington had firmly presented itself as the party of order in relation to labour unrest, unashamedly nativist and enthusiastic for Prohibition. The FLP already supported Prohibition, and it could hardly advocate strong measures against labour. Democrat and FLP votes combined could not defeat the Republicans; it is unrealistic to ask why they did not win in 1920. A far more productive question is why such a successful start failed to establish an ongoing political presence for labour? In part this chapter has already begun to give an answer that is developed further in Chapter 7.

Compared to New York, the Seattle FLP had firm roots in the official labour movement. Chicago had even stronger roots with the unqualified endorsement of the Illinois State Federation of Labor. It was not just a matter of official endorsement; many at the centre of the SCLC were able to enthuse their union branches into FLP activity. The party used union offices and resources, none of which were available to the New York party. There the union progressives lost their influence in the central labour body at an early stage, and with it official endorsement and resources. The progressives at the centre of the SCLC had firm roots in the 'federated unionism' of Seattle. They had substantial support in the local movement, and were not easily undermined by conservatives. Without the problem of a strong socialist competitor and with a popular progressive newspaper backing them, they also had a lengthy experience of intervening in municipal politics. None of these advantages applied to the New York union progressives.

However, some of these factors did apply to the Chicago movement. Fitzpatrick and his allies had firm roots in the official movement at state and city level. Indeed, Fitzpatrick's influence ran deeper than Duncan's in his state federation. Paradoxically, the fact that the Chicago labour movement's industrial muscle was stronger than Seattle's might explain the less cohesive political intervention by the CFU. Of course Chicago was more ethnically diverse than Seattle, and powerful party machines opposed labour. While this is important, there still remains the problem that often the unions were not able to put their weight fully behind the new party. This was not necessarily a matter of syndicalism. The problem was the amount of time taken up defending sizeable union organization. In Seattle many union branches had lost members, many even becoming mere shells. It is possible that this gave the remaining local officials the time required to agitate politically. There is no doubt that the defeat of the General Strike gave political action a boost in Seattle. Many Chicago officials had no such luxury in this period; political defeat had occurred in advance of industrial action. Meanwhile the city's labour movement became involved in a bitter industrial struggle lasting several more years.

However, this still leaves the question of why Chicago did not do as well in its first election campaign as Seattle. Accepting that Chicago faced stiffer competition from the main parties, the new party also faced the problem of entering a major election only a few months after its formation. In Seattle, labour prepared itself with interventions at a whole series of municipal elections before entering the general election of 1920. It had a well-established record of political progressivism, especially with its newspaper the *Record*. The Chicago movement produced its political newspaper only months before its first major election campaign. Perhaps a more established political tradition a year or so before the election could have delivered a larger vote. The fact that progressivism was stronger in Seattle than in Chicago gave the former an advantage that the latter lacked. All things considered, the Chicago movement was stronger than that of New York. But its electoral results were not enough to convince those looking for an alternative in 1920 that a vote for the FLP was not a wasted one. In contrast, the Seattle party had, by the general election, a whole series of impressive results.

5 Unity and Independent Political Action in New York 1921–24

Whatever the assessment of the New York Farmer Labor Party's (FLP) electoral performance in the 1920 General Election, many contemporaries saw it as disastrous. Dudley Field Malone, the most successful of the FLP's candidates, left the party and did not stand on its platform again. The general election of 1920 saw the end of the New York FLP as an effective organization. In the Fall of 1921 the party stood only a handful of candidates in municipal elections. By mid-1922 it lost its independence as the New York Socialist Party (SP) effectively took control.[1]

Between 1922 and 1924 the SP replaced the progressive trade unionists of the AFL in the attempt to build the New York labour party. In this period the Socialists stressed the importance of working with labour and other progressives. Although they won tens of thousands of votes for La Follette in 1924, they received nothing in return. This sacrifice did nothing to help the FLP, which sank without trace. This chapter outlines why the Socialists changed their attitude towards the FLP, and why it failed in spite of this additional help.

The optimism felt by many workers and the left in 1919 was short-lived. Unions lost the protection of a wartime Democratic administration, and not only did the unions suffer an offensive from the employers but also from injunctions against strikers, the arrest of militants and mass unemployment. These factors led to a decline in strikes and union membership.[2] None of this negated the argument for a labour party; on the contrary it strengthened it, for it proved that the Democrats were not the workers' friends. The leaders of the FLP were not slow to point out that Democrat administrations proved just as hostile to the working class as Republican ones. However, many workers wishing to protest against the anti-working class measures of the Wilson administration felt that the FLP, denied AFL national support, was not a credible alternative. In most other cities, including New York, it was the Republican Party that benefited from the backlash. Industrial defeat turned into its political counterpart.

The New York FLP had entered the 1920 election with little support from AFL unions, Socialists or progressives. In the bleak circumstance of working-class and trade-union movement retreat the New York FLP was unable to establish itself. Its poor electoral showing further increased its isolation. The FLP response in early 1921 was to reorganize itself. Jerome T. De Hunt, President of the New York Harbor District Council of the Railroad and Steamship Clerks representing some 20 000 men, became the chairman of the city committee. Indicative of the growing isolation and weakness was the failure of the party to find new allies. Frank Walsh declined to help the New York Party due to the pressure of work and illness.[3]

Unable to obtain new support the Party began to lose the support it already had. The NYWTUL was the party's most solid supporter, but by early 1922 it had distanced itself from the FLP. The NYWTUL had problems of its own; the Central Trades and Labor Council (CTLC) in early January 1921 refused entrance to Maud Swartz and Miss Coffin at a regular meeting. However, on 7 March 1921 they were reseated at a regular meeting.[4] Between 1921 and 1922 the depression caused many branches of the NYWTUL to fall away and it could ill afford to lose official union support in New York. Circumstances relegated the FLP to a low priority in the mind of NYWTUL leaders. In June 1922 a regular meeting of the NYWTUL voted eleven to eight against supporting a labour party. There is no doubt that fears of antagonizing the CTLC had led to the NYWTUL abandoning the FLP.[5]

THE ROAD TO UNITY

In spite of an extensive platform for municipal reform the party only stood three municipal candidates, none of them as well known as Malone, Schneiderman or O'Leary, in the 1921 elections. De Hunt was nominated candidate for Mayor, Ben Howe, author of a plan for credit union banks, for Controller, and Abraham Lefkowitz, Vice President of the Teachers Union, for President of the Board of Aldermen. Several hundred delegates, including 20 women, attended the meeting to launch the FLP's election intervention, but the *New York Times* and the *Call* studiously ignored the FLP campaign. Final proof that the game was up came with the FLP's election results. They were so poor that the *New York Times* did not report them and it proved to be their last independent election intervention. However, the factors that had combined to make the FLP weaker were not discriminatory:

the Socialist's vote also declined. Within six months the two groups went into alliance.[6]

THE SOCIALISTS

Though the Socialists went into decline nationally, in New York City their electoral performance from 1919 to 1921 remained substantial. This was in spite of the New York SP (NYSP) suffering considerable losses of membership. In 1920 the NYSP had completely ignored the FLP. However, by 1921 the Socialist vote was stagnant and New York Socialists began to reappraise their attitude to the FLP.[7]

In 1920 the New York Socialists' factional struggle with those who had formed communist parties affected their attitude to the FLP. Having lost their most radical element to the Communists the Socialists swung to the left, putting all their effort into campaigning for Debs in the 1920 presidential campaign. They gave little thought to an alliance with the FLP. However, the result of the campaign was disappointing. Nationally Debs polled 915 302 votes, his largest vote ever. However, it was only 3.5 per cent of votes cast, compared to the 6 per cent polled in 1912. Though a remarkable achievement for Debs, it meant electoral decline for the Socialists. The result was a watershed as many Socialists became aware that they were no longer advancing – indeed in some areas organization had collapsed. Although the NYSP vote was better than elsewhere, it could not escape the growing sense of crisis. A debate on the way forward for the Socialists began to dominate the *Call*'s party page.[8]

The Socialists' Ninth Annual Convention in June 1921 signalled a change of direction for the New York Party. National membership had fallen to 17 000, 10 000 down on the average for 1920. Something had to be done. Hillquit, from New York, moved the resolution that ended the party's swing to the left and launched it on a trajectory back towards the right. The party was to waive its 'traditional policy of aloofness' and seek cooperation to beat the old parties. The aim was to create a federated unity of labour organizations, each keeping its own identity but uniting for electoral purposes. He cited the British Labour Party as an example to illustrate the proposal. However, the national executive committed itself only to canvassing the opinion of other labour organizations and then reporting to the next annual convention. In spite of the slow pace of proposed change, the *Call* proclaimed that the resolution would end the Socialists' isolation.[9]

The change in policy came too late to make any major difference that year. For by early July 1921 the NYSP had already made its main nominations. During that July the *Call* carried much news of Socialist electioneering, but none of the FLP's. It was the National Executive Committee's September meeting that prompted the New York Socialists to repeat their unity proposal to the local FLP. For in the midst of an important election campaign, the New York Socialists started taking the issue of federation, and their own decline, seriously.[10]

Realizing that the election results would not be different from previous ones, new strategies were required; the Socialists began to look forward to the development of a labour party. Thus in the middle of the campaign the *Call* noted that the painters' union had endorsed the FLP and that William Kohn believed that Johnston of the International Association of Machinists (IAM) was moving in a similar direction. Those opposed to Gompers might unite into one similar organization on the same lines as the British Labour Party. However, the *Call* continued to ask its readers to vote the straight Socialist ticket and ignored the FLP candidates.[11]

When the election results came they were bad news for Socialists and Republicans alike. The Socialists lost their aldermanic seats in a Tammany landslide. The *Call* complained that there was an added reason for Socialist defeat. In the races they had won in the past, they usually faced a three-cornered fight. This time, opposed by fusion candidates, with either Democrat or Republican standing down, they had lost in straight fights. Though the Socialist vote was respectable, approximately 50 000 votes city-wide, the overall total was slightly down on the year before. Although they came second in 12 assembly districts a flood of criticism poured in. W. M. Feignbaum took on the task of refuting it. He noted that the FLP and the smaller left-wing organizations had received only 7000 votes at the maximum. He looked beyond the labour vote to the high vote for the Democrats, which, he argued, proved that workers had not yet learnt to vote for themselves. Therefore uniting with others would not provide easy solutions or gains. Members should carry on with the hard task of making the party worthy of working-class support.[12]

However, hard work did not arrest the decline and party organization in the 5th Assembly District changed from weekly to fortnightly meetings to save expenditure on rent. Simultaneously the party organization of the 7th Assembly District in the Bronx met to discuss the election and to practise self-criticism. The poor election results gave impetus to the shift towards unity and independent political action.

Increasingly the tide of party opinion turned towards the need for cooperation and a change in strategy.[13] The pressure for unity was growing but the FLP had rejected the Socialists' previous advances, though that was before its disastrous election results. Now its supporters had nowhere else to go, and increasingly the *Call* carried news of individuals who, once prominent in the FLP, now cooperated with the Socialists. For example, the CTLC delegated Thomas J. Curtis, Vice President of the State Federation and the Labor Party's first electoral candidate in 1919, to the *Call's* Labor Conference Circulation Committee, a body formed to extend the newspaper's influence in the official labour movement. The *Call* interpreted the CTLC's endorsement as meaning that unions representing 750 000 workers in New York City were behind the paper. Nonetheless the support was not empty rhetoric as the CTLC agreed to a fund drive among union affiliates.[14]

The Socialists' shift to the right paid dividends as old friends, and even old enemies, responded to their unity call. Of course the CTLC would not agree to independent political action; however, it dropped its hostility to the *Call*. The *Call* gained extra union sponsors. In addition to the usual progressive or needle trade unions, it received support from some craft unions. It gave the ailing Socialists a sense of substance that their elected officials (aldermen etc.) had provided in the past. The fact that some of the sponsors were unionists like William Kehoe and John P. Coughlin, who had defeated the progressives, did not bother the Socialists at all. Sponsors also included defeated union progressives such as Lefkowitz and Curtis.[15]

The past year had seen an onslaught by the bosses against the unions and they had received little support from city government. There was even talk of bringing in state wide anti-strike legislation. Now Coughlin and his allies needed to show their independence from Tammany. They needed the threat of militant action to prevent such legislation, and the *Call* was an ideal vehicle for carrying news of the campaign. Thus the right wing of the CTLC made left-sounding noises just as the Socialists moved right.

However, the Socialists still needed to pursue the matter of unity with the FLP. FLP reticence on the issue disappeared and opposition to cooperation with the Socialists melted away by the spring of 1922. A national decision of the SPA's 10th annual convention further smoothed the path to unity, going beyond its previous policy of just canvassing opinion and deciding state groups could 'federate'. This meant they could affiliate with farmer labour organizations, but keep their independence and integrity by not participating in Democratic or Republican primaries. The New York Socialists wasted no time and on 24 May 1922 they held a joint conference with the New York FLP. The conference issued a call for a joint campaign of Socialists, FLP and the unions in the Fall election. There was no mistaking that the FLP was the junior party in the new venture, for the Socialists' convention went ahead and nominated its main candidates for governor and other state-wide positions. A few nominations were left open for joint agreement with the FLP, clearing the way to unify the electoral intervention of the two organizations.[16]

The new-found unity did not get the blessing of the *Call*'s new friends, the leadership of the CTLC. William F. Kehoe, Secretary of the CTLC, complained to Gompers that a number of New York labour leaders had signed the call for 'an official labor non-partisan' political convention. Kehoe sent a letter informing every signer that they did not have the authority to support independent political action. But Gompers took no action, apart from asking the signers for their reaction to Kehoe's protest. Nonetheless Kehoe's actions alerted the New York labour movement that the CLTC was not supporting the initiative.[17]

On 15 July 1922 over 300 delegates representing 250 000 union members and 200 000 FLP and Socialist voters attended the unity convention. Delegates excluded the communists from participating by a vote of 204 to 15. At first the convention called the party the Independent Labor Party but later renamed it the American Labor Party (ALP).[18] Because of election laws the name of the new party could not appear on ballot papers. The old titles of Socialist and FLP were used instead. The new party also agreed to work inside the Conference for Progressive Political Action (CPPA) for an independent party, but with its own distinct platform. The platform commenced by stating that workers by hand or brain faced a crisis: unions, free speech and liberties were under attack, especially from 'the open shop drive'. The invisible 'monied' interests controlled the two main parties. Therefore workers had to 'destroy old parties'. A long list of demands that were standard FLP policy followed. There was nothing particularly revolutionary about the platform, though it did oppose US foreign intervention. It also supported the ongoing miners' strike and called for the release of all political prisoners. The platform ended with proposals to increase democracy by measures such as referendum and recall, proportional representation, and the putting of constitutional amendments to referendum. The newly formed ALP sent out a call for trade unions to back a labour party on the British model to the national committee of the CPPA. Ironically, the Socialists now promoted a programme for which they had criticized the FLP in the past.[19]

The reconstructed ALP was weaker than the party formed in 1919. It did not have the support of the CTLC, the WTUL or even as many unions as before. The Socialists were also weaker. The original party had formed at a time of growing militancy and trade union membership; now it was relaunched in a situation of few strikes and declining union membership. Unemployment in some sectors, in spite of economic recovery, remained high. Thus in more difficult circumstances than those of 1919, the Socialists turned to a strategy of labourism. Socialist support for the FLP in 1919 may have established a substantial minority presence for the party, and prevented the defeat of the progressives in CTLC. But in 1922 they needed more powerful allies than the shadow of the old labour party movement to revive their fortunes.

THE ELECTION CAMPAIGN

Suddenly doors previously closed to FLP activists opened. The facilities of the clothing workers' unions that had been cool to the party in 1920 now became available. Financial support and meeting rooms also became available. A women's organizer was appointed, and speakers despatched to union meetings. The new party did win some substantial union endorsements. For example, delegates of the Amalgamated Sheet Metal Workers Local 28 representing 2000 men unanimously voted for affiliation. They also directed their delegates to raise affiliation at the trades council. The largest typographers' local in the country also gave its support. A few weeks earlier the International Typographers 67th Annual Convention placed itself on record as favouring the formation of a 'political Labor Party'. The resolution had not mentioned the FLP or the ALP, but this was enough to encourage 400 members of Typographical Union No. 6 to endorse the ALP.[20]

The Railwaymen's Non-Partisan League of Kings County endorsed several ALP candidates in Brooklyn, including De Hunt in the 10th Congressional District. Nevertheless this was not a complete break with non-partisan politics, as they also endorsed Democratic candidates. The journal of the Amalgamated Clothing Workers was even more circumspect, stating it would not choose between Socialist, labour or workers parties (Communists). Instead it advised its readers not to vote for the two main parties but to vote as workers. Having no intention of breaking with non-partisan politics, the CTLC felt under enough pressure to endorse 31 ALP candidates. However, this was on the basis of questionnaires returned by all candidates; they also endorsed 64 Democrats and 13 Republicans as 'fair to Labor'. However, the 31 labour nominations did nothing to soothe the tension between the two warring sides in the New York labour movement. For the nominations were not distributed even-handedly. Only one 'Socialist–FLP' candidate obtained endorsement in the Tammany labour stronghold of Brooklyn. Not prepared to let bygones be bygones the Brooklyn CTLC officials refused to endorse De Hunt. Thus in Brooklyn the bulk of those nominated were Democrats, with a few Republicans.[21]

Though Abraham Lefkowitz was among those endorsed, he still raised the inconsistency of the non-partisan method of backing candidates. Many 'Socialist–FLP' candidates were considered not favourable to labour, yet Democrats and Republicans were endorsed. He believed this was ludicrous, for the ALP candidates stood on a pro-worker platform, while the others stood for the parties of big business. However, *Labor*, the campaign magazine of the Rail Brotherhoods, gave De Hunt a warm recommendation for congressman. Gompers went beyond the CTLC by personally endorsing Meyer London for the 12th Congressional District. In addition the Party got support from those Jewish organizations that normally supported the Socialists. Poale Zion of Greater New York called on all Jews to vote for the ALP and the Jewish *Forward* issued a special edition to support the federated election campaign.[22]

Union backing for the ALP was less, even with some support from the CTLC, than in 1920. Without its own newspaper and ignored by the mass circulation press, its profile remained low. The ALP had only a handful of non-Socialist candidates standing and no FLP candidate stood for a major position such as governor. Since the defection of Dudley Field Malone and the WTUL, no well-known member of the FLP was available to stand. The *Call* gave the ALP some limited publicity with news of its rallies, though the keynote speakers were usually from the SP side of the alliance. The balance shifted even further towards the Socialists when De Hunt, candidate for the 10th Congressional and a founder of the ALP, joined the Socialists. Edward F. Cassidy, the Socialist candidate for governor, headed an all-Irish list of speakers in support of Ben Howe. Howe a leading member of the New York FLP, stood in the predominantly Irish and German 18th Congressional District. Ironically this major effort by the Socialists to help the FLP in this district was two years too late. In 1920 the FLP candidate Jeremiah O'Leary might have won but for the diversion of 5000 protest votes to the Socialists.[23]

Three thousand supporters attended the new party's first major rally at the Lexington Theatre. Hillquit told the crowd that if the ALP succeeded in New York then a labour party would become an accomplished fact nationally. The main speakers were mainly leading SP members, though Lefkowitz did speak. In Brooklyn 5000 attended the ALP rally, with De Hunt the first to speak; not surprisingly, he made the rail strike the thrust of his speech. The Party made clear its commitment to striking workers, promising that both Socialists and the FLP would give their fullest support to striking rail workers, as would trade unions affiliated to both parties. They reasoned that action by Attorney-General Daugherty against the strikers showed the need for independent political action. The ALP condemned the judicial assault on rail workers and called for an assault on the ballot box.[24]

THE END OF THE BEGINNING

The election proved a massive landslide for the Democrats that undermined the Socialists. Meyer London, perhaps the most prestigious candidate, failed to win, and Cassidy's vote for Governor was 20 000 down on the 1920 result. In the 18th Congressional District the Socialist–FLP fusion candidate, Howe, got only 2376 votes. In 1920 the FLP vote alone had been 9998, and in addition the Socialists got 5668. The *Call* believed that the delay in 'organizing' the ALP was decisive. This was a weak excuse for the two parties had amalgamated in the July, before the nomination of most candidates. The other participant in 'federation', the FLP, fared even worse, failing to get the 25 000 votes required to get onto the ballot in the future. They provided only an extra 6887 votes towards Cassidy's total. None of the original FLP members won a seat, though De Hunt received a respectable 6532 in Brooklyn's 10th Congressional District; Abraham Lefkowitz got 2659 in Manhattan's 13th Congressional District. Each of the candidates came third. The ALP had gained little by uniting with the Socialists but the funeral would not take place until two years later.[25]

It is unlikely that leading SP members like Oneal and Hillquit were unaware of the scale of defeat, but they had another vehicle to achieve their aims, the CPPA. Nevertheless the empty shell of the FLP was a convenient way of furthering the Socialists' unity offensive. It also provided a few extra delegates at labour conventions, and a more respectable face to show to conservative trade unionists. If they were not sincere about the ALP, they were sincere in their desire that the CPPA should become the basis of a third party. The CPPA came about in early 1922; the AFL did not oppose the CPPA, but refused it official backing. Therefore it was a quasi-official body led by the International Association of Machinists and the Rail Brotherhoods. The link between the two was, of course, the fact that the IAM organized the Rail Shopmen, and that both had suffered badly since the railroads had returned to private ownership. During 1921 and 1922 the railroad employers cut wages several times and in some areas tried to bring in non-union workers. Striking railworkers faced intransigent employers who often turned to the courts to stop solidarity action. The use of the courts, and the failure of any sizeable section of Congress to stop the passage of the Esch-Cummins Bill, drove the conservative brotherhoods towards political action which, in this case, meant only a more aggressive form of non-partisan activity. However, at times, in order to sound more threatening, CPPA leaders, William Johnston in particular, spoke in third-party terms. Johnston often threatened that the CPPA would lead to a British-style labour party. The aim of this threat was to persuade progressives in the two main parties that if they did not provide more support then labour would go it alone. This vague promise was intended to draw in more militant workers and progressive groups such as the FLP, the Socialists, the Non-Partisan League and the Cooperatives.[26]

A series of defeats inflicted on the miners, railmen and the unions in general had the effect of disillusioning many with the AFL's non-partisan stance. Neither of the main parties had intervened to support workers against the onslaught. At the same time workers were not in the confident mood of 1919. Nonetheless sections of labour still desired political change, not on the basis of workers' activity and growing confidence, but on a foundation of resentment and enforced apathy. However, this was not the analysis of the Socialists. They could see only the radical side of the equation. To them the advent of the CPPA was proof not only of the desire for a third party, but also that events were pushing substantial sections of the union leadership to deliver one. A labour party could only succeed if a substantial section of the official union movement backed the project, therefore they had to work inside the CPPA to win it for independent political action. The ALP's electoral performance diminished its importance, thus the CPPA became central to the Socialist strategy of creating a third party.

When the CPPA first convened, the New York Socialists believed that forming a labour party was uppermost in the minds of delegates. Only a day later they concluded the opposite; the majority of delegates had voted against a new party and for a policy of rewarding friends and punishing enemies. In other words this was a non-partisan policy, albeit more active, identical to that of the AFL. However, Oneal and Hillquit made it clear that the SP would not enter the old party primaries. The 16 rail unions stood as a unit against those wanting independent political action, but local branches could decide how to put the policy into practice. Hillquit criticized the convention declaration as not showing any way forward. Nonetheless, he believed that there was progress, because the various organizations had come together in Chicago. The Socialists regretted the failure to form a party, but accepted that most probably the majority of the larger unions' members would not join it. For a while this muted Socialist enthusiasm for the CPPA. However, the disappointing election results of 1922 spurred both the Socialists and the CPPA into fresh activity.[27]

Once again the New York Socialists, with De Hunt and Gerber supporting them as delegates on behalf of the ALP, prepared to argue for a labour party at a CPPA convention that December. The Socialists also supported the barring of the Workers Party (the Communists) from the convention. Once again the Socialists suffered disappointment as the delegates voted 64 to 52 against, with the railroad unions united in opposition. Socialist Party delegates, the needle trades and typographers voted in favour of it. The defeat did not dismay Hillquit and Oneal, as both believed the impetus was still towards a labour party, though it would be a long and hard road.[28]

The refusal of the CPPA to back a third party created tension between it and the FLP nationally. However, in New York there was almost complete accord between the cadre of the FLP and the New York Socialists. The New York labourites faithfully supported the Socialists in every twist and turn they made inside the CPPA. They did not follow the FLP's national walk-out when the CPPA rejected third-party politics. They clung to the Socialists, both believing that the CPPA was the key to creating the new party.[29]

THE FINAL LAP: 1923–24

The years' 1921–22 had seen the relationship between the CTLC and the Socialists improve, but the election of Al Smith as Governor soon broke up the alliance. Smith carefully avoided taking the Tammany unionists' support for granted, and wooed them with many promises. Indeed, his proposals on compensation laws, labour injunctions and opposition to the Lusk Committee (an anti-red investigative body) even generated a favourable response from original supporters of the ALP such as Thomas J. Curtis and Henry R. Linville. Curtis described the proposals as progressive stating it was the best message ever, as far as he was aware, from a governor to a state legislature. The increasingly good relationship between the old guard and Smith undermined the CLTC's limited support for the Socialists. The CTLC's support for the *Call* proved to be a brief marriage of convenience.[30]

The Socialists, however, believed that the CPPA could overcome local AFL opposition to third-party politics, even though the CPPA had rejected this path. They based their hope on a concession made at the CPPA convention. Not wanting to alienate their more radical allies, the CPPA had sanctioned the calling of state conferences. These miniature versions of the CPPA would decide at a local level how to intervene in elections. Theoretically, this left the door open to third-party politics at the state level. Oblivious to the domination of the New York State AFL by those opposed to all independent political action, the New York Socialists grabbed enthusiastically at this possibility.[31]

Hillquit, convinced they could win over a state convention of the CPPA to supporting 'federated' action, explained the strategy for the months ahead at the ALP's Second Convention. The fact that the conservative Rail Brotherhoods were at the centre of progressive political action proved to him that the offensive against labour was forcing even the most conservative leaders leftwards. The two main parties would stand presidential candidates unacceptable even to the rail brotherhoods, forcing them to realize the logic of independent political action. It was only a matter of time before the more backward New York leadership would follow suit. The CPPA nationally had created an opening in which the Socialists could make progress towards a new party. They would not force the issue, but would wait until they could convince a majority of New York unions to their side.[32]

Convinced by Hillquit's reasoning, the ALP voted to stay in the CPPA. Convinced of the need not to frighten their more conservative allies it also decided against sending a delegation to the national FLP convention (initiated by Fitzpatrick and the CFL) to take place on 3 July 1923. As an affiliated member of the CPPA it had a duty to explore every possibility of building state wide through that body.

They shared the hopes and desires of the FLP but opposed its methods. New York FLP members, though loyal to their party, also believed it was unwise to attend the Chicago conference. It might imply they were withdrawing from the CPPA. Thus the Socialist Party strategy of waiting for the CPPA leaders had the support not only of their creation the ALP, but also of the New York FLP. Indeed the New York FLP was more loyal to the aspirations of the New York Socialist Party than to its leadership in Chicago.[33]

This is not the place to detail the failure of the Chicago FLP initiative, but there is no doubt that if the Socialists had supported the 3 July Convention it may have been more effective. Also the Workers Party would have failed to capture it. With the two most powerful labour centres of progressive and Socialist politics divided over the strategy for independent working-class politics, it was impossible to launch a serious national alternative to the conservatism of the AFL leadership.

The New York Socialists soon discovered that union conservatism was not as easy to shift as they predicted. At the end of July the long awaited convention to launch a state wide CPPA took place. Delegates, representing half a million workers and 100 000 Socialists, gathered at Albany. From the start the precarious position of the Socialists was made obvious. The Socialist and ALP delegates had to wait on the pavement as the 16 sponsoring Railroad Brotherhoods discussed whom they would admit. Although eventually admitting the Socialists the convention barred the Workers Party. Later on the Socialists were expelled from the convention. Moreover the Socialists claimed that the delivering of this coup de grace was a great surprise. Yet the composition of the convention should have alerted them. It consisted of members of the Rail Brotherhoods and organizations affiliated to the ALP; there were very few delegates from any other source. The placing of leading Socialists on various committees probably reassured them that everything was going well.[34]

Hillquit requested on behalf of the majority of the organization committee that the CPPA Conference be put on a permanent basis. An unexpected two-hour attack on the Socialists by the Rail Brotherhood leaders followed his speech. They accused the Socialists of trying to gobble up the convention. The Socialists refused a request that they should withdraw and the railmen voted to disown the convention that they had actually called, deciding to reconvene on their own. This resulted in a failure to set up any organization. Incredibly, Hillquit declared that a labour party was still inevitable. He believed it was the insistence of conservative union leaders that labour operate through the old parties' primaries that caused the split. For the Socialists there could be no compromise on independent political action. Though the situation was not going well in New York, Hillquit still believed that nationally there was a drift to independent political action. This was not completely fanciful. In Minnesota the Rail Brotherhoods supported the Farmer Labor forces, and even *Labor*, the national newspaper of the Rail Brotherhoods, supported them.[35]

Forced to enter the 1923 municipal elections without the mass weight of labour behind them, the Socialists contented themselves with the fiction of the ALP, although the ALP's name could not appear on the ballot paper due to electoral regulations. In the last election the organization polled as Socialist-FLP. Now the ALP had to sail completely under the Socialists' banner. None of this stopped the Socialists from behaving as if they were responsible for a fully fledged labour party. They carefully passed resolutions that did not raise too many issues, sticking 'wisely' to those issues that directly affected New York men and women, including housing and traction. The shift to the right did not stop with the kind of reformist campaign they had criticized the FLP for in previous years. *In their effort to turn themselves into a mainstream labour organization they prepared to divest themselves of the* Call, *the only English-language Socialist daily in New York*. Historians have suggested that this was due to financial difficulties; however, no attempt to raise funds to save the *newspap*er was made. Indeed the change was presented as a great political opportunity. Instead of being the voice of the New York Socialists it was to be the voice of labour. If this was intended as a solution to financial problems it turned out to be a very ineffectual one.[36] The Socialists believed that the new paper would be an official newspaper for the ALP in New York. The problem they failed to envisage was that the trade unions, even Socialist and progressive ones, did not have the commitment to politics that they themselves had.[37]

Even before the new paper appeared, the amount of news about the Socialists began to decline. On 1 October 1923, the *New York Leader* made its debut with two pages of sports news and a dully presented page of official union news. Its attacks on the Workers Party were not something new; the Socialists and the *Call* had considered it a hostile grouping that was a fair target. What was new was the uncritical reportage of AFL policy with Gompers' views regularly published without criticism, although the paper took him to task for not supporting the CPPA.[38]

However, the AFL convention took such a reactionary stance on the issue of a labour party that the *Leader* had to respond. Even Johnston of the CPPA and the Machinists had joined in the 12 to 1 vote against a labour party. John H. Walker of Illinois, a founder member of the FLP, spoke against the party. This one-time Socialist endorsed the conservative Matthew Woll as well as Gompers on the issue. Woll in turn had linked William Z. Foster and the Communists with the Labor Party. Max Hayes, representing the typographers, made a principled speech in its favour; Walker rewarded him with a nasty personal attack. As far as the AFL was concerned, a labour party was further away than ever. This was too much even for the now moderate *Leader* and it mildly rebuked Walker for being taken in by the Communists. A labour party was essential to dealing with the questions of the mines and railroads. Such criticism of AFL leaders was the exception rather than the rule. The new attitude of the *Leader* towards the AFL and its leadership did not go unnoticed by its readers. The editor admitted he had many letters attacking the paper's view on the AFL. He agreed that AFL leaders, such as John L. Lewis of the miners' union, had wrongly attacked progressives, but that they must continue to work inside AFL. This defence was somewhat disingenuous as most readers of the *Call* worked with or inside the AFL. It was the increasing emphasis on the 'official' side of the AFL, and the decrease in political criticism, which was the real issue.[39]

Though a major backer of the 'new' paper was the non-AFL Amalgamated Clothing Workers, it was not a solid advocate of a labour party. Its members had split between support for the Socialists and the Communists. The ALP was an additional supplicant for the ACW's support. The ACW solved the problem by supporting all working-class parties while opposing the Republicans and Democrats. Joseph Schlossberg, the editor of *Advance* and treasurer for the *Leader*, made this position clear. He praised the latter paper but argued it was mistaken to advocate voting for any one particular party. He claimed he had always abstained from telling his members to vote for any one party, though he had urged voting for working-class candidates. He wanted to make it clear that though he was treasurer of the *Leader*, he did not wish that to be taken as endorsement of the paper's political line. Perhaps Schlossberg had a bad memory, for in 1920 *Advance* had attacked the FLP and declared that Debs was their candidate.[40]

Indeed the ILGWU, which put far more effort into supporting the Socialists and the ALP, was involved in a serious faction fight with the

Trade Union Education League (TUEL) and its Communist supporters. The ILGWU leadership intended to purge the union of the TUEL and by implication the Communists. This probably explains their enthusiasm for the ALP; it was a useful left cover for their purge of the Communists. Of course the Socialists had always had a good relationship with the ILGWU, and the case was the same for the ACW, but it was the non-AFL union that was cooling towards them. It was the ACW that had more weight in the New York labour movement. The ACW's central role in the reorganized *Leader* explains why the paper's campaigning for the ALP and the Socialists was somewhat muted compared to the propaganda the *Call* had provided at election time.[41]

The New York Socialists entered the 1923 elections in an extremely weak position with reduced membership, no newspaper and without the wholehearted support of the ACW. Attempts to get broader forces behind them had achieved very little. The *Leader* formally, but not very enthusiastically, called for an ALP vote. Much was made of the fact that the Citizens Union had endorsed a handful of ALP aldermanic candidates. Yet it did not mention that they had also endorsed a far larger number of Republicans. The *Leader* was proud that the Citizens Union had endorsed Socialist candidates; it claimed that the fact that non-Socialists were endorsing them was the sign of a breakthrough.[42]

Unfortunately the breakthrough never came. No banner headlines heralded election day in the *Leader*. The main coverage of the election was about Tammany. It was Jacob Pancken, a well-known Socialist municipal judge, who got the best results for the joint Socialist and FLP alliance, with 35 000 votes for the post of Greater New York City Associate State Judge. The *Leader* admitted that the rest of the results were disappointing. Not a single Socialist or ALP candidate won an aldermanic or assembly seat. More bad news rapidly followed the poor election results. Without any warning or appeals for money the *Leader* announced 'LEADER SUSPENDS WITH THIS ISSUE'. It claimed that though circulation had doubled from 10 000 to 20 000, the cost of maintenance was still too high. The *Call* had run for 15 years; the *Leader* had not lasted 15 weeks. The Socialists were too weak to relaunch the paper straight away, leaving them without an English-language newspaper in the whole of New York. Putting the *Call* in the hands of the labour movement had proved a serious error. Taking into account Schlossberg's attitude, the central role of the ACW may have been particularly damning. By mid-January 1924 the Socialists managed to launch a new English-language newspaper, but only on a weekly basis. Named after the British Labour Party organ of the same name, the *New Leader* was firmly back in the hands of the Socialist Party.[43]

In what was a presidential election year the prospects for the Socialists and the ALP did not look good. Nonetheless, James Oneal believed that it was still forging ahead. The 'magnificent showing of the British Labour Party' had inspired the Socialists. In addition election returns, at state and national level, indicated that a substantial block of American voters supported labour taking independent political action. Thus it was on the basis of vicarious success rather than any concrete achievement that the Socialists looked forward to the events of 1924.[44]

THE ROAD TO LA FOLLETTE AND OBSCURITY

If the actual strength of the New York Socialists and the ALP had been the criterion for launching an independent presidential campaign in 1924 it is reasonable to suggest that it would not have happened. The odds of any major force inside the New York labour movement supporting an independent campaign were remote. Once again the CTLC became strongly allied to Tammany, and the State Federation to Governor Al Smith. But the chance of a campaign taking place was not just dependent on the balance of forces in New York. National events changed the odds.

The decision of the Democrat and Republican conventions to nominate candidates that were unacceptable to the most conservative sections of the AFL and the Rail Brotherhoods threw the traditional non-partisan policy into crisis.[45] Coolidge was unacceptable to the rail brotherhoods for his actions against the rail strikers and his support for the Esch-Cummins Bill. Neither was better treatment expected from Davis. The railmen had hoped that William G. McAdoo would be the Democratic candidate, but his implication in the Tea Pot Dome scandal ruled him out. With La Follette failing to get the Republican nomination the CPPA had no alternative but to ask him to stand. La Follette's acceptance letter arrived at the CPPA convention on 4 July 1924, but he made it clear that he stood as an independent, not as a candidate of a third party.[46]

For the Socialists this was a mixed blessing for they had predicted, for several years, that the reality of the US political system would force conservative labour to break with the two main parties. In one sense they were proved right. La Follette was an independent candidate, but he did not represent a third party. The Socialists had attacked him on numerous occasions for not breaking with the Republicans; they also made it plain that they would not be part of a non-partisan campaign. Indeed, just before the CPPA 4 July Convention the ALP overwhelmingly passed a resolution committed to an independent party of labour composed of industrial, agricultural and professional workers. The Chairman of the ALP, De Hunt, made the intentions of the Executive Committee clear. In the event of the CPPA convention not adopting this policy, the delegates of the ALP would have no further function in the convention. Reality turned out to be the complete opposite; the Socialists fully capitulated to the La Follette bandwagon.[47]

The capitulation at the CPPA convention was presented in a heroic light. The Socialists claimed they had prevented the steamrollering of the convention into immediately endorsing La Follette. Hillquit had persuaded the conference to defer its decision until 4 p.m. The very next day he seconded the nomination of La Follette. He praised La Follette's labour record but argued the real achievement was that the new alliance had come together. He believed it spelt the beginning of a new political movement, of which the great masses of organized labour were the backbone. A convention would take place the following January to 'crystallize these forces into a lasting movement'. Hillquit's action contravened the policy of the ALP, but the party concurred without dissent, ignoring its own policy to the contrary. The basis of abandoning that policy was the promise of a convention after the completion of the election campaign. Hillquit had played an invaluable role in selling the package to Socialists and labourites in his own camp, some who were dubious about the La Follette bandwagon.[48]

The Socialist Party did not wait to see which way the AFL would jump. Delegates at its 12th National Convention voted, by 115 to 17, to endorse the action of the CPPA. A minority opposed, arguing that although prepared to cooperate in building a labour party, they believed the promise to form a party the following January was too vague not to nominate their own candidate for president. Debs, not at the convention, sent a telegram stating it would not be wise to nominate a Socialist candidate for president under the circumstances. The telegram contributed to making the decision almost unanimous. Debs announced, after the decision, that the party would have thrown away the greatest opportunity of a lifetime if it had made an independent nomination. The *Leader* claimed that it was not dropping the banner of independent labour politics. On the contrary, several million organized workers were associated with the Socialists in holding the banner aloft. They were stepping back a pace or two to meet the main army of labour so that they could march forward together.[49]

Nearly a thousand members of the Greater New York Socialist Party met to overwhelmingly endorse the La Follette candidacy. The ALP also announced its support for La Follette although not everyone in the ALP agreed with the new policy. FLP member Robert Ferrari declined the ALP nomination for the 13th Congressional District. Since the La Follette campaign was not a third party, he believed it was a choice between isolation or fruitful cooperation with a congenial political group. Therefore he decided to back Coolidge. He was particularly scornful that it was the Socialists who had nominated him, as they had 'declined in principle and deteriorated in action'. However, among leading FLP and ALP members Ferrari was an exception; the rest enthusiastically supported the campaign. Lefkowitz and Nathan Fine served on the state wide La Follette Campaign Committee for the FLP; De Hunt and MacDonald sat on it from the ALP.[50]

The AFL leadership did not respond as rapidly as the Socialists and the CPPA, but by 5 August, having received rough treatment at both Republican and Democrat conventions, it issued an appeal supporting La Follette. The executive made it clear that it was supporting an individual, not a third party. They were free from obligation to any party machine. Neither Republicans nor Democrats provided a platform that labour could support; the La Follette platform with its end to the evil of injunction was one they could endorse. The logic of events had dictated support for independent candidates, as the two traditional parties had lost all vestige of claim to the support of the American people. The campaign was to be non-partisan in the manner of all previous campaigns.[51]

In theory non-partisan politics meant independence from the two main parties, but in New York it usually meant more support for the Democrats than the Republicans. For some AFL officials it also meant a very close working relationship with the Tammany Democrats. A few officials did support the Republicans, but for the most part it was the close relationship with Tammany that underlined the hostility to independent political action. These officials were very keen to block the progress of the FLP, and had allied with Gompers to do so. What appeared as loyalty to Gompers and the AFL in 1920 was revealed as loyalty to the Democrats and sectional interest in 1924. It was not even the case that the AFL wanted the New Yorkers to drop support for Al Smith and Mayor Hylan; they could still endorse them.

It was only the Democratic presidential candidates that the AFL opposed. However, Tammany's commitment to the Democrats was so total that the leadership of the CTLC and the State Federation refused to back the official AFL La Follette campaign. This meant that Gompers suffered the embarrassment of the leaders of the AFL's largest state and city central bodies opposing AFL policy. The opposition of these officials had serious repercussions for the La Follette campaign in New York.

Initially it appeared that the labour movement, Socialists and liberals had united under the auspices of the CPPA. At Albany 45 presidential electors, representing every section of the movement, were nominated. Members of the Progressives, Socialists, ALP, FLP, trade unions and the WTUL were on the list. The committee for the campaign was even broader, including members of the NAACP, the United Hebrew Trades, Fiorello H. La Guardia and numerous representatives of the Railway Brotherhoods. At first sight it appeared impressive. The promise of labour's endorsement had united the majority of liberals and progressives behind an independent campaign. This was something the FLP had not done.[52] Unfortunately New York labour was not as united as appearances suggested.

The CTLC sent letters to affiliated unions advising withdrawal from the city-wide CPPA convention, claiming that the city-wide division of the CPPA lacked the authority to call such a convention. The La Follette headquarters replied that the meeting would go ahead, arguing that the CTLC's action was a trivial matter that was the result of a misunderstanding. At first it seemed that La Follette's supporters were right, for the CTLC endorsed the AFL's election campaign at its next meeting. The only vote against was that of the Longshoremen's delegate. However, John Buckley, head of Local 856 of the Longshoremen's association, claimed: 'Nine tenths of our men are voting and working for La Follette – no former officers of our organization who are now holding political jobs can deliver our rank and file.' Labour support for the campaign increased at a meeting of the State Federation, with only the Longshoremen opposing. Formally, the CTLC and State Federation were supporting the progressive campaign.[53]

Yet the ink was hardly dry on the reports of these decisions when a number of AFL officials and bodies began to oppose the campaign. At a national level, Berry, President of the International Printing and Pressman's Assistants Union, announced that the AFL could not bind members to voting for La Follette. The AFL had not committed itself to any party or candidacies, thus he would support the Democrats and Davis. As the election drew nearer opposition intensified. On 7 October the executive of the Building Trades Council of New York City decided to endorse the Democrats for state and national tickets. The Brooklyn Council came to the same decision. James P. Holland, President of the State Federation of Labor, declared that Gompers could not control labour and swing its vote to La Follette; no one, including himself, could do that. Labouring men would vote for whom they individually wished. He also attacked Coolidge, clearly hoping labour would vote Democrat.[54]

Worse was to follow. On 31 October the *Times* front page proclaimed 'CITY LABOR COUNCIL WITH 700 000 VOTERS SWITCHES TO DAVIS'. The *Times* reported that a number of CTLC officials believed that La Follette could not win and feared his campaign would aid Coolidge and Dawes. Thus they praised and endorsed Davis, claiming that the shift was in response to constant demands by their members. However, it was not a full meeting of the CTLC that had taken the decision but a number of its leading officials. It was not an official decision of the CTLC, but the *Times* article made it appear so. One of the signatories, Curtis, had made the transition from supporting the FLP to backing the manoeuvres of Tammany in the CTLC.[55]

Defections from La Follette to the Democrats continued when 'officers' of the New York City Allied Printing Trades Council and the New York State Printing Trades Council endorsed Davis. The Council spokesman declared that no member of labour in their right mind would support Coolidge and Dawes, but a vote for La Follette would split the opposition resulting in their election. The *Times* gleefully used these examples to undermine support for La Follette. It gave the impression that the rebels represented official union policy. In most cases the anti-La Follette forces represented individuals or groups of officials. Rather than oppose the La Follette campaign at open delegate meetings they had bided their time, making their opposition known later. As leading figures in the New York labour movement their opposition was significant. Whatever the official status of this opposition, labour appeared split and unable to deliver its vote to La Follette.[56]

Gompers informed the press that the CTLC statement of support for Davis did not represent the CTLC or its executive board, but was the outcome of a rump meeting. Six of the 14 present attending the meeting refused to sign the document as it was in violation of the direct instructions of the Central Labor Council. Thus the statement only represented the machinations of a few individuals. Not only Gompers rebuked those not carrying out AFL policy. Johnston, the President of the IAM and Chair of the CPPA, denied that New York City labour had split over La Follette. The executive council of the longshoremen's union rebuked the New York City Council of Longshoremen for defying AFL election policy. Timothy Healey, President of the International Brotherhood of Stationary Fireman and Oilers, left his sickbed to visit La Follette and assure him his members were backing him 'almost to a man'. He claimed that the CTLC officials represented only a few Tammany men, and that there was no real sentiment for Davis in the organization.[57]

Clearly the New York trade union leadership was divided over the election. The anti-La Follette rebels, apart from expressions of disapproval, escaped discipline. Indeed Gompers had an escape clause in the event of being unable to enforce the endorsement of the La Follette campaign. For he had stated, at the National Convention, that the AFL consisted of organizations enjoying full autonomy and that the central body could only make a recommendation. Yet the AFL executive often threatened the disaffiliation of bodies that ignored its will or even withdrew the salary of dissidents.[58]

Those campaigning for La Follette in New York had the handicap of a substantial opposition, even in the pursuit of official AFL policy. Nonetheless, official endorsement enabled them to build a more effective campaign for an independent presidential candidate than on previous occasions. Also the CTLC had a formal commitment to La Follette's candidacy. It was not until the very last week that its officials abandoned the campaign. Thus the CTLC nominated 12 speakers to aid La Follette; most of the speakers nominated remained loyal to the campaign.[59]

For the first time in several years the ACW put its national support behind candidates in a general election, asking its 140 000 members to back La Follette. They declared that the action of the CPPA in endorsing him was a big step forward in workers' consciousness. A few days later delegates from 127 unions attended a meeting to launch the New York City campaign. The campaign got an added boost from Fiorello H. La Guardia, who forsook the Republican ticket for the progressive party campaign of La Follette. The Socialists and the ALP agreed not to oppose La Guardia. In return La Guardia accepted that the Socialists would nominate him on their list. A La Follette Clerical Workers Progressive League (WPL) carried out propaganda among the city's clerical workers, including bank clerks, insurance clerks, stenographers, typists and accountants. As well as urging a vote for La Follette, the WPL leaflets stressed the need for white-collar workers to join unions. Much was made of the fact that La Follette had fought for higher wages for postal employees and federal clerks and that he stood for the workers of hand and brain. In comparison, Davis had repeatedly opposed organized labour and Coolidge had vetoed the bill increasing the salaries of postal clerks.[60]

A women's welcoming committee for Mrs La Follette, which included Socialists and progressives, was formed. Although the NYWTUL supported the campaign, it did not support the ALP but the nonpartisan campaign. Thus it supported La Follette for President and Al Smith for Governor. The NYWTUL played a central role in organizing a La Follette Women's Division in New York City. It distributed propaganda to attract women, not just as voters, but as workers. Leaflets urged women who laboured, 'with hand or brain in office, factory, school or home', to support La Follette. The women's campaign offered cheaper rents, food, clothing and heating, and the promise of a better life for women and their children with clean and honest government.[61]

Dudley Field Malone also returned to independent politics, speaking in support of La Follette on the All Party Progressive League Platform. On 18 September the campaign organized a massive rally at Madison Square Garden. An estimated 20 000 were present; thousands more who could not get in heard the speeches relayed on outside speakers. Norman Thomas, Socialist candidate for Governor, got the opportunity to address the vast crowd prior to La Follette.[62]

WEAKNESSES OF THE CAMPAIGN

A major problem for the campaign in New York was the constant need to refute the propaganda of the union officials supporting the Democrats. But La Follette's headquarters argued that the local executives concerned did not reflect rank-and-file opinion, and that straw polls among workers put La Follette ahead of the Democrats in New York City. They also claimed that unions representing 450 000 members in New York City supported him. It was not just the progressive unions of the needle trades that supported La Follette. Support included members of the largest print-workers' union, the Big Six (the largest typographers local), the Barbers' Union, 36 locals in the painters' group and the Electrical Workers Union, as well as many others.

However, Teamsters, Transit Workers, Building Trades, Longshore-men and Marine Workers were absent from the published list of supporters. The absence of the first three organizations is hardly surprising, as their leaders were well known for hostility to third-party activity. It is harder to assess the importance of the missing Marine Workers – in the past they had supported the FLP – as no reason for their absence was given. Whatever the reasons, it indicates that the campaign failed to maximize potential support. Thus in the closing stages of the campaign La Follette's supporters had to concentrate their fire on an internal opposition of AFL conservatives.[63]

An added weakness was insufficient financial support. AFL unions did not have a tradition of raising vast sums for electoral campaigning. By 1924 the unions were also weaker in terms of membership and finance. Many members had suffered long drawn-out strikes and wage cuts. The ACW had survived major lockouts, and by the time of the election its weekly newspaper appeared only fortnightly. The Socialists no longer had a daily newspaper. Nonetheless there were other weekly newspapers campaigning for La Follette. The railworkers' magazine *Labor* and the AFL national newsletter campaigned on his behalf. *Justice*, the weekly newspaper of the ILGWU, campaigned enthusiastically for La Follette, as indeed did most official union newspapers. The New York mass circulation Jewish Socialist press also supported the campaign. Thus the support of the trade unions, inside and outside the AFL, cannot be calculated purely in terms of the money donated to the main campaign.

THE RESULT

La Follette received 281 527 votes in New York City: 133 024 of La Follette's votes appeared on the Socialists' ballot, and 148 503 on the Progressives'. The city vote for La Follette was 20 per cent. This was 3.5 per cent above the national average and nearly 6 per cent over the New York State average. In no borough did La Follette get a majority. His best results were 100 746 in Kings (Brooklyn) and 86 664 in New York County. Coolidge's plurality in New York City was 136 240, garnering 626 111 to Davis's 489 871. There is no doubt that the Socialists, trade unionists and progressives had made quite an impact on New York politics. However, the Socialist candidates fared very poorly with Norman Thomas receiving only 44 852 gubernatorial votes from the whole of New York City.[64]

Thomas's poor showing was not a freak; he was too busy campaigning for La Follette to push his own candidacy. He agreed not to mention the Socialist campaign when on La Follette's platform. In almost every congressional district where the Socialists stood, they polled half or less than in 1920. Ironically, the only district where the vote held up was the 20th Congressional where the Socialists polled 42.7 per cent. However, it did them no good, as the victor was La Guardia for whom they had stood aside. In fact when Hillquit stood in 1920 he had obtained a slightly higher share of the vote (42.8 per cent), although not elected as he faced a fusion candidate. The fact that the Democrats and Republicans remained divided in 1924 gave La Guardia a majority of some 3700 votes. The Socialists had made a major contribution to the Progressive vote, but in doing so they had neglected their own profile. Their allies had benefited from their intervention, but the Socialists had gained little in return. The Socialists were the only part of the alliance genuinely committed to independent political action but were too weak to stop their allies from deserting the cause.

CONCLUSION

La Follette's New York City vote was 2 per cent more than he won in Chicago, but 17 per cent less than in Seattle. That New York did better than Chicago is somewhat surprising as the CFL had remained united for the La Follette campaign. The fact that one in five voters broke with the main parties is quite impressive. This raises an interesting point: New York was as ethnically diverse as Chicago, but had delivered a higher progressive vote. Indeed unions that represented 'foreign' workers, such as the needle trades, had played a central role in supporting the campaign and delivering their members' vote. How could this be explained?

Though there are several differences between New York City and Chicago, the one that is most relevant to this question is the existence of a strong Socialist tradition in the City. The Socialist tradition in Chicago was weaker. It is reasonable to assume that if New York's official labour bodies had united behind the La Follette campaign, the vote could have been even higher. However, the chapter on Chicago which follows will demonstrate that electoral success is not just a matter of official trade-union support, but of political organization. Indeed larger workplaces and more industrial-style unionism does not guarantee political results. Though New York's La Follette vote was less than Seattle's, the difference between the two cities was less pronounced than the case had been for the presidential election campaign of 1920. La Follette's vote increased in urban areas generally, and in New York State particularly. Indeed the vote was even higher in New York City. A Socialist tradition, urbanization and trade-union organization combined to give New York greater political success than Chicago. As Chicago was also urban and had a strong trade-union tradition, it was political tradition that was the key difference between the two cities. These factors are considered further in the chapters that follow.[65]

6 Two Steps Back: Red Flag to White Flag – Chicago 1921–24

In May 1924 John Fitzpatrick announced he had given up hope on political activity. Instead he praised the union label campaign as the way forward. He briefly mentioned the FLP, but only for the purpose of attacking factional behaviour. How could a man who had been a thorn in Gompers' side for so many years now mouth banal craft routinism as a political way forward? The answer is not to be found in the psychological make-up of Fitzpatrick but in the experience of the CFL and the labour movement he led. The transformation of Fitzpatrick was also the transformation of the politics of the Chicago labour movement. This chapter deals with that transformation, analysing the factors that caused Fitzpatrick's dramatic surrender and destroyed the Cook County Farmer Labor Party (CCFLP).[1]

Fitzpatrick and the CFL's commitment to building a third party ended just before the Robert La Follette presidential campaign began. This had repercussions for both the campaign and independent political action in general. This chapter will focus upon three major themes: the collapse of the CCFLP; Fitzpatrick's and the CFL's surrender to AFL policy; and finally the experience of the La Follette campaign. The high point of electoral success for the Cook County Labor Party was Fitzpatrick's mayoral vote of 1919. However, the vote was not sufficient to give the new party credibility. In electoral terms the Party was still-born and never recovered from its inability to challenge the established parties. From the peak of 1919 the trajectory for the CCFLP was down-hill. Electoral returns diminished until they were almost non-existent. At the end of 1922 the CCFLP suspended most of its electoral activity, intending to conserve its strength for a big push in the 1924 election campaign. In the 1924 presidential election campaign a third candidate, Robert La Follette, did achieve a vote higher than any other independent labour candidate had obtained in Chicago. Ironically this occurred at a time when the Chicago Federation of Labor had completely abandoned independent politics. The Chicago party had briefly performed better than its counterparts in

New York, but it never became a second party as the FLP had in Seattle. Though the New York party did poorly, it managed to sustain electoral activity right up to 1924 by uniting with the Socialists. In Chicago the antipathy between these two parties meant that no such lifeline was available. Thus, between 1921 and the demise of the Party in May 1924, there is little of importance to say about the CCFLP.

This being the case, why devote a large section of this chapter to the activities of the CCFLP? Irrespective of its electoral achievements the CCFLP was the vehicle through which the CFL chose to pursue its goal of independent political action. The Party's lack of electoral success did not break the CFL's commitment to building a labour party. The CFL pursued its goal in the face of both voter apathy and fierce opposition from sections of the AFL. Yet the CFL finally abandoned this strategy at a time when sections of the unions were moving towards independent politics. Thus the events leading to the abandonment of the CCFLP are central to understanding why the CFL ended its commitment to independent political action. The failure of the 1920 FLP election campaign, locally as well as nationally, forced FLP activists to assess the reasons for their defeat. Fitzpatrick concentrated on organizational explanations, and forced through changes of personnel and organization. Fitzpatrick believed that the 'greatest handicap' in the 1920 General Election campaign was that the FLP Illinois state secretaryship and national secretaryship were combined. This, he concluded, meant that neither the national nor state branch had the services of a full-time secretary. He proposed that Jay G. Brown become the national secretary, and that Frank J. Esper relinquish his national duties and concentrate on the state branch.[2]

Brown was an able organizer, former International President of the Timber Workers Union, a former secretary of the National Committee to Organize Iron and Steel Industry, and friend and colleague of W. Z. Foster. Brown's appointment became one of the causes of the split between left and right in 1923, but this was not foreseen in late 1920. Esper protested against Fitzpatrick's plans, arguing that the combining of the Illinois and national organizations was 'one of the greatest assets' in the campaign. The Illinois Farmer Labor Party had been the main source of funding for national expenses. He singled out only one county branch for criticism, that of Cook County. It had a permanent secretaryship, yet had not paid one cent to the state or national organization. Fitzpatrick's motion meant opening up a national headquarters, duplicating all costs of administration. Esper protested in vain, and by early December, Brown replaced him to push organizational work throughout the country.[3] Thus the main response to the failure of the 1920 general election campaign was organizational. The theme found echo in the rallying call of S. T. Hammersmark, Secretary of the CCFLP, to the Cook County FLP membership. Now was the time to build party organization. However when Hammersmark resigned the secretaryship in June 1921, the Party was almost non-existent.[4]

The new secretary, Gifford Ernest, believed that fighting unemployment and the open shop should be the main thrust of rebuilding the Party. Where ward organization did not exist, the county organization would direct the campaigns. Whether the issue was the Constitutional Convention or unemployment and the open shop, the *New Majority* did not give these matters priority in the first few months after the Fall election. Editor Robert Buck, and to a lesser extent Fitzpatrick, believed that internationalism was the key to winning over workers, especially those from an East European or Irish background.[5] The front page of the *Majority* regularly led on the crisis in Ireland; inside articles protested at US Russian policy. There were still many articles on issues of local concern, but these were usually the smaller items. Fitzpatrick, heavily involved in campaigning for Irish Freedom, believed that if the FLP was perceived as the most principled organization on the issue, then it could break the Chicago Irish from the main parties. Fitzpatrick told the Irish that only the FLP was 'foursquare for the recognition of the Republic of Ireland'. He urged a boycott of English goods and a support of the FLP as the way forward. As the year progressed, the balance between international and domestic issues changed. Increasingly the paper led with domestic issues and put international issues on the inside, for by late January 1921 the ferocity of the open-shop campaign and the threat of unemployment had grown. The *Majority* exposed the secret open-shop plans of employers' associations. The CFL intended to take 'aggressive' action against the open shop. For the most part this meant educating workers about the threat of union busting, and recruiting and retaining members.[6]

Fearing unemployment would become a threat to union organization Fitzpatrick called a special delegate conference on 21 February 1921 to discuss the issue. One solution advocated was trade with Russia. The *Majority* was emphasized as the best way of educating workers on the need to fight unemployment and the open shop. Indeed the threat became even more serious as the Meatpackers (the employers) moved to reduce wages and get rid of the eight-hour day.

Twenty-five thousand stockyard workers attended a union meeting to protest at wage cuts. As attacks on the unions grew, the ability of the FLP to intervene politically diminished. By the spring of 1921, the situation was so serious the CFL devoted a major part of its meeting to the future of the *Majority*. Robert Buck claimed that the finances were so parlous that publication might cease. He was bitter that W. Z. Foster had resigned as business and circulation manager. This, he claimed, forced the acceptance of advertising as a form of revenue. Buck also complained that the unions affiliated to the CFL were not sincere in pushing the paper. The only solution that resulted from the discussion was the CFL's offer to work with the *Majority*'s staff to find ways to induce unions to take subscriptions. The debate had been lengthy, the solution short and simplistic. In reality, it was yet another call for increased support based on will-power, and no different to previous failed attempts.[7]

BACKS AGAINST THE WALL

The issues concerning the *Majority* were for the most part the same as the concerns of the CCFLP. Moreover, there were few reports of activity from the precincts. Reports came from the joint county and Illinois branch secretary, but not from activists. Reports in the *Majority* claimed that the county party was attracting interest. Quarterly conventions were reported as well attended, but no figures were given.[8] Internal correspondence painted an entirely different picture. In April 1922 Gifford Ernest wrote to the Executive Committee of Cook County FLP, urging that they meet as the last meeting was 'non quorate'. On the very day that the Cook County primaries took place, due to executive committee failure to obtain a quorum, the Delegate Convention authorized the committee to select a committee of five. The calibre of candidates standing could not explain the apathy: they included Ed Nockels for Sheriff, Hammersmark for County Clerk and Gifford Ernest for County Superintendent of Schools. Even these candidates, well-known in the Chicago labour movement, could not inspire the executive committee. Was this apathy a matter of obstruction?[9]

It is unlikely, for the explanation lay elsewhere; the party's key activists were also leading activists in the trade unions. With the unions under attack these activists were central to organizing the defence. The stockyards strike of December 1921 ended in defeat, and by early 1922 the packing plants were effectively operating as open shops. In response to the bosses' open-shop campaign, at the beginning of 1922, the CFL organized a massive demonstration. Fitzpatrick wanted a demonstration large enough to deter the employers from taking any further anti-union action. This was not a favourable time for organizing such action. The movement was reeling from defeat after defeat. In July that year, due to a lack of enthusiasm, the CFL decided not to organize a Labor Day Parade. Therefore to ensure that the demonstration succeeded a massive propaganda and educational campaign took place. Leading activists such as Fitzpatrick, Hammersmark and Arne Swabeck were central to the campaign. These were the same activists centrally involved in promoting the CCFLP.[10] The concentration of resources on the demonstration paid off, with 'scores of thousands' marching. The turnout was a tribute to Fitzpatrick and his colleagues, but there is no evidence that their activity fed back into building the CCFLP. If it did, the Fall election results gave no such indication.[11]

Of the 19 districts where the Party could stand for the Illinois Legislature, it stood in only three. The six candidates got a total vote of 6086, of which 3105 were won in the 25th District. The Socialists did far better. In several districts a single Socialist candidate outpolled the total FLP vote. The first reaction was that although Chicago was the 'most difficult kind of a field' the FLP should have done better than a 'measly 6000 votes'. A more considered reaction was to revive the Chicago labour movement's interest in the party for the 1923 city elections. By mid-January 1923 this became considered over-ambitious. The Party decided to forgo intervention in the 1923 city elections in order to prepare for the 1924 elections. This decision marked a major retreat, yet the usual reports of growing membership and better-attended conventions continued to appear.[12] The key to the claim of better attendance lay with the Workers Party (the Communists), which had a tradition of working inside the CFL. At the October 1922 Cook County FLP Convention they had sent 12 delegates from unions; another ten non-Communist union delegates attended. This represented a total of 17 unions with 9000 members. Cook County contained the majority of the CFL's membership, yet only a tiny fraction of these sent representatives, which demonstrates how weak the party was. As the political interest of the Communists moved from abstention to involvement in the FLP, so the size of Cook County Conventions grew. However, even with increased Communist participation, in June 1923 the delegates only represented 25 000 union members.[13]

It is difficult to explain why Fitzpatrick, having persisted with the CCFLP for so long, dropped it so quickly. The explanation does not lie entirely in Chicago. However, it is not the intention to detail here the national events that led to the collapse of the FLP and the formation by the Communists of the rump Federated Farmer Labor Party. It is the repercussions that followed this fiasco that are central to this account. Fitzpatrick had intended to build a national progressive coalition inside and outside the AFL. The Cook County party gave him a base independent from the AFL for this project. (Fitzpatrick's support for the CCFLP was similar to the New York Socialists, who supported the American Labor Party (ALP) in order to pursue their aims inside the CPPA. Ironically Fitzpatrick opposed the CPPA, but in 1924 the bigger irony was that he and the Socialists dropped their insistence on a third party before backing La Follette.) As Fitzpatrick intended to relaunch the FLP in mid-1923, it was not the time to abandon the CCFLP. Neither was Fitzpatrick prepared to abandon the FLP in favour of the CPPA. He had welcomed the launching of the CPPA, but he led the FLP's national withdrawal from the CPPA in early 1923. The reason for leaving was the failure of the CPPA to break with non-partisan politics.[14] In early 1923 Fitzpatrick tried to relaunch the FLP on a broader basis. This was in contrast to the FLP's national executive decision a year earlier to reject a unity proposal from the Socialists. Fitzpatrick called on all labour, farm and political groups to attend a national convention to participate in forming a 'program for unity of political effort by the workers'. Fitzpatrick hoped to profit from the CPPA's refusal to launch a third party. Although the talk was of unity, the July convention took place under the banner of the FLP.[15]

The attempt to build influence on a national scale was doomed from the beginning. In spite of their earlier calls for unity the Socialists, fearful of alienating conservative trade unionists inside the CPPA, refused to take part. In a contradictory sense the existence of the CPPA was evidence of a radicalization, but it also served to isolate Fitzpatrick and his allies. It became the focus for those disillusioned with the AFL's political strategy rather than the FLP. This led to one of the major centres of left-wing trade unionism, New York City, refusing to join Fitzpatrick's initiative, preferring to work inside the CPPA. Moreover, with the Socialist unions boycotting the national FLP convention, it meant that the only organized force prepared to back the FLP was the Communists. Fitzpatrick, outvoted by the Communists at his own convention, lost control of the attempt to relaunch the FLP.

DESERTION AND SURRENDER

The capturing of the FLP by the communists forced Fitzpatrick and his allies to disown the new party. Nationally it was a serious setback, but the consequences were even worse for the Cook County FLP, leading to Fitzpatrick deserting a Party he had defended through thick and thin. Gifford Ernest, the long-time secretary of the CCFLP resigned but remained secretary of the Illinois branch. Meanwhile his wife, Ruby H. Ernest, a committee member of the Illinois party, demanded the resignation of J. G. Brown for his support of the July convention. Only six members of the FLP's National Committee voted for Brown's removal, and 19, including Fitzpatrick, opposed it.[16] The Ernests then got the Illinois state executive of the party to demand Brown's resignation by 25 November 1923. The National Committee rejected the demand and the state executive committee seceded in protest. The executive of the CCFLP refused to follow the seceders. This caused Ernest's supporters to resign from the Cook County Executive Committee. The county chairman, David A. McVey, and Fitzpatrick severed all connections with the Illinois branch and set up a provisional body in its stead. The atmosphere became so bitter that the party executive passed a resolution barring from office and conventions party members who owed allegiance 'to any group or organization in active conflict with the Cook County FLP'. Whether this action was aimed at the Communists or the supporters of Gifford Ernest is not clear.[17] What was clear was that the Communists and the progressives of the CFL had split. The progressives still supported the CCFLP but opposed the FFLP. Communist attempts to gain CFL support for the FFLP failed as they were in a minority.[18]

It was not the Communists who had split the Illinois party or divided the Cook County branch. It was Ernest and his supporters who did that in the belief that Fitzpatrick and the executive were too soft on the Communists. They wanted to stampede Fitzpatrick into taking a hard line against the Communists. Thus the CCFLP had not just split in two, but in three, with progressive or non-Communist supporters also divided among themselves. From the beginning the AFL executive had tried to stop CFL support for the new party but with the majority of CFL progressive delegates and the State Federation supporting the party Fitzpatrick would not comply. Now his supporters were in disarray. The difficulties caused by the failure of the 3 July convention and the ensuing splits had demoralized even the most determined. Whether it was by conviction, or loss of will power, some of the party's founder members, including the State Federation, withdrew support and began to persuade Fitzpatrick to do the same.

The abandoning of the FLP by the State Federation was the crucial blow and it gave Gompers the leverage he needed against Fitzpatrick. Walker, making no concessions to the fact that he had been an FLP activist, launched a major attack at the AFL national convention on those supporting the FLP. He declared that if as much energy had gone into supporting AFL policy as building the FLP, more would have been achieved. Only a small number of delegates voted for the Labor Party, and they suffered defeat by a 12 to 1 margin. The success of Walker's attack was proof of Fitzpatrick's and the FLP's isolation. The realization of this fact is the most convincing explanation of why Fitzpatrick dropped his party-building activities like a hot brick. The Communists became the scapegoat for the failures of Walker and Fitzpatrick.[19]

It took a leading Communist, James P. Cannon, to objectively analyse their blunder. The Communists had broken the united front with the progressives by splitting away to form the FFLP. The progressives, terrified of being labelled communist, united with the reactionaries. Cannon believed that the 'Gompers Machine' had been unable to beat the Communists and progressives combined. The Communists managed to isolate themselves, with reaction given a boost. The same threat of isolation drove Fitzpatrick into the hands of the conservatives. Subsequent events confirmed Cannon's analysis. At the State Federation Convention, Fitzpatrick personally denounced resolutions moved by the Communists. That the resolutions contained policies the CFL had always supported, including a labour party and amalgamation of the unions, made no difference.[20]

Why did Fitzpatrick make no attempt to rescue any of his policies from the wreckage? Of course he could justify his attack on the Communists by noting their treachery at the 3 July conference. However, Walker had already decided to abandon the cause well before this meeting. Fitzpatrick was under intense pressure to abandon his progressive stance before his conference was 'hijacked'. Therefore the defection of Walker must have affected Fitzpatrick before the Communists had hijacked his conference. Fitzpatrick had stood up to enormous pressure from the 'Gompers Machine' over the previous five years. After several years of threats, the AFL executive stopped paying half of Fitzpatrick's salary, but he refused to surrender.[21]

The key to his surrender was the fact of the removal of Illinois State Federation support. For he had continued supporting a third party several months after losing his wages. He had been undeterred by the lack of electoral success. Faction fighting from both left and right, the financial drain of running the *Majority* and the deprivation of AFL funds were serious blows. However, the removal of State Federation support was the last straw. Fear that isolation from the national and state union machines could spread to the CFL impelled Fitzpatrick to ally with the conservatives. The role of the Communists should not be over-exaggerated. Like Henry VIII's divorce, they were the excuse for a change of faith, not the real underlying cause. Their sacrifice provided the blood to cement unity between former enemies.

The Illinois Convention's decisions were a major watershed for the CCFLP. It could only exist, at least formally, with the support of the CFL. This it did for a few more months, but the loss of State Federation support was too much for Fitzpatrick to bear. On 18 May 1924 he delivered the final blow: he stated that there had only been one genuine FLP in existence and that had been sponsored by the CFL. He described his own candidacy as a 'burnt offering', which in the right circumstances he would do again; they had held the flag alone long enough. He also argued that the situation was confused, with numerous political organizations trying to exploit the political hopes of workers and farmers. It was, he believed, a situation of hysteria and mania for control. It left the CFL with no choice but to cease all FLP activities and to throw in its lot with the AFL. Two delegates spoke against, but the decision received overwhelming support. The CCFLP was well and truly dead. It had not survived as long as the labour parties of New York and Seattle, and played no role in the 1924 general election.[22]

Once Fitzpatrick abandoned the attempt to build a labour party he had little to put in its place. For years he had ridiculed the AFL's non-partisan policy. He had stayed aloof from the CPPA, and now he was in conflict with the Communists. Apart from the fact that he would no longer oppose the AFL's policies, he had little else to offer. No trace remained of the once insurrectionary policies of the CFL. The *New Majority* became the *Federation News*. However, a change of name was not enough. Robert Buck, its editor, accepted that the FLP had to suspend activity. What he could not stomach was full acceptance of the AFL's non-partisan policy. He argued that the CFL's acceptance of non-partisan policy and the FLP's suspension of activity were two different things. He believed the Party and its leaders had not abandoned their principles. They were still committed to independent political action but were simply making a tactical withdrawal. Buck was wrong and the CFL insisted that the *Majority* 'adhere strictly to the policy of the AFL.' The policy of the AFL was total opposition to a third party, not waiting for a suitable time in which to launch one. Buck had no option but to resign. With Buck gone, there was nothing to stop the CFL's newspaper from making a massive shift to the right.[23]

On 16 August 1924 the *Federation News* appeared, its change of title and policy a direct result of the CFL's adoption of the AFL's non-partisan policy. The first edition declared: 'The *New Majority* has gone – long live the *FEDERATION NEWS*.' With it had gone all aspirations to independent political action. Nonetheless, the new paper supported the La Follette campaign. Even before the change, the *Majority* enthusiastically reported news of the La Follette campaign. In the past it had criticized the CPPA for not committing itself to a third party. Now the CFL's organ was an enthusiastic supporter of a campaign that gave no guarantees of a new party. However, the *Federation News*'s enthusiasm did not win uniform reciprocation from the former CCFLP men; some, such as Buck, abstained. However, several former party supporters became heavily involved in the campaign. It is true that Fitzpatrick did not play as prominent a role in the 1924 campaign as in previous elections. Nonetheless, the CFL and *Federation News* gave more than token support. As will be seen, sections of the CFL enthusiastically supported the campaign.[24]

THE CHICAGO ROAD TO LA FOLLETTE

In early 1923 the FLP broke with the CPPA, but CFL support for the CPPA's La Follette campaign in 1924 did not come completely out of the blue. Fitzpatrick was closely identified with the FLP's break with the CPPA. He was not as closely associated with the return to the fold. However, signs of a thawing of relations between the CPPA and the CFL, and even the FLP, were obvious by early 1924. The Illinois branch of the FLP agreed to meet with the Illinois CPPA. They also agreed to send delegates to the national CPPA convention on 4 July 1924 to discuss backing La Follette's candidacy. The joint Illinois conference did not come to any agreement, but relations remained friendly and the FLP did not withdraw. When the FLP, nationally and at county level, made it clear it would not be standing in the 1924 election any further obstacles to unity were removed. At the same time the CFL agreed to return to the AFL's non-partisan policy, yet it delayed until 17 August 1924 before endorsing the La Follette campaign. Although Johnstone of the Painters Union and the Workers Party spoke against endorsement, the policy passed by 132 votes to 18.

The slowness in adopting the policy was probably a matter of caution. In the aftermath of factional fighting it is likely that Fitzpatrick wanted to present support for La Follette as endorsing State Federation policy. Thus the issue was not presented as endorsing La Follette, but as supporting the State Federation's political policy.[25]

The delay in endorsing the campaign was not mirrored by the CFL's newspaper. From the very beginning it was full of enthusiasm, not waiting for AFL endorsement to rally behind the CPPA's candidate for president. It also gave the impression that a labour party would result from the campaign. From the first announcement of La Follette's standing, to the day of the election, the *Federation News* campaigned fervently for 'fighting Bob'. Even with a new editor, they ran ahead of the AFL and CFL in supporting La Follette. By mid-August both the state and city federations were supporting the La Follette campaign.[26]

On 25 August the CFL's Non-Partisan Political Campaign Committee moved into action with both Fitzpatrick and Nockels present. Fitzpatrick explained that the AFL wanted every possible effort made to ensure the campaign's success. The committee formed a corps of speakers. They concurred with the State Federation by not encumbering the La Follette ticket with any other candidates. Whatever the outcome of the campaign the CFL clearly intended to take it very seriously. Though Fitzpatrick did not stand as an Illinois elector for La Follette, Nockels and W.E. Rodriguez did.[27] The CFL's campaign organizer was Anton Johannsen, a leading anarcho-syndicalist and friend of W. Z. Foster. Johannsen was part of the progressive bloc inside the Carpenters' union, which in 1919 had enthusiastically campaigned for the Labor Party. He threw himself into the campaign, stirring the CFL to action, visiting affiliated unions, organizing rallies and parades. Johannsen's centrality undermines the contention that those who had supported the CCFLP in the past did little for the campaign.[28]

Organizing meetings were inspiring events, with leading political speakers addressing large numbers of volunteers; enthused, they agreed to canvass on the day of the election. A large number of delegates, including Johannsen, passed a resolution that all local unions should declare a holiday on election day. Unions should do everything to convince workers and their families of the importance of election day, persuading them to spend as much of the day as possible overlooking the polls. Here was excitement similar to that which heralded the CFL's first independent political electoral intervention.

The campaign did not let up as the election neared. In the final weeks of the campaign the CFL held yet another spirited organizing meeting. Johannsen addressed representatives from every ward in Chicago. The local chairman of the Cook County La Follette–Wheeler campaign committee spoke, announcing messages of support from La Follette, Wheeler and Gompers. During the final days of the campaign the *Federation News* led with the AFL's call for the unions to redouble their efforts for La Follette.[29]

By the end of the campaign the CFL had raised $11 215.80 for La Follette, an amount that does not compare unfavourably with the $12 791.89 raised for Fitzpatrick's 1919 campaign. Taking into account that the CFL, in terms of membership and finance, was weaker in 1924, the figures demonstrate serious commitment to the campaign.[30] It is more difficult to assess Fitzpatrick's personal contribution, as he was not as prominent in the campaign as in previous elections. Nonetheless he was a sponsor of the 'Fola La Follette Unit' (Fola was Robert La Follette's daughter). It consisted of labour women honouring Fola La Follette's support of striking women household linen workers in 1921. They reminded women workers that Fola had stood on the picket lines. Compared to the major parties, the funds and resources received by the La Follette campaign were minuscule. However, in Chicago, the unions were major contributors.[31]

Unlike the New York campaign, there was no major opposition within the CFL to support for La Follette. The Illinois State Federation was also firm in its support for La Follette, and the central bodies remained united in their support. The Ladies Garment Workers Union (ILGWU) was particularly enthusiastic about the campaign. When La Follette came to Chicago in October he addressed a crowd of 11 000. Afterwards there was a parade of 4000 on which 'Garment Workers predominated'. This included 700 'Bobs' – women garment workers who wore their hair in a bob to demonstrate support for La Follette. In Chicago unions considered conservative in New York supported the campaign – these included the Teamsters, most of the building trades, as well as the progressive unions. Thus the *Federation News* and Gompers did not waste their time counteracting an internal opposition, as was the case for La Follette's supporters in New York. However, there was one section the progressives were unable to convince.[32]

Although Du Bois and the NAACP supported La Follette, the *Chicago Defender* did not. Instead it enthusiastically campaigned for Coolidge and Dawes. However, the La Follette campaign and the *Federation News* made no special effort to win black votes.[33] Though

La Follette's denunciation of the Ku Klux Klan impressed the NAACP, it made little impact on the *Defender*. It preferred Coolidge, who did not mention the Klan. It also gave star treatment to General Charles G. Dawes, Coolidge's running mate. The *Defender* knew that union labour detested Dawes. Nonetheless it defended him against the accusation of anti-trade unionism on the basis that not everything the unions did was desirable.[34]

THE RESULT

La Follette came third in Chicago, narrowly behind Davis, but way behind Coolidge who out-polled the Democrats and Progressives combined (see Table 6.1[35]). In a few wards La Follette narrowly beat Davis, but in most cases he came third. In the urban areas of Cook County, La Follette polled 17.9 per cent of the vote, slightly higher than in the country towns and Illinois state as a whole (see Table 6.1). However this urban vote was 2 per cent less than La Follette had garnered in urban New York City. The Illinois vote of 17.5 per cent was higher than the New York State vote of 14.6 per cent, but both figures were substantially lower than the 35.8 per cent La Follette vote of Washington State.[36]

A comparison with New York City suggests that the Socialist Party made a difference to the vote there. But in the state of Illinois the support of the State Federation and the tradition of FLP voting gave the La Follette vote the edge over New York State. These figures are of course general and do not take into account geographic and class breakdown. If we disaggregate the vote into different wards in Cook County we discover notable differences (see Tables 6.2[37] and 6.3[38]). In Table 6.2 most of the results are slightly above or around the average, whereas in Table 6.3 the vote is well above the average. The wards that gave La Follette support above his state and city average were in

Table 6.1   City and Cook County vote

	City	*Country Towns*	*Total*
Coolidge	561 584	104 776	666 360
Davis	208 512	15 767	224 279
La Follette	168 476	24 804	193 280
Total Vote	938 572	145 347	1 083 919

Table 6.2   Wards in Cook County where Polish voters predominated. (La Follette's percentage share of vote cast shown in brackets)

Ward No.	Democrat	Republican	La Follette	Total
4	2826	19 989	2355 (9.3)	25 170
8	4446	14 887	4323 (18.3)	23 656
11	4313	5 569	2238 (18.5)	12 120
16	4500	8 854	3731 (21.8)	17 085
17	3869	13 890	3316 (15.7)	21 075
27	4379	8 314	3357 (20.9)	16 050
28	4162	10 145	4213 (22.7)	18 520
29	6642	10 997	5274 (23.0)	22 913

Table 6.3   Wards in Cook County where La Follette polled above average

Ward no.	Democrat	Republican	La Follette	Total	La Follette share (%)
15	7113	12 586	6456	26 155	24.68
23	5119	7 707	4172	16 998	24.54
24	4040	5 057	2840	11 937	23.79
34	3540	4 806	4139	12 485	33.15
35	1813	8 941	4206	14 960	28.11
43	2204	7 889	4435	14 528	30.52

working-class areas such as the 'back of the yards' and South Chicago. The wards in Table 6.2 have been selected on the basis that they had sizeable Polish populations in the 1920 general election. Unfortunately Kantowicz does not provide a ward breakdown for the 1924 presidential election. Over 14 per cent of Poles who voted in Chicago did so for La Follette: this was more than 3 per cent below average. Thus in wards where Poles predominated La Follette received a smaller share of the vote. However, Poles were only 11 per cent of Chicago's overall population, so this does not entirely explain the result. More Poles voted Democratic at 47.8 per cent compared to 21.9 per cent of the city average. However, this was less than 50 per cent of the Polish community; the majority of Poles had not voted Democrat. It could be argued that the Polish vote for La Follette was surprisingly high. In two Polish wards La Follette had polled as high as 18 or 19 per cent. Even the average of 14.41 per cent was higher than the Polish vote previously given to Socialists or the FLP; it was second only to the showing of Theodore Roosevelt. However, the Poles had given less support to La Follette than the city's population as a whole.[39]

The explanation for this difference is not just that the majority of the Polish press ran a virulent campaign against La Follette. There was nothing unique about that: all major newspapers had opposed the campaign. However, propaganda that La Follette was pro-German during the war, and was still a supporter of the German point of view may have affected Poles more than other sections of US society. That being the case, it is remarkable testament to those Poles who ignored nationalist arguments and voted for a reform candidate. It is not the case that the Poles voted as a coherent bloc in the 1924 election. Over 37 per cent had voted Republican. It would not be until 1928 that the Polish vote became a solid block, with nearly 80 per cent voting for Al Smith.[40]

CONCLUSION

The progressives took slightly more votes from the Republicans than from the Democrats. However, Coolidge's vote outnumbered both parties combined; thus La Follette's intervention was not the cause of the Democrats' rout in Chicago. It was in the urban areas of Illinois that La Follette performed best. His city vote was 17.9 per cent as against a country vote of 17 per cent. On average, one in five voted for La Follette, and in some areas it was one in three. Taking into account that a high percentage of workers did not vote this was a significant insurgent voting movement. Of course it was not as successful as the Bull Moosers in 1912, but Roosevelt and his allies had split the Republican party, thus managing to obtain much of its resources and membership. The La Follette campaign of 1924 did not split either of the main parties.[41]

Nonetheless, the campaign did not live up to expectations. In the early days of the campaign Chicago and New York newspapers had held straw polls showing La Follette in second place or even in the lead. After a large La Follette rally in mid-October, a poll claimed his support in West Chicago had risen to 49.9 per cent. The same poll put Coolidge at 40.8 per cent and Davis at 9.9 per cent. The *Tribune* claimed this showed that Democrats were flocking to La Follette. It also warned that the West Side figures could not be generalized to the whole of Chicago. Just before the election the polls finally began to indicate that La Follette was beginning to fall behind and that Coolidge was heading for a large majority. Thus, it was only a week before the election that Republicans felt confident of victory.[42]

So why did the early potential of La Follette's campaign not become realized? As stated above, La Follette lacked a party machine. In Chicago, this meant depending on the unions and some progressives. The two main party machines in Chicago remained intact; there were no major defections to the progressives. However, in 1924 this was also the case in Seattle and New York. Yet Chicago, with a stronger, and more united trade-union tradition, fared worst. However, this formal appearance of strength hides important weaknesses. For the Socialist and progressive tradition was far weaker in Chicago. Thus, CCFLP supporters failed to enter into any effective political alliance outside of the CFL. When the CCFLP died, it died alone. In reality by 1922 the CCFLP, without a Socialist or progressive political tradition to lean on, was defunct. The high point of the 1919 election result had not been substantial enough to convince workers of the possibility of independent political action.[43]

The CFL, aware that its political strategy was not working, endeavoured to spread industrial unionism across Chicago. This meant that many of the more syndicalist-minded activists concentrated on this activity at the expense of the political. This may not have been, for the most part, a conscious choice. Besieged by employers and courts determined to weaken the unions, real choice was too limited to be tangible. To create a class-conscious working class that did not retreat into ethnic or sectional boundaries, it was necessary to involve all workers, irrespective of colour or origin, into the unions. Fitzpatrick and the CFL tried to do just that in 1919 and 1920.

The strategy had some success. Old world immigrants and some blacks did join the unions. Some of these voted for Fitzpatrick in 1919. However, the gains made by workers in terms of organization and confidence were rapidly lost. Fitzpatrick's strategy of creating a type of industrial unionism by drawing unskilled workers into 'federated unions' was unable to overcome the conservatism of some of the unions in the steel and packinghouse industries. The employers were strong and the AFL was handicapped by a craft organization that it

would not or could not change. This led Fitzpatrick away from his old
concept of federated unionism and for a time he pursued the aim of
amalgamation.

By 1922 beset by defeats the CFL passed a resolution asking the
AFL to call a conference of international unions to discuss amalgamating all unions in the respective industries into one organization. It
is hard to believe that Fitzpatrick and the CFL had any illusions that
the AFL would help. It was an attempt to shift the blame for failure to
where they believed it really lay. Gompers became infuriated by the
resolution; it angered him far more than the CFL's attempt to form a
labour party. Whether Fitzpatrick was serious in pursuing the resolution or not, he suffered a vitriolic onslaught from the AFL executive.
He rapidly dropped the idea and accepted the decision of that year's
AFL annual convention.[44]

However, the damage was done, with Fitzpatrick linked to the
Communists who were actively campaigning on the issue. It hardened
Gompers' resolve to finally break Fitzpatrick's power. Keiser believes
that Fitzpatrick's support for the resolution, and his subsequent dropping of it, stemmed from his experiences in the stockyards and steel
mills. Since defeats made the possibilities for success unlikely, even
with AFL support, he was not prepared to carry on fighting for the
concept. Though Fitzpatrick abandoned the issue, it did not deter
Gompers from intensifying his attack on the CFL leader.[45]

Fitzpatrick was caught between the devil and the deep blue sea. If he
supported issues advocated by the Communists, the AFL attacks on
him intensified. If he distanced himself from the Communists, he had
to drop principles he believed in, confuse his own supporters and
strengthen the conservatives. In the end, deciding he could not survive
without AFL sanction he chose the latter course. Thus he surrendered
his opposition to non-partisan politics.

At the time of the election of 1924 the Chicago FLP activists were
isolated in every sense. They refused to ally with Communists or
Socialists even though, deserted by the CFL, their own political organization had disintegrated. The CFL had suffered from the bosses'
attacks on the one hand, and the conservatism of the AFL on the
other. No longer the strong confident organization of 1919, it capitulated to the orthodox politics of the AFL.[46]

There was a massive gap between the early impulse for La Follette
and the actual outcome. Any explanation of that gap must take into
account the collective weakness of the Chicago working class and the
concomitant weakening of the CFL. Of course ethnic divisions and

loyalties to the established party machines also played a role. But nothing is static or determined in advance, for in 1919 a sizeable minority of ethnic voters broke with their community leaders. Even in 1924 the difference between Polish workers and the rest of Chicago was not that enormous. Nor had the ethnic vote solidified into hard voting blocs by 1924. It is true that a majority of the black vote was Republican, but this would begin to shift towards the Democrats in the next decade. Patterns may have been emerging but were not yet fixed.

During the 1924 election the situation was volatile, with opinions changing rapidly. What is the explanation for these dramatic shifts in support between the candidates? Local and ethnic considerations are important, and the national situation does not translate uniformly into the local one. But there was one national trend: this was early support for La Follette followed by decline, accompanied by an increase in support for Coolidge. Moreover, early predictions of Democratic Party humiliation were revised. La Follette was squeezed between a solid Republican vote and a recovering Democratic one. With some regional variations, it was these later predictions that became the reality. The same straw polls that predicted success for La Follette correctly predicted Coolidge's landslide victory.

The impulse for La Follette turned out to be far greater than the outcome. I have argued that the Chicago working class and its unions were far weaker in 1924 than in 1919. At the same time, the political impulse was far stronger in 1924, as of course was the outcome. Yet if the AFL had supported the move for a third party in 1919, and a stronger presidential candidate had stood in 1920, the vote might have been considerably higher. The experience of Seattle, where well-known candidates did well in 1920, would appear to support this contention. However, the reality was that the 1924 result was more substantial than that of 1920. This may appear to contradict the argument outlined above. But the correlation between working-class militancy and the desire for political change is a complex one. Defeat as well as victory can affect workers' political consciousness. There are no simple equations that can explain workers' political actions. Each situation must be studied in relation to its specificity and conjuncture. The working class was stronger in 1919, yet the political outcome weaker. With working-class organization weaker in 1924, the political outcome was stronger. Though generalizations are possible from these conjunctures, hard and fast rules are not easily applied.

When workers engage in collective action they may become less interested in political activity. It was the defeat of workers' collective action, especially of those working on the railroads in 1922, that led to the political radicalization of the rail brotherhoods. The radicalization of the conservative brotherhoods led to the eventual endorsement of La Follette by the labour movement. Thus it was the weakness of labour that led to the AFL breaking with its own policy of pure non-partisanship. This was true on the local level as well as the national; in other words, the increasing weakness of the CFL made it dependent on the AFL nationally. As some sections of the AFL became more radical, the CFL became less so. What was a radical move for the AFL was a conservative one for the CFL. Thus the CFL and AFL converged, backing a third candidate, not on the basis of independent politics but on the basis of non-partisan politics.

The problem for the La Follette campaign was that it had no party machine. La Follette rejected any move towards a third party until after the election results became known. Thus he depended, in the main, on interest groups to carry his campaign. The most important of these groups were the unions, but they had no party machine either.[47] The CFL, for a variety of reasons, had failed to build a party. By the time of the La Follette campaign it had given up the attempt altogether. Perhaps if the AFL had supported the CFL's efforts, there might have been a small but credible party in existence. Such a party might have been able to organize and sustain the La Follette impulse in its early stages. But the AFL leadership had insisted on the complete elimination of the FLP. Thus the unions campaigned as a diverse group without a party for the election. Although the AFL leadership called on the unions to provide full-time officials for the campaign, some did while others refused or were in no condition to do so.[48]

Without a party machine or an effective national press, the La Follette impulse was at the mercy of those who did. Arguments that La Follette meant chaos and an end to prosperity began to find a resonance amongst a working class that had come through the 1920 depression. Having suffered defeats workers were not ready for conflict. That is why many looked to the third candidate. They wanted Congress to improve their lot, not strikes. But now their electoral solution became equated with conflict and an end to prosperity. It was clear that La Follette faced formidable opposition, and that he was only an individual without a party. How could he carry out his programme? Thus it was not just a matter of the opposition to La Follette, but the perceived weakness of his ability to effect change. A vote for La Follette was a vote for an individual and nothing more. As arguments and scares against La Follette intensified, the absence of an organized party, rooted in the localities and that could argue back, took its toll. In such a vacuum, geographical, ethnic and individual loyalties become more important than collective ones.

Given this situation it is remarkable that so many workers nationally, and in Chicago, kept to their original impulse and voted for La Follette. No doubt campaigning by the CFL unions contributed to the vote of one in five. Without the CFL the vote would have been far less. But for the most part unions are most active in the workplace and least effective in the community. Therefore at a time when workers were lacking in confidence and fearing a return of depression, they retreated even from reformist aspirations at the ballot box. Without a party to effectively refute the scaremongering of the press and with a weakened union movement, workers took the line of least resistance. At the same time the CFL's abandonment of third-party politics ensured that votes for change were nothing more than protest votes. The CFL was no different to the other central labour bodies in this book in abandoning third-party politics. Only the Seattle body maintained its commitment to the FLP as long as Chicago. There are many similarities in the circumstances that led to the two bodies surrendering to the AFL leadership. However, there was one major difference: James Duncan's personal refusal to abandon his belief in independent political action. This difference, and the reasons behind it, are dealt with in the following chapter on Seattle.

7 Duncan's Last Stand: Seattle 1921–24

By the end of 1920 the Seattle Farmer Labor Party (FLP) had become the city's second party. This distinguished Seattle from the other two cities, where electoral success had not been forthcoming. However, second place had delivered very little with the FLP only returning three members to the state legislature, none of them from Seattle. William Short believed that supporting the FLP had cost the Washington State Federation of Labor (WSFL) every ounce of its political prestige. Prospects were not good for the new party, not entirely due to the electoral situation, but because of the growing hostility of the WSFL. The WSFL's endorsement had been an important factor in the FLP's electoral success. But, after the 1920 general election, the conservatives of the WSFL began to remove its support of the FLP.[1]

The main barrier to abandoning the FLP was the Seattle Central Labor Council (SCLC). James Duncan and his allies remained in control of the SCLC refusing to abandon the FLP. Driving the progressives out of positions of influence in the central body proved to be a difficult task for AFL conservatives. Duncan resisted the AFL conservatives as determinedly as John Fitzpatrick in Chicago. Short was wary of directly opposing Duncan and his allies. It was not until early 1921 that he began his offensive. Duncan and his supporters did not surrender without a powerful struggle. Ironically, their defeat came just before the launching of the La Follette campaign. It meant that Seattle's workers entered the campaign without their own independent organization.

This chapter outlines the civil war between the SCLC and the WSFL and the reasons for progressive defeat. It also evaluates the consequences of this defeat for independent political action. In terms of the FLP and the La Follette campaign, Seattle was electorally the most successful of the three cities. This chapter will identify the factors that account for this difference. First it is necessary to outline the reasons for the progressives' defeat.

The year 1921 saw the SCLC badly prepared for the conservatives' attack. Rather than concentrate on defending themselves from the WSFL, council members spent their time attacking each other. This lack of unity convinced the conservatives that the time to strike had come. The cause of the in-fighting was not an outbreak of insanity but the hostile environment that Seattle's trade unionists operated within. Though the defeat of the Seattle trade-union movement occurred a year earlier, the progressive and radical factions had remained united. Perhaps the moderately successful electoral campaigns of the SCLC had kept the various elements together. However, by the end of 1920, in spite of gaining an impressive vote, labour had little to show for its efforts.

Dissension broke out over 'labor capitalism'. By 'labor capitalism' the radicals meant those business enterprises run and managed by members of the trade-union movement. These included a labour-run laundry, a finance company, a property company and a deep salvage company. The *Union Record* stood at the centre of the controversy. Its sales declined after the defeat of the General Strike and the subsequent rise in unemployment. Big business also ran an advertising boycott against it. Thus the *Record* welcomed the new 'labor capitalists' as a ready source of advertising revenue. The radicals led by Phil J. Pearl saw things differently. They believed that the labour capitalists were exploiting workers and diverting trade-union money into the pockets of the directors. Matters came to a head when the *Record*, desperate for funding, announced it would raise $10 000 in stock. Labour had little capital, and the radicals and some of the progressives refused to give. The issue drove the SCLC into a serious crisis and changed the alignment of forces inside the SCLC. Both sides began to recall delegates to the SCLC in the struggle for control. Conservatives recalled several radicals, and Duncan was recalled by radicals in his own union. However, he obtained credentials from the Auto Mechanics Union and continued attending the SCLC.[2]

The ferocity of the conflict saw Duncan and other progressives enter into alliance with the conservatives. Duncan now depended on the conservatives to keep control of the SCLC. This dependence became his undoing for increasingly the dispute strengthened the conservatives. Short seized the opportunity to weaken the progressives in the WSFL. He sent a referendum to all affiliated unions calling for the election of the Federation's officials by balloting through the locals rather than at the annual convention. He also proposed, on the grounds of economy, to combine the offices of President and Secretary-Treasurer. Short's proposals carried by a vote of 4763 to 926. This ended the traditional compromise of electing Short as President, and a progressive as Secretary-Treasurer.[3] Buck, who had given the FLP much support from this position in 1920, suffered defeat by 7179 to

1854. Phil J. Pearl lost his position as First District Vice-President. Besieged Duncan turned to the conservatives of the WSFL to help him beat the left but he paid a heavy price. The conservatives gained total dominance of the State Federation. Even more seriously, the balance of power changed in the SCLC.[4]

During July the radicals tried to recoup their losses, campaigning furiously against the incumbent officers of the SCLC. A coalition of conservatives and progressives defeated the radicals by a margin of 20 per cent. Demoralized the radicals and their support dwindled. Not content with defeating radicals the conservatives passed a resolution requiring every delegate to the SCLC to sign a loyalty oath declaring that they did not belong to any organization that conflicted with the American Federation of Labor. Business meetings of the council became private, the number of visitors that could attend open meetings restricted, and sessions had to adjourn by 11 p.m. The radicals had suffered a serious defeat. It was the end of the progressive–radical alliance and would have serious consequences for the Seattle FLP.[5]

Short did not make a major attack on the FLP at the 1921 WSFL convention, but restricted himself to a report critical of independent political action. The convention dealt mainly with the labour–capitalist controversy. One major controversy was more than enough; an attack on the FLP might have split the conservative–progressive alliance, nor was 1921 an important year for elections. Short preferred to wait for the right moment. The *Record* noted that although the conservatives were in control, they had not taken any political action. Probably relieved at its vindication at the convention, it did not consider the consequences for the FLP.[6]

THE STATE OF THE PARTY

Unlike the situation in New York and Chicago, the Seattle FLP was not in dire straits after the 1920 election. Immediately after the contest, state chairman David Coates declared his belief that the FLP, as the second party in the state, could win in 1922. He reasoned that if every supporter for their ticket got a second person to vote with them the party would sweep the state. Perhaps this explains why Coates put a major emphasis on education and propaganda as the way forward; he also proposed producing a Farmer Labor newspaper. The only concrete legislative proposal put forward was for a Marketing Bill which would cut out the middlemen in the sale of farm produce, reduce prices to the consumer and increase profits for the farmer. Apart from petitioning for the Marketing Bill there was no mention of any other issue to campaign around. However, if it only required just one more push at the polls, then it was not an unrealistic strategy. There was no portent of the impending problems of losing the WSFL's support.[7] Duncan endorsed this strategy though he opposed the creation of a party newspaper, believing that a separate organ would undermine the *Record*.[8]

As 1920 came to a close the opportunity to put Coates' strategy to the test arose when the Thirty-Seventh Senatorial seat became vacant. The King County Labor Party swung into action. The *Record* enthusiastically campaigned for labour candidate Joe Smith. He was well-known in Seattle political circles not as a labour activist, but as a progressive. However, the *Record* was clear about the benefits of the candidate, depicting him as a hero of the Spanish War, cruelly denied a place in the First World War due to old age. The *Record* stressed it was all-important to get Smith to the legislature; failure would mean the end of the Municipal Markets Bill. It was a straight Republican–FLP fight; the Democrats did not stand a candidate. Though the *Record* gave much prominence to the campaign and the Municipal Markets Bill, it did not manage to fire public imagination in District 37. The poll was low, and the Republican won by 2672 to 982. Smith took the eight precincts where the FLP had done well in 1920, but all other precincts went Republican. It was not a disastrous vote, but it did not confirm the Coates' 'one more shove' strategy.[9]

The report of the County Convention, which took place at the end of January, showed no concern about the progress of the party. Though it declared there would be a membership drive, it concerned itself with constitutional change. County FLP organization would be integrated into state and national bodies. The *Record* believed that by adopting a new constitution and electing the appropriate committees to carry out the work of forming locals in the precincts, the party could be put on a healthy footing.[10]

King County FLP enthusiastically carried out reorganization. By 22 February 1921, it reported that it had amalgamated city locals into districts. This rationalization would enable activists in various precincts to get together. It would also help overcome the weakness of areas where there were few members. Subsequent meetings took place to inform members which district they were in and where boundaries were drawn. It was a top-down approach, with the committees telling members where to go. The FLP would not be involved in electoral activity until late 1922, as municipal elections were non-partisan and parties could not be involved. The party was all dressed up with nowhere to go.[11]

During the spring council elections the party contented itself with petitioning for cheaper streetcar fares. The campaign did not originate from the SCLC, Doyle or the FLP, but from Oliver T. Erickson, a conservative labour maverick. Meanwhile the SCLC endorsed Charles W. Doyle as labour's champion in the municipal elections.[12] Doyle did not mention the FLP in his campaign, but he did join in on the low car-fares bandwagon. Ironically Doyle's moderate attempt to win favour blew up in his face. Councillor T. H. Bolton, who considered himself a labour candidate though the SCLC refused to back him, probably feared losing his seat. Rather than jump on what now was an over-crowded bandwagon, he decided to attack Doyle for using the streetcar fares as a political issue. On 6 March Bolton's resentment boiled over as he linked Doyle with the SCLC 'reds'. He denounced the 1919 General Strike, which he had opposed and Doyle had supported. The attack was obvious nonsense. Even William Short came to Doyle's aid. However the damage was done: Doyle came last with a substantial 15 017 votes; Bolton got a larger vote of 19 073, but lost his seat.[13] He had damaged Doyle with his red smear, but it is probable that he alienated enough union men for his own vote to drop.

Independent political action had gained little out of the election. The streetcar issue, overshadowed by the split between union men, saw the SCLC's nominee come last. The FLP had not been able to intervene effectively because of the non-partisan nature of Seattle elections. Labour was divided and unable to achieve positive results at the ballot box. The 1920 election result was losing its lustre. Short's claim that the FLP was causing labour to lose political power was finding reso-nance, and support for the party declined further.

Even after the failure to push ahead in 1921 and the resulting infighting, the Seattle FLP remained active and enjoyed the support of the SCLC. At the beginning of 1922, the Seattle party continued to petition on streetcar fares and workmen's compensation. In the sum-mer the King County FLP organized a picnic attended by an estimated 30 000 men, women and children. Yet, in spite of the optimism and reorganization, the FLP and the SCLC did not stand their own candid-ate for mayor in the spring municipal election. An even more dramatic indication of the decline in labour's political activity was the fact that the SCLC did not endorse a single 'councilmanic' candidate, some-thing unheard of since at least 1910. Instead the SCLC concentrated on defeating Walter F. Meir, an anti-union mayoral candidate.[14]

Another indication of the decline of labour's political influence was the referendum on the Erickson streetcar fare plan. The plan was outvoted 40 000 to 15 000. Though the *Record* believed the vote was quite an achievement, it was yet another example of electoral failure. Nonetheless the vote indicated that there was still a substantial minority in Seattle who supported the reform proposals of the FLP.[15]

In this period of unrealized expectations and little progress, the phoney war between the SCLC and the WSFL finally ended. Short launched a war of attrition against the SCLC to restore the AFL's non-partisan policy. Encouraged by the Seattle Building Trades Council Short attacked the council for its continued support of the third party. He claimed that a number of unions endorsed a Federation letter asking that action on political matters be deferred until after the state convention. He maintained that Duncan and the SCLC renewal of support for the FLP, in spite of the Federation's letter, was proof that the SCLC was trying to usurp the state body.[16]

In effect Short was warning Duncan that he did not want the FLP intervening in the 1922 state elections. He had started the battle early to try and prevent the FLP deciding a course of action before the Federation met. He wanted to remove Republican Senator Poindexter, and to do this he needed to involve the labour movement in the Republican primary. He feared that the FLP would nominate their candidate first, presenting the convention with a *fait accompli*. This is exactly what the FLP wanted when it nominated Duncan before the convention took place.[17]

Duncan refuted Short's claim that the SCLC's policy was unrepresentative arguing that the SCLC had numerous new delegates and therefore adequately represented the rank and file. He accused Short of trying to undemocratically destroy the policy agreed at Yakima in 1920. Short replied he had letters from three times as many locals supporting the Federation's position as from those who had voted for the SCLC policy. As for the accusation that a few officials were undemocratically blocking the membership from deciding the Federation's policy, he maintained that the exact opposite was the case. He wanted the membership to discuss and vote on the issue at the convention. Disquiet over the present policy threatened division. Therefore he was not changing the policy, but enabling a discussion to take place so that the membership could decide.[18]

The temperature heated up with Short issuing a circular entitled 'Answering the Bunk of Jimmy the Dunc'. The controversy spilled back into the SCLC. The conservatives and the moderates had combined to defeat the radicals. Now Short's attack, on Duncan, signalled his determination to rid the SCLC of its political policy. The Boilermakers suggested they should divorce economic and political affairs, and stick to the former. Duncan offered to debate Short in public. The Barbers, Blacksmiths and Bakers all supported Duncan. The Bakers held a joint meeting, with their drivers, supporting the Council's case, and opposing Short. The attempts by the Building Trades Council, supported by the Teamsters and the Culinary Crafts Councils, to reverse the policy failed.[19]

Short's onslaught was halted, but the problems it created lingered. For his offensive not only caused a stir in the SCLC, but at the heart of the Labor Party itself. His arguments were beginning to affect even those close to Duncan and the FLP. Harry Ault, editor of the *Record*, and David Coates proposed that the FLP move closer to organized labour and wait until the State Federation met before taking any decision on political activity. For Duncan, this smacked of Short's policy; instead he proposed the FLP's programme be presented to the conventions of the various organizations. Duncan prevailed, supported by many of the old enemies of the *Record*. Although Duncan's view won, Ault had the newspaper.[20]

The tension between Duncan and Short put pressure on the relationship between Ault and Duncan. Ault tried to keep both men happy, but this meant less support for the FLP from the *Record*. The stage was set for a serious blow against the Party. As Duncan refused to broach any compromise with Short, it is fair to surmise that he had underestimated the strength of the opposition. The moment of truth came at the WSFL's Annual Convention, Short, in his opening address, urged all labour and progressive groups to unite behind the one political policy. On 13 July a resolution was moved that the WSFL should adopt the AFL's non-partisan policy in the coming election. It is not the case that everyone who spoke for the motion was overtly hostile to the FLP. George Maston, the state chairman of the Railwaymen's Political Club, stated he did not oppose the FLP but he wanted them to 'lay off' the senatorial race.[21]

FLP supporters at the convention put up a fierce defence of their party and the non-partisan resolution was not put until the following day. When the vote finally took place, Short won by 110 to 48, with the majority of the pro-FLP vote coming from Seattle delegates. Delegates from Seattle also voted 49 to 25 in favour of non-partisanship and against the standing policy of the SCLC. A majority of these anti-FLP delegates represented non-SCLC locals. The convention endorsed

Short's plan to unite all labour and progressives to defeat incumbent senator Miles Poindexter inside the Republican primary. The extent of Duncan's surprise at this decision is measured by the fact that he immediately offered cooperation. Even though two-thirds of the convention had rejected affiliation with the FLP, he believed that cooperation was possible. Short, however, refused to meet with Duncan or any other FLP representative.[22]

During the state convention the SCLC delegates returned to Seattle for a council meeting. They decided, by a two-thirds majority, to give preference to union business of a distinctly local character as too much time was spent on 'matters extraneous' to the interests of Seattle organized labour. It is possible that not only conservatives supported the rule, but also the syndicalists, who complained that too much time was spent on political rather than economic matters. If it was meant to be a conservative measure it backfired. The WSFL provided details of its non-partisan campaign which the council promptly filed and ignored. Short and his supporters discovered that Duncan had tricked them, as the new by-law became used to block WSFL policy. Of course Duncan and his supporters were now a minority in state, and perhaps even in city, terms. Short must have believed that he had solved his problems with the SCLC for good. Nonetheless Duncan and his supporters carried on resisting from their besieged position. Short turned to Gompers for support in enforcing his policy.[23]

Gompers asked the SCLC why it was not lining up with the State Federation over election policy. He requested that a special meeting be devoted to the issue, and that Short address it. The CPPA also urged the SCLC to unite to defeat Poindexter. Instead of complying with Gompers, the SCLC appointed a committee of three to present the facts to Washington labour. Duncan announced he was standing as an FLP candidate for Senator. He argued that the FLP was still the second party in Washington, and that more producers supported it than in any other state. The Democrats were the third party; Poindexter would undoubtedly win the Republican primary. Therefore he believed the best-placed party to challenge Poindexter was the FLP. Meanwhile Short continued trying to pull the SCLC into line with Federation policy.[24]

The dispute between Short and Duncan put the *Record* in an embarrassing position. It depended on both the WSFL and the SCLC for support, yet it enthusiastically supported the FLP. Ault also worried about the increasing isolation of the FLP. With Duncan unopposed, his primary was a mere formality and all attention focused on the Republican contest. This gave Ault an excuse: he was not arguing against support for the FLP, but merely saying that it was Short's campaign to defeat Poindexter that mattered most. The *Record* concentrated on the Republican primary, almost to the exclusion of all else. The FLP almost disappeared from its pages, and to all intents and purposes it appeared that the *Record* supported the non-partisan policy of Short.[25] Unfortunately for Ault and Short, Poindexter won the primary, and therefore the issue became whether to support the FLP or the Democrats.[26]

The Democrats were extremely weak in Washington State, and this explains why Short had planned to defeat Poindexter inside the Republican Party rather than outside of it. Opposed to independent political action, it appeared that the WSFL had no choice but to switch its support to the Democrats. Most progressive support went to the Democratic candidate Clarence C. Dill. Unable to carry on with his previous ambiguous attitude, Ault returned to the FLP fold. The *Record* would make every effort to secure the election of FLP candidates. For a few months Ault had had the luxury of being on the same side as Short. Ault was back in the opposing camp, but was saved from further embarrassment when Short declared that he wished to avoid further controversy in the ranks of labour. Therefore the Executive Council of the State Federation would not make any recommendation for the senatorial race.[27]

This was not a victory for the FLP since the State Federation had withheld its endorsement. Short officially remained neutral, but behind the scenes he worked for Dill. Towards the end of October most of the locals in the state were supporting Dill. However, the SCLC remained loyal to Duncan, as did several of its affiliated branches. Duncan took his two weeks annual holiday in order to campaign. Two Carpenters locals deplored the action of the Building Trades' Council in endorsing the Democrat candidate for Senate. Boilermakers' Local 104, which earlier had been critical of the SCLC's political policy, made a donation and deplored those trying to nullify the action. Meat Cutters Local 81, claiming they had received an insulting letter from the State Federation over the FLP, confirmed support for the FLP, and declared they would leave the Federation if similar letters followed. Martin Flyzik, District President of the United Mine Workers, announced that Duncan had the support of miners throughout the whole state, claiming that miners were raising money for the campaign and holding mass meetings in their camps. He also scorned press reports that the miners were supporting the WSFL's policy.[28]

The day before the election, the *Record* urged support for the FLP. But unlike previous elections, labour and progressive voters were divided. Most progressives supported Dill and the Democrats, and the SCLC no longer could claim support of the State Federation, or even of some of its own affiliates. Dill's victory and the overall results confirmed that the FLP had fallen from second party to third. Even in King County, where Duncan polled best, the FLP ran behind the Democrats. This was a serious setback for Duncan and the FLP. In 1920 he had won 33 727 votes in Seattle; in 1922 he received only 12 034 in King County.[29]

The result was a boon for Short and a blow for Duncan. It meant the conservatives had the upper hand, and Short could return to his war on Duncan and his followers. Duncan's defiance of Short now stood on very weak ground. Perhaps Duncan was not aware how much his union base had disintegrated. For example, Carpenters Local 131, a founding affiliate of the Seattle FLP that had enthusiastically backed the party, by the spring of 1922 was no longer supporting the FLP. It ignored all political activity, including the Federation's non-partisan political campaigns.[30] Local 131 had provided keen FLP activists; now they were quiescent. This suggests that Duncan's support had become increasingly removed from the grass roots, and now mainly existed at the meetings of the SCLC. However, as there was a direct relationship between union activists and the SCLC, he was unable to ignore the lack of support permanently. Nevertheless, immediately after the election Duncan had no intention of surrendering. He called on the members of the FLP to keep up the fight. The FLP had got more than the 10 per cent required to keep it in the primaries. Unfortunately for Duncan, the main fight in the coming months was not that of spreading the influence of the FLP, but of survival against the onslaught of Gompers and Short.[31]

Almost immediately after the election, the AFL executive council acted on a complaint from the President of the United Association of Plumbers and Steamfitters. He claimed that several of his locals in Seattle had protested at the SCLC's refusal to agree with the AFL's non-partisan political policy. Gompers was empowered to turn the Seattle Central Body into a 'bona fide' trade union organization, 'complying with the constitution and principles of the AFL'. He ordered the SCLC to pledge loyalty to the constitution and the policy of the AFL. Unless the SCLC complied with the AFL's instructions it would lose its charter. The SCLC discussed the AFL's ultimatum on 18 April 1923; it had sixty days to comply or have its charter removed.[32]

Duncan suggested they should reply with a mild but firmly worded letter, denying the charges and putting the record straight. However, rather than take Duncan's advice, the SCLC appointed a committee to draft a reply. The committee's reply created further friction between Duncan and the AFL executive. Gompers wrote to the SCLC that, since its reply effectively admitted the charges against it, there was no need for further investigation. He demanded that the SCLC abide by the constitution of the AFL and adhere to its policies. His letter would be read before the full SCLC. He did not consider further action necessary, and the AFL executive council would ignore Duncan's attempt to 'dissemble'. The executive expressed gratification at the SCLC's professed intent to obey the laws, constitution and principles of the AFL. Copies of the letter were sent to Short and to the executive officers of the international unions.[33]

To all intents and purposes Duncan was called a liar and the threat of the removal of the SCLC's charter was implicit. Although Duncan did not resign for two more months, and the SCLC did not purge itself of third partyism until the Fall, the SCLC immediately became very cautious in its political activity. Delegates ignored a request to attend the FLP convention, in Chicago to relaunch the third party.[34] This denied Fitzpatrick's project support from the Seattle union movement. Although acting cautiously, and despite the draconian action of the AFL, the third-party supporters still refused to surrender, making Short determined to see the charter removed immediately. The SCLC protested its loyalty, offering to comply on all issues except the FLP.[35]

Short immediately rejected the SCLC's response, stating that it was tacitly complying but in reality not carrying out its responsibilities. He claimed that SCLC meetings had become smaller: whereas 250 delegates used to attend now only 95 gathered. Short believed it would be easy to defeat Duncan and his supporters. As proof he pointed to the result of the State Federation election of officers the previous week, in which he had run unopposed and his entire slate had won. Duncan had even failed to win election as a teller. However, Duncan was not completely without support as some results were close. In King County, Short's candidate for Vice-President received 1383 votes to the 937 of William McGuern, a Duncan supporter. Short's vote for president was 4749; Duncan's vote for teller was 2141. The top vote for teller was 3754. Thus Duncan still enjoyed substantial support in Seattle and throughout the state. But not substantial enough to deter Short from seeking the complete crushing of Duncan and his allies.[36]

The third-party supporters in the SCLC attempted to rally support to defend themselves from further blows. In advance of the annual State Federation Convention they printed and published the full correspondence between the SCLC and Gompers, who received 25 copies. A further 5000 were distributed to Seattle unions, central labour bodies and state federations. Members of the SCLC visited other states to put their case. The SCLC put up a far more vigorous fight inside the AFL in defence of the FLP than either the CFL or New York third-party activists.[37]

Gompers, not to be hurried by Short, bided his time. No doubt he wanted to see the result of the AFL's and WSFL's conventions before acting. All attention now turned to the State Federation Convention with the expectation that controversy would erupt. For 15 minutes acrimonious debate ensued, but the explosion never came. Martin J. Flyzik of the miners tried to rally support for the SCLC. When Robert Hesketh, a conservative city councillor, spoke against, all was set for a major row. Then a delegate moved that the matter be postponed indefinitely without prejudice to anyone. This received vocal unanimous support, and the moment of crisis passed. This was not as even-handed as it appeared, for it meant that the SCLC would have to face the wrath of the AFL on its own.[38]

The next day Duncan announced his retirement from the SCLC. Short had won a total victory. With nobody of Duncan's stature left to continue the fight against Gompers and Short, no serious obstruction remained to prevent the AFL turning the SCLC into a 'bona fide' union organization. In late September Gompers addressed a conference of presidents, secretaries and other officers of the Seattle unions. He stated that if the SCLC, like the Chicago Federation of Labor and the Illinois State Federation of Labor, disavowed its opposition to the principles of the AFL and declared for its policies, all would be well. However, to prevent the revocation of the charter, those present must attend the SCLC, and make sure that delegates loyal to the AFL also attended. He was quite clear that if this did not happen, a central body loyal to the AFL would be formed.[39]

Several weeks later Gompers triumphantly wrote to the executive council that the SCLC had decided to unreservedly comply with the AFL and all its rulings. He enthused on the good relations between the two bodies and the splendid work the SCLC were doing. The council sent a letter to Gompers pledging its opposition to dual unionism, and loyalty to all aspects of AFL policy. The signatories did not just include the moderate C. W. Doyle, but two of the FLP's firmest supporters,

Martin Flyzik and Phil Pearl.[40] This was the end of the SCLC's affiliation to the FLP and to any form of militant independent political action. Duncan and a few others remained loyal to the FLP, but became removed to the margins of organized labour. The conservatives who took control of the SCLC had little taste for any political action. This became evident in the subsequent campaign for La Follette in which the SCLC leadership played a passive role.[41]

THE SCLC AND THE LA FOLLETTE CAMPAIGN

Neither the WSFL nor the SCLC played a leading role in the La Follette election, and though formally endorsing the campaign, they gave little support. However, the official response of the WSFL and the SCLC does not tell the full story. This section describes the formal response of the two bodies and, more importantly, the activities of those unions and individuals who did actively campaign.[42]

The AFL's endorsement of La Follette came too late for consideration at the WSFL's Annual Convention. For the first time in several years the convention passed by without any controversy over independent political activity. FLP members were present, but remained silent on the issue of a national party. The more assertive of them were pinning their hopes on the La Follette candidacy, but made no effort to raise the issue of a third party at the convention. Duncan, though still supporting the FLP, had retired from union activity and was not there to raise it either. It was a matter of waiting for La Follette to do the job for them.[43]

State leaders determined not to endorse La Follette in advance of the AFL nationally. Therefore the convention discussed state candidates, not national ones. Leading FLP members Phil Pearl and Martin Flyzik did not challenge the non-partisan strategy of the Federation. Thus the Federation was late in turning its attention to the La Follette campaign. The executive finally found time to take its decision on 19 October 1924. Its endorsement of La Follette, when it finally came, was full and warm-hearted. Short rushed out a circular to affiliates, demanding an active campaign. He supported La Follette and had already supported the campaign before the executive decision.[44]

The failure of the WSFL and SCLC in giving a lead was not typical of Seattle's labour attitude in general. Although labour and progressives split over support for the state and local candidates, most supported La Follette. The Railroad Brotherhoods supported some FLP candidates, and the FLP opposed some CPPA-sponsored candidates. When it came to the presidential race there was complete unity between the main forces of labour and the progressives. The FLP split between the Communists, who supported their own candidates, and the rest of the old SCLC third-party activists who went with the La Follette campaign. The Communists bolted, but the original FLP members stayed and offered their support to the CPPA. The Communists received a tiny vote, and had little effect on the campaign.[45] The *Record* campaigned hard for La Follette from the start. It did not wait to see which way the official union bodies jumped. Progressives, labour men and the railwaymen's political club in particular started organizing unionists for La Follette in Seattle, forming a Trade Union La Follette Club of King County. They agreed not to endorse any other candidates and to concentrate on building support for 'Fighting Bob'.[46]

As well as the trade-union committees, there was a Seattle La Follette for President Club. A meeting of 250 appointed its committee, which in addition to local progressives had a member of the FLP as secretary. The FLP in Seattle not only played a prominent role in the La Follette campaign, but also stood its own candidates in the locality. Though the SCLC was slow in acting, as the campaign progressed more and more local unions took part. The Cooks and Assistants Local 33 appointed a committee to raise money for La Follette. The streetcar men organized a public meeting to support La Follette. The International President of Seattle Painters, at a mass meeting, urged his members to support the campaign. The Railroad Brotherhoods distributed 150 000 copies of a La Follette campaign special throughout the state of Washington. Carpenters 131, who had been founders of the Seattle Labor Party, sent money to the state campaign, as did a millmen's local. In the absence of the SCLC's official presence the King County CPPA intervened to coordinate and extend union support.[47]

Unlike New York, there was no major division between union officials over support for the campaign. At no time did the state or city bodies oppose it. There was only one serious opponent, Martin J. Flyzik, who came out for Coolidge. But his opposition may not have counted for much, for his miners' membership had declined due to unemployment and a series of defeated strikes.[48]

In spite of the local union's campaign and La Follette's popularity among trade unionists and progressives, the SCLC remained passive. It was not until Frank Morrison, Executive Secretary of the AFL, visited the council that it finally called a trade-union rally. A diverse platform of trade-union speakers, including Short and the maverick Robert Hesketh, addressed a large crowd.[49] On the day before the election 3000 attended Seattle's largest rally of the campaign. The platform included Democrat Thomas R. Horner as well as John C. Kennedy of the FLP. The campaign had ended on a high note and the *Record* was full of optimism for the result.[50]

THE ELECTION RESULT

La Follette garnered 30 102 votes in Seattle, 36 per cent of the total and double the national average. There was little difference between his vote in Seattle and in King County or Washington as a whole. His state average was 35.8 per cent compared to 37.8 per cent for King County. The slightly higher vote in King County probably reflected the fact that farmer organization was more radical there. The urban bias towards La Follette that had occurred in New York State and Illinois was not apparent in Seattle. Support for La Follette was fairly even throughout the towns and countryside of Washington State (see Table 7.1).[51]

Table 7.1   1924 Presidential vote

	Republican	*Democrat*	*La Follette*
State wide	220 224	42 842	150 727 (35.8%)
King County	60 438	7 404	41 146 (37.75%)
Seattle	47 451	6 023	30 102 (36.0%)

However, a comparison of the result with the 1920 mayoral and general elections reveals an interesting feature: La Follette's vote in Seattle was lower than Duncan's in 1920 (see Table 7.2).[52] Duncan had got 40 per cent of the poll in 1920, 4 per cent more than La Follette's share (though it was a mayoral election).[53] Also if we compare the votes with King County in 1920, we see that La Follette received just 1.35 per cent more than the FLP vote for governor. It is true that La Follette garnered 11 per cent more than the FLP presidential candidate of that year. The little known Christensen ran well

Table 7.2   A comparison of the 1920 Labour vote with La Follette's vote

	Bridges FLP governor (1920)	Duncan mayoralty (1920)	FLP presidential (1920)	La Follette (1924)
State wide	121 371 (30.5%)	—	77 068 (20.0%)	150 727 (35.8%)
King County	39 034 (36.0%)	(Seattle only)	26 768 (25.0%)	41 146 (38.0%)
Seattle	N/A	34 049 (40.1%)	N/A	30 102 (36.0%)

behind the whole of the FLP ticket in Seattle and Washington State as a whole (see Table 7.2).

Scholars have not noticed that Duncan did better than La Follette or, to put it another way, that the La Follette result was actually a sign of the *decline* of third-party voting in Seattle. Duncan, the hard-nosed trade unionist and fervent prohibitionist, had done better than the 'fiery' but more diplomatic La Follette. The comparison demonstrates that in Seattle, and to a lesser extent in King County, there was a solid trade union–progressive alliance that could win a substantial vote without La Follette. The poor performance of the 1920 presidential campaign was due to the fact that the candidate, Parley P. Christensen, was not as well-known as Duncan or Bridges. However, in less urban areas La Follette did far better than the 1920 FLP candidates. The state wide figures in Table 7.2 highlight this.

The Seattle experience demonstrates that well-known candidates are central to success. There is little difference between La Follette's, Duncan's or Bridges' vote – but they all polled well ahead of Christensen. Still, La Follette was a more substantial candidate than Duncan or Bridges, and therefore should have done better. It is probable that several years of AFL anti-third-party activity, plus the decline of the trade unions, meant that in Seattle the vote stagnated. In New York and Chicago the third-party vote started from such a low level that it was not difficult to improve on previous results.

How are we to find the answer to La Follette's failure to do better than Duncan did in 1920 Seattle? We could become lost in a number of complex tentative solutions. Perhaps Seattle's citizens preferred a hard-line prohibitionist, or maybe La Follette was not 'nativist' enough. The two men's stand on the First World War was identical but Duncan had faced a far more hostile press; at least one more

Seattle daily newspaper had supported La Follette's campaign. There is one major difference between the two persons: the nature of their campaigns. This is not a reference to the propaganda involved, but to the actual organization. Duncan's was more of a trade-union grass-roots campaign. The SCLC and its affiliates enthusiastically built support for it, far more than the alliance of progressives and a less centrally organized labour movement did in 1924 for La Follette. Five thousand had attended a pro-Duncan Rally in 1920; the largest La Follette rally had 3000 present. Thousands were locked out of the 1920 FLP presidential rally.

Of course the difference may not just be due to the attitude of trade-union organizers and their rank and file. It is also the case that the trade-union movement was weaker in 1924 than in 1920. Union membership had seriously declined. In 1920, the year Duncan stood, Seattle's claimed union membership had been over 21 000. This was probably an exaggeration, but even the next year the figure was still 15 335. However, by 1924 it was down to only 12 320. Membership losses had been heavy, strikes fewer and union leaders more conservative. Miners' District 10 had suffered several defeats and, in the 1924 election, its leader supported the Republicans. It was a far weaker Seattle labour movement that took part in the 1924 election.[54]

It was also less radical, not just at the top, but also at the grassroots level. The more radical metal trade workers from the shipyards became lost to the movement when the yards closed. Ironically it was the more conservative rail brotherhoods who became the firmest adherents of independent political action. It was these railway workers and their comrades in the Machinists that put their backs into the La Follette campaign in the light of SCLC passivity. The Railroad Brotherhoods even insisted on standing their own candidate for Governor under the old FLP banner. It was in Washington State that the real FLP made its last and gallant stand. Though they only received 40 000 votes state wide, the 6000 plus votes in Seattle were just over 8 per cent. Considering that the SCLC and the WSFL had refused to endorse the FLP, this was not a humiliating outcome. As a beginning it might have been a useful result, but for a party that had been in second place, third place meant its final attempt.[55]

In 1922 Duncan found consolation in the fact that the FLP had got over 10 per cent, a result that ensured an automatic place on the ballot. He had issued a rallying call to rebuild for 1924, but starved of official trade-union support the party declined rapidly. After 1924 it withdrew from all active political life. There is no doubt official union support was essential. The conservative wing of the Seattle labour movement was well aware of that, hence its collaboration to break Duncan's grip on the SCLC. Brewery workers were particularly hostile, and backed Short in his attempts to undermine Duncan and the SCLC.[56]

The SCLC's experiment with independent political action ended by 1923. Cast adrift from the official union movement there was nowhere else to go. Within the SCLC, Communists and the IWW had no influence. Those loyal to the AFL dominated the body. Even when Duncan and his allies dictated policy, they still remained loyal to the AFL. Seattle had the same kind of federated unionism as Chicago. Like Fitzpatrick, Duncan had tried to initiate a more formal industrial unionism, and like Fitzpatrick suffered defeat. Unable to deliver industrial unionism within the AFL, Duncan had no alternative but to stay inside the AFL. This demoralized his more radical allies who became increasingly disruptive.

In reality Duncan, similarly to Fitzpatrick, had no powerful base outside of the SCLC itself. Necessarily he turned to the conservatives for support. They willingly gave it, and then turned on Duncan himself. In some ways Duncan remained truer to himself than Fitzpatrick did. He refused to disavow the FLP, remaining loyal, even though this meant his ousting from the labour movement. Perhaps it was Duncan's Calvinist background that kept him from recanting, and Fitzpatrick's Catholicism that led him to seek redemption in the fold of the AFL. However, religious ideology as an explanation for the differences between the two leaders is not a satisfactory reason. The trade-union aims of the two men had been almost identical. The main difference was the degree of integration into the AFL and its structures. Fitzpatrick had a close working relationship with the Illinois State Federation of Labor, and considered himself part of the national organization. The AFL's national office paid half his salary. When Fitzpatrick faced the abyss, rather than push him, state officials persuaded him not to jump. When Duncan stood on the brink the WSFL conservatives pushed him over.

Duncan had always been at odds with his State Federation. The SCLC, unlike the CFL, rarely enjoyed the support of its state body. Even though SCLC membership was at least half of the Federation's membership, it was never a major influence at its conventions.[57] This was for two reasons. First Seattle was surrounded by a host of small unions, whose voting power outnumbered it because of the delegation system. Secondly, the SCLC delegation rarely acted as a united force at conventions. Duncan could not even count on full support from Seattle trade unionists. Fitzpatrick had the backing of a broader range of like-minded officials and activists. It was Fitzpatrick's far deeper roots in the movement that kept him in the AFL, but it also meant that he disowned all he had ever fought for as a progressive trade unionist. When it came to dealing with the CFL and the SCLC, the AFL had played a waiting game. It was not until the progressives became isolated from their state federations, and to some extent their own central bodies, that the knife went in.

8 Conclusion: the End of a Dream

> There is a tide in the affairs of men
> Which, taken at the flood, leads on to fortune;
> Omitted, all the voyage of their life
> Is bound in shallows and in miseries.[1]

While specifically concerned with three cities, this book has not ignored national events and trends. Indeed, the three cities were central to working-class politics in this period, if only for the fact that between them New York and Chicago contained 25 to 30 per cent of the AFL's entire membership. If the respective state federations' members are included, this figure is even higher. Seattle's membership did not make it a major centre. However, its general strike and the fact that its FLP achieved second place in electoral terms makes it significant.

National events were central to the decision to launch labour parties in the three cities. As demonstrated in Chapter 2 the initiative flowed from the desire to participate in postwar reconstruction. Labour party activists wanted to maintain, or even extend, wartime legislative gains. The AFL's policy of non-partisanship became discredited as both Democrats and Republicans proved, in office, to be hostile to workers. Thus, discontent with the two national parties, combined with confidence gained due to increased union membership, spurred the formation of labour parties. It is important to remember that though each locality responded differently, each also related to national events and to each other. Thus the experience of the three cities was an interaction between local and national politics.

The rising tide was not restricted to the USA: nationalist uprisings in Ireland, revolution in Russia and Germany and the growing success of the British Labour Party further encouraged the third-party activists. It appeared a good time to start their project. Thus national, international and local events combined to spur independent political action. An understanding that it was this combination of factors that motivated the participants in what proved to be a very difficult time is essential. Otherwise it is arguable, with hindsight, that it was the wrong time to start a labour party. The participants

162

did not have the benefit of hindsight; the opportunity was there for the taking. As events turned against them, their project still made sense. The hostility of the two national parties and of the courts to labour proved more than ever the need for independent working-class politics.

Armed with the knowledge that state power could benefit workers and the example of the British Labour Party, a significant section of the AFL battled not only against the US electoral system but their own union leadership to build an independent party. It was the spirit of the times, the doubling of AFL membership and the occurrence of industry-wide strikes, that gave these activists an impetus that sustained them through the lean years. They were not isolated individuals. In Chicago and Seattle they controlled the local city central bodies and enjoyed substantial support from the state federations. It is important to appreciate the depth of this support because it affects our perception of the AFL. Gwendolyn Mink's assumption that 'American Trade Unionism explicitly rejected the idea of independent labor politics' is undermined by the concrete experience of the three cities in this study.[2] The labour movements of these three cities contested the AFL's political policy. They did not reject independent politics; rather they embraced them. The explicit rejection refers only to the national leadership. The claim that 'rejection' applies to the AFL as a whole ignores the reality of the civil war that raged between reformists and conservatives. It took Gompers and his supporters six years to fully defeat the supporters of independent labour politics. Ironically, Gompers' victory came at a time when the vote for La Follette showed the desire of many in the AFL and beyond for an alternative to the two main parties. Therefore rather than accepting the notion that American labour explicitly rejected third-party politics, this book has sought to explain why it was the advocates of independent politics that failed.

A comparison of the three cities has contributed to answering this question, as the different experience of each case has allowed the testing of different hypotheses. For example, if the answer is simply lack of electoral support, we face the problem that the Seattle party achieved a significant vote. Yet it was unable to maintain its organization any longer than Chicago or New York. Thus electoral results, though important, cannot on their own explain the failure to create a labour party. To establish the key variables, it is necessary to systematically assess the various major factors that may have weakened or strengthened the labour party movement in each city.

Chapter 2 considered the industrial structure of each city. Clearly each city was different, but the difference in workplace sizes was not the most crucial factor in determining trade-union membership and militancy. If large workplace and industry-wide unions are essential for militancy and radicalism, then Chicago certainly fitted the bill. Seattle also fitted this model, for a brief period, with the growth of shipbuilding. Also in both cities the progressives controlled their respective central labour bodies in a period of militancy and union growth. It is also the case that they lost control as union membership shrank and industrial militancy declined. The Seattle Central Labor Council (SCLC) continued with its reformist policies long after the decline of the mass unions in the shipyards. If the theory that large-scale industry is essential to unionization is correct, then New York should have had a weak trade union centre. Yet its unions recruited large numbers in aggregate across small industries. Workers in small workplaces struck just as often as those in large, including shipbuilding and the docks. Nonetheless there was a problem in New York of the split between 'progressive' and 'craft' trade unionism. The failure of the New York FLP supporters inside the AFL to build links with those outside of it had more to do with their own political traditions than with the structure of industry. For the New York progressives created problems for themselves, failing to make the right overtures to possible allies outside of the AFL.[3] Yet in Chicago and Seattle, the central bodies enjoyed close working relations with many of the unions outside of the AFL.

Chicago and Seattle also had a stronger tradition of 'federated unionism', although the differences between the cities should not be exaggerated. New York had several industry-wide organizations, including printers, marine workers, carpenters and clothing workers. Proto-industrial type unionism did exist, in places, in New York; therefore the political tradition of those who led these unions was as important as the structure of industry, though perhaps a more important structural explanation is found in the nature of the AFL itself. New York's central body had often been more radical than the State Federation, but conservative AFL officials used the predominance of small locals outside of the city to defeat the city body. Chicago and Seattle had the same problem, but far later and to a lesser extent. For most of the period covered by this book the Chicago Labor Party activists enjoyed the support of their State Federation. The Seattle Labor Party also had a degree of state federation support in its first two years. However, in both cases the opposition of the respective state federations proved decisive. All three city bodies were under-represented at a state level. State officials used the state organization as a barrier against the more radical city centres. In Illinois, however, upstate unions, especially miners, often proved to be a source of support. Yet none of the three cities' central bodies were able to dominate the state federations. Once the state federations moved against the FLP in Chicago and Seattle, support for the party crumbled. The fact that the New York central body never secured state federation support for the FLP meant the initiative was stillborn. Conversely the support of the state federations had a beneficial effect: the Seattle FLP performed at its best when it enjoyed the support of the Washington State Federation.

However, the level of state federation support and union organization did not prove to be the only important factors in the La Follette campaign. New York, with its more craft-based industry and more opposition from the State Federation than Chicago, actually gathered more votes for La Follette. The difference here is that the Socialist Party had a strong political tradition in New York and a weak one in Chicago. This begs the question as to why the Socialists had more influence in New York than Chicago. Though the answer is beyond the scope of this book, it is worth noting that the more industrial nature of Chicago gave nurture to syndicalist ideas that failed to take root in New York. Leading syndicalists such as W. Z. Foster put their energy into Chicago, not New York, and for the most part were disparaging of electoral politics. This also affected some of the Socialist Party membership who preferred direct action to political activity. I have already argued against an over-deterministic view of structural differences, although it is true that New York did not have the great organizing campaigns around steel and meatpacking that attracted the syndicalists to Chicago. However, if this is an important factor, it stands on its head the theory that industrial unionism was essential to creating a third party. For in 1924 it was New York that obtained the higher vote for La Follette.

Syndicalism is not necessarily a barrier to building a third party. In Seattle, with its form of 'federated unionism', Duncan's alliance with syndicalist activists helped the new party to achieve its best results. This brings us full circle. In other words, even though we cannot ignore the industrial structure of each city, it is the structure of the AFL and the political tradition of its constituents that is more important. This affected the outcome of events in all three cities more than the nature of industry.

POLITICAL MACHINES

One factor affecting the success of independent political action is the local political tradition. During this period party machines could not automatically count on certain sections of the population for full support, nor, with the state playing a smaller role, did they have as many spoils to offer. In Chicago a majority of the black population had a commitment to the Republican machine. However, such commitment was not the rule during this period. As we saw with the Poles in Chicago, hard and fast party lines did not exist. Ethnic factors are discussed in greater detail below. The issue here is the party machine as a barrier to the growth of a new party.

In New York, Tammany held many trade-union officials in its grip. Even at the height of the Republican ascendancy it kept the loyalty of a substantial number of New York's voters. Neither of the two major parties in New York suffered major defections. In Chicago the two major parties dominated the political scene. Even when split, these were able to win elections. It was in Seattle, where progressivism crossed party lines and the Democrats in 1920 all but collapsed, that the FLP faced the least severe opposition. But though the FLP could beat the Democrats, the Republicans proved to be far too hard a nut to crack. New York and Chicago in the negative, and Seattle in the positive, prove that the two-party system makes it very difficult for a new party to progress. This is not unique to the USA. The British Labour Party faced the same problem: it was only the rapid decline of the Liberal Party that catapulted it into second place. In a sense the same thing happened to the Seattle Labor Party with the temporary collapse of the Democrats.

Though it is idle to speculate what would have happened in New York or Chicago had the main party machines been weaker, it is not unreasonable to suggest that the FLP could have done better. In Seattle, it was the tradition of the *Union Record* and the SCLC that enabled labour to win the leadership of the progressive movement and take the FLP to second place. Neither the New York nor Chicago labour progressives were in a position to emulate the Seattle movement. Unlike New York and Chicago, the Seattle Socialists had no presence at all. Thus it was the Seattle movement that faced the fewest political obstacles.

The movement in Seattle also existed in a political environment that was more democratic than that of the other two cities. However, it is also possible that the early benefits of a non-partisan system later became a barrier in itself. It allowed labour an easy entry into local politics, but at the same time blunted the edges of party organization. In other words, reforms were achievable by individuals or coalitions, as well as parties. This meant that at times the profile of the Seattle Party was difficult to establish in the maelstrom of municipal non-partisan politics. Thus, the very factor that allowed labour to do well was the same factor that made it difficult for a new party to establish roots. This did not matter as much to the main parties, who had national profiles to keep them in the voters' memory. However, once the FLP lost its official union support many progressives returned to the Democratic fold. The recovery of the Democrats saw the immediate decline of the FLP. In the 1924 election the Democrats had still not solidified their vote, which collapsed when many Democrats backed La Follette. But by then the Seattle FLP was too weak to benefit from this switch.

Indeed Seattle explains why even with a high vote it is very difficult for a new party to make headway in the United States. Though the party's vote was high, it was not high enough to win it any posts. Even the Democrats driven into third place still had electoral representatives from previous elections. This enabled the weakened Democrats to survive until their voting fortunes recovered. But the leaders of the Washington AFL were not impressed with second place, or the fact that Labor's vote was higher than the Democrats. They wanted influence immediately, so they turned to the Republicans; when that failed they helped to resuscitate the Democrats. Of course to do that they had to destroy the Labor Party. This of course was exactly the same rationale that guided Gompers and the AFL leadership.

RACE, ETHNICITY AND GENDER

If Seattle benefited from a weaker Democratic Party in comparison to Chicago and New York, it suffered from the strength of the Republican Party. The FLP was never able to secure enough votes to topple the Republicans from first place. Even if the FLP had completely won over the Democratic vote, in most cases it would not have been enough for electoral victory. Seattle was the most homogeneous of the three cities, with a majority Protestant native population. This may have given the FLP an advantage in that the other parties could not depend on ethnic voting enclaves. Some scholars have argued that Duncan's Calvinism, prohibitionism and opposition to Japanese immigration cost the party

Catholic or ethnic support.[4] If one of the causes of Republican dominance in Seattle was nativist sentiment, it could explain the FLP's use of similar sentiments in the pursuit of building a working-class party. However this was in response to the accusation of un-Americanism. Indeed, the SCLC on one occasion did run an extensive 'Americanism' campaign. It is possible that this alienated Catholic and immigrant groupings, but they were not substantial enough to be a decisive factor in elections.

We should not assume that the FLP attracted the xenophobic vote. The FLP opposed racism, believing in equality for all Americans, naturalized or native. It campaigned against voting regulations that made it difficult for naturalized or first-generation Americans to vote. It was internationalist in character, supporting the Russian Revolution, and opposed the deportation of militants. In Seattle its support for Prohibition was class-based, motivated by the belief that drink weakened working-class solidarity and militancy. It also complained that Prohibition did not apply equally to the rich.

It is true that the SCLC supported a ban on Japanese immigration. This was not couched in racial terms but on the grounds that labour was imported to cut wages and militancy. Ironically, John C. Kennedy believed that one reason that the FLP did not do better in 1920 was that the party became characterized as the 'Japanese Labor Party'.[5] Yet the FLP candidate most closely associated with being pro-Japanese did better at the polls than any other of the Party's candidates.

The situation in New York and Chicago in ethnic terms was very different to that of Seattle. There is clear evidence that racial and ethnic patterns affected the outcome of party politics. In Chicago a substantial section of the black community supported the Republicans, while the Democrats enjoyed substantial Irish support. In New York, Tammany and sections of the AFL leadership enjoyed Irish support. The Socialists had substantial Jewish support, and many immigrant groupings supported particular parties or candidates.

There were political loyalties based on race and ethnicity. However, where workers from different backgrounds joined unions there were successes in breaking sectional loyalties. In Chicago, Polish workers joined the meatpacking unions in large numbers, as did a substantial minority of black workers. Italian workers and Jewish immigrants joined the clothing workers' unions in both New York and Chicago. Thus immigrant workers did not just relate to community organization, but also to the workplace. Polish workers, sometimes in larger numbers than Americans, voted Socialist and FLP. La Follette received a substantial portion of the Jewish vote in New York. Class loyalty, for some, did play a role in voting behaviour.

In other instances Nationalist concerns affected ethnic political loyalty. The Irish did not slavishly vote Democrat. In 1920 there was much dissatisfaction with the two main parties' refusal to oppose British foreign policy. In New York City Jeremiah O'Leary narrowly missed becoming an FLP congressman in a predominantly Irish-German district. Ethnic voting patterns were not strictly defined in 1920, nor fully settled by 1924. The FLP did not suffer ferocious opposition from Catholic or Irish organizations. In Chicago, Fitzpatrick had good relations with a range of Irish organizations. The most important trends determining voting patterns were national and international ones. Thus, Poles and Irish did not behave that differently from the rest of the population; they also turned against the Wilson government.

Political allegiances were fluid in the opening years of the 1920s. In Chicago the FLP made a considerable effort to persuade ethnic groupings to vote for it. Although it organized a black party branch and stood one black candidate, it made less effort, in political terms, among African-Americans. It was not just the black vote the FLP failed to win, but most votes. The reasons for different minority sections failing to vote for the FLP in Chicago may not have been much different to the rest of its population. Potential voters probably believed the Party could not achieve anything in the short term. It is difficult for a new party to achieve success at the polls at its very first attempt, especially in a first-past-the-post system, but to admit that is hardly likely to inspire support. Those who argued that they should sink roots before intervening at the polls were ignored. No doubt there was an impulse for a new party in 1919 and 1924 that went far beyond the actual vote delivered.[6] However, in 1920, a party with little experience and a presidential candidate unknown to most people was not able to turn enthusiasm into electoral support. Thus the failure of the labour party to win immigrant or black voters was, for the most part, integral to its overall failure.

The originators of the labour parties supported women's suffrage and believed that women should be in unions. The latter belief often brought them into conflict with conservative elements in the AFL. For example, the AFL ordered Duncan to refuse recognition to the women barbers. Duncan fought long and hard to keep these women in the AFL. Progressive trade unionists in all three cities worked with women trade unionists and, in particular, the WTUL. The labour parties and the La Follette campaign directed propaganda specifically at women.

In all three cities women stood as FLP candidates in prominent positions and played a central role in organizing election campaigns. However, a higher percentage of women voted for the two main parties than for the FLP. But fewer women than men voted in the early years of extended suffrage. Given that the two main parties received fewer women's votes than men's, a newly created party with limited resources had even less chance of winning women's votes. Therefore the failure to win women's vote was part of a general problem.

Although I have argued that the effects of workplace size on union organization should not be assessed deterministically, the structure of the workforce and the AFL did have an effect with regard to women and independent political action. Though the numbers of women in the workforce were increasing, the majority remained outside of the workplace. Most of those who did work were not AFL members. There were some exceptions, as in the teachers' and clothing workers' unions. Overall union density was lower among women than men. In Chicago and Seattle there was a clear correlation between membership of a union and voting for the FLP or La Follette. In other words, there was an organic link between membership and voting behaviour. In the case of women this link was far weaker, and it is not unreasonable to expect a lower vote. Women were a minority of the AFL, but they were not the only section of society outside of its orbit. The AFL did not organize the unskilled, or most black and foreign workers.

This derived from the AFL's policy of concentrating on recruiting skilled workmen. This was not a matter of simple prejudice, but a defensive strategy that unions adopted in response to hostile employers. This policy left many outside of the organized working class. The failure of the AFL to extend its membership to all sections of employees had implications for its ability to intervene politically. Nonetheless, where AFL trade unions supported independent political action support for the FLP and La Follette was greater than elsewhere. Union membership influenced the way workers voted in their geographical communities. The actions of the streetcar men in Seattle or Polish meatpacking workers in Chicago prove the case. Where the organic link was weak, for example with black workers or women, then the response to independent political action was weaker. Therefore the density of the AFL affected its ability to influence workers' political preferences. Before the war union membership was low, but the war and its aftermath saw AFL membership grow. In some areas recruiting the unskilled became possible. It was this expansion of the AFL that convinced leaders like Duncan and Fitzpatrick that independent political action was possible. They also believed it would be possible to extend trade unionism to the unskilled, to women and black workers.

The failure of industrial unionism was not their fault. Nor was it the case that workers did not respond. Thousands flooded into steel, meatpacking, clothing, telephone and other white-collar unions. Teachers' unions in New York and Chicago were the most fervent supporters of the new party. However, the employers set out to destroy the union shop. Fitzpatrick and Duncan were well aware that the structure of the AFL was inadequate to deal with such an offensive. They were also aware that without extending union membership they could not succeed in building a labour party. Unfortunately, it became increasingly difficult to extend union membership as the bosses went on the offensive. Forced on to the defensive, conservative strategies of exclusiveness, restricting work to those with particular skills and accepting wage cuts in return for union recognition came to the fore. In such a situation it became difficult to maintain independent political activity. This was clearly the case in Chicago, where even those activists who agreed with political action had their time taken up with defending basic union organization.

The experience of American workers was different to that of European workers. However, their aspirations were not very dissimilar. American workers faced an intransigent ruling class, unwittingly aided by a union structure that failed to appreciate the need for change. The leadership of the AFL had developed at a time when defensive strategies were effective. They had the experience and the loyalty of a layer of officials and activists around them. Those that joined in the wartime upsurge had no such experience or base. However, there was a counterbalance to this conservatism provided by officials at a lower level in the city central bodies. Thus the battle to establish a labour party and extend the AFL was not only a fight against the employers and the established political system, but a battle between contending forces inside the AFL.

That being the case, the question arises why did one side win rather than the other? Why was it that the politics of the craft-orientated and conservative wing prevailed over those who wanted to break down craft barriers and bring about reform? The argument that the right wing represented the ideology of the membership more closely than the left is not adequate. If the membership was always conservative then why, at times, did the conservatives speak in radical terms? In New York City there were times when the Tammany trade unionists supported the FLP or the socialists. In Seattle and Chicago it was not until after 1922 that the conservatives dared to confront the insurgents. If the left had no base for their politics it is unlikely that they could have held off the right for so long. This is proved in the negative by the New York experience, where the base of the reformers was far weaker than in the other cities. Here they became isolated before the end of 1920.

There was also a sentiment for radical change in union structure among workers typified as conservative. Thus, railroad and marine workers built unofficial rank-and-file structures, and went on industry-wide strikes against the wishes of their leaders. Even in New York this kind of action was commonplace. The problem for the insurgents was that these unofficial joint organizations did not become part of the power structures of the official AFL machine. Thus this informal move towards industrial unionism came up against the barrier of the more conservative state and national union structures. There were times when the membership went well to the left of its leadership. Railwaymen demanded election of their officials and supported the Labour Party. There are examples of this radicalism, and its effects, in all three cities. In Chicago, New York and Seattle, political action gained endorsement not just from the left, but from the right as well. The AFL had to relaunch its traditional non-partisan policy in a vigorous fashion. In 1924 it had no choice but to endorse the La Follette campaign. This was not a case of leading but of following and then outflanking the radical impulses of sections of the membership until safely controlled and defeated.

This still leaves a key question unanswered: why did the left suffer defeat? The above argument discounts ideology on its own as an inadequate answer. Terms such as 'conservative' do not adequately describe the membership of the unions involved. At times, as already stated, the membership went to the left of their leaders. It became involved in campaigns to unionize blacks and women. It attended mass rallies in support of the FLP and La Follette. At other times it was passive and gave little support to the reformers. The ideology of workers is not static. It is possible for workers to hold conflicting ideas, and those ideas can vary.

There is no doubt that victory and defeat affect which ideas are likely to prevail at any given moment. In a period of militancy and state intervention in labour relations, third-party ideas can enjoy wider currency than in periods of little struggle. This relationship between struggle and ideas is not a simple one. Defeats on a large scale, or aggressive action by employers and government can also have a radicalizing affect. Defeats in the industrial field or anti-union legislation can turn workers' minds to political action. For example, in Seattle it took the defeat of the General Strike to create enthusiasm for political action. In Chicago strikes increased following the failure of political action. However, the general trend between 1919 and 1920 of rising struggle saw the left in control of the three cities' labour movements. It was precisely when the high tide of militancy receded that the left's domination of the central labour bodies became undermined.

It was not simply a matter of ideas; in a period of economic recession, with the unions under attack from the employers, the left faced a conundrum. It wanted to oppose the leadership of Gompers and his supporters, but at the same time it needed the support of the official AFL machine. Under attack from the employers, it needed the protection of the AFL trade card. A fight to the death against the conservatives by the reformers would have deprived them of this protection. Gompers made it quite clear to Duncan in Seattle that persistence with the third party would mean the revocation of the SCLC's charter. Fitzpatrick and the CFL faced a similar threat. With workers on the defensive and struggle at a low ebb, neither Duncan nor Fitzpatrick felt able to continue opposing the AFL leadership.

The AFL's reformist left was not prepared to break with craft unionism. They wanted to reform it, not be outside of it. Increasingly they began to modify their demands, dropping plans to industrialize the AFL. This found them under fire from the Communist and syndicalist left. Forced to choose between the radicals or the risk of losing AFL endorsement, they went into an alliance with the conservatives to defeat the former. The FLP had failed to build a sustainable party culture independent of the AFL. In the absence of an independent base they became prisoners of the right wing and were forced to drop their own reformist ideals. The key to this defeat was not just the left's lack of an independent base or of ideological consistency, but the conditions of retreat forced on the labour movement by recession and the employers' offensive.

This stark choice had not confronted them when protected by the militancy of the membership. But from 1921 onwards the unions were in decline. With the defeat of major sections of workers, the loss of union income, and with many former members and activists unemployed, workers became increasingly indifferent to the activities of the party builders. However, apathy does not equal conservatism. That workers felt that strikes and independent political activity could not succeed does not mean they were reconciled to the situation. The events of 1924 demonstrated precisely this as millions of workers rejected both Democrats and Republicans.

Life is not as simple as the Shakespeare quotation at the beginning of this chapter. Tides and the actions of men do not easily correlate. At the high tide of 1919 New York and Chicago reacted by announcing a third party, while Seattle let the moment pass. In New York the Socialist Party ignored the high tide and yet as the tide receded it relaunched the third-party initiative in far less favourable conditions. At the end of 1923 the FLP was no longer sustainable, due to the removal of any serious union support. Yet, in 1924, there was great feeling among workers of the need for independent political activity. It was the Conference for Progressive Political Action (CPPA) that became the focus for those dissatisfied with the main parties. Now, those who had acted conservatively in the past, most notably the railroad unions, launched a campaign of support for La Follette. The candidates of the two main parties were too conservative even for Gompers to stomach, and so the AFL joined in the campaign. This was not a break with non-partisanship, though many who supported La Follette longed for a new party.

Ironically those who had tried to create a third party in the past were to miss the tide yet again. Many had become demoralized, and allowed the La Follette campaign to pass them by. Others were uncritical of the campaign and dropped any demand for a third party. The worst culprits were the Socialists of New York City, allowing their own party machine to disintegrate and abandoning their own daily newspaper. They almost believed that the AFL and the La Follette progressives would do the work of building a third party for them. But the leaders of the CPPA and the AFL had no intention of building a third party. When the result of the election became known, they declared the building of a third party a lost cause.

The La Follette campaign should not be considered in isolation from the activity of those who had advocated the FLP. Many of the unions that had supported the FLP also backed the La Follette campaign. They may not have attracted a substantial vote for their project, but they had established the idea of a third party in the minds of many trade unionists. It was partly as a concession to a growing desire for a new party that the CPPA, and even the AFL, broke with the presidential candidates of the two main parties.

The contention that the AFL leadership ditched the campaign or provided it with few resources is not sustainable. The AFL never provided massive cash injections for political activity. Its resources were its officials and its press. In all three cities such resources were given to the campaign. As we saw in Seattle, only a few days before the actual election Frank Morrison attended the SCLC to urge more action. Gompers denounced the right-wing rebels of New York and reaffirmed the AFL's commitment in the dying days of the campaign. Labour newspapers such as the *Seattle Union Record*, the *New Leader*, *New Majority*, *Labor* and the clothing workers' press all agitated for La Follette. The case studies at the local level have contradicted the view that labour was not central to the La Follette campaign. Of course there was a problem with the AFL's support. It was not as fulsome as it might have been. This was not due to insincerity on the part of the AFL's leadership but a logical consequence of its non-partisan politics. For years the leadership had attacked independent political action; motivated by the needs of the short term, they sacrificed the long term for alliances with Democrats and Republicans. Thus the AFL opposed independent political action because it could not achieve pro-labour legislation, nor stop Prohibition or deregulation of the railroads. Ironically the AFL's non-partisan policy did not stop the latter either.

Nineteen-hundred and twenty could have been a good year for the AFL to have supported a third party. The backlash against the Democrats was immense, and the Seattle labour movement proved that the FLP could benefit from it. It is unlikely that Chicago or New York would have done as well as Seattle but, as 1924 proved, they would have improved their performance. AFL support and more substantial candidates in 1920 could have made a difference. It also means that a tradition and a party machine could have existed by the 1924 election.

Even though the AFL switched to supporting La Follette in 1924, this was yet another example of short-termism. Unable to gain effective support from the main parties it turned to an independent candidate. This was only possible because there was broad sentiment for such action in the labour movement. But the AFL remained committed to its non-partisan policy of opposing a third party. The contradictory nature of the AFL position made it difficult to discipline those who would not follow its lead. By insisting that the campaign did not support a new party, voters were asked to back an individual who could not possibility achieve anything in Congress. In spite of all this, a large section of the AFL supported the campaign and many workers voted for La Follette. It is unlikely that La Follette could have stood at all without the pledge of the CPPA and the subsequent backing of the AFL. Organized labour was the only substantial force La Follette had behind him. Progressivism enjoyed a brief resurgence only because labour had acted.

La Follette attracted nearly five million voters, but after the election they had nowhere to go. There was no organization of any substance to which they could turn. The AFL leadership remained true to its short-termism, and recoiled in horror at the fact that a lost campaign gave them no influence in Congress. Immediately repudiating its own actions, the AFL returned to a policy of supporting the main party presidential candidates. The CPPA acted in the same manner, withdrawing all support from any proposed third party. Neither organization looked to the possibility of relating to the five million insurgent voters.

Sadly the left of the movement had nothing to offer either. The remnants of the old FLP and the Socialists had failed to warn of the treachery that would follow the election. Perhaps these activists had genuinely believed that La Follette's vote would be so large as not to allow any room for retreat. Whatever their reasons, their abandonment of their own organizations during the election left them in no position to salvage anything from the post-campaign wreckage. Millions were left stranded on the beach as the tide receded yet again.

This returns us to the issue of inevitability discussed in the introduction. Was this outcome inevitable or one of the 'great missed opportunities' of history. For Marx, men make history, but not in circumstances of their own choosing.[7] It cannot be denied that circumstances were unfavourable for the party builders, and it is most unlikely, in the period outlined here, that the labour party could have become a national second party. But if the AFL had supported the party at the height of the anti-Wilson backlash it would have achieved very much more. Indeed the 1920 Seattle results point in that direction. At least a minority organization based on the unions could have been built, leaving different options open in 1924. If the local leaders had been able to sustain their parties until 1924 then they may not have remained passive and uncritical in the face of the La Follette campaign. The fact that five million people voted for a candidate clearly associated with labour is remarkable, but they were deserted before the counting of their ballot papers. The AFL leadership, wedded to the past, turned its face against change, arguing that the building of a workers' party could never succeed. If it had supported those advocating a labour party then it is possible that small changes could have come about. These as I have suggested could have made an important difference on a later occasion. The failure of the labour party movement was not 'inevitable', but rather it was the product of conflicts between supporters and opponents of the movement. If the AFL had used its organization in an attempt to hold these people together something may have been salvaged. A small party with roots in the unions would have been well placed for future upheavals. After all the mass struggles of 1936 were only 12 years away. I quoted Richard White at the beginning of this book and make no apologies for ending the book with a quotation from him:

> Small changes in one period can yield significant differences in another. Contingency is not the whole story, but it is part of the story.[8]

Appendix
Labor's Fourteen Points[1]

FOURTEEN POINTS OF LABOR SWEEP COUNTRY

Platform Adopted by Chicago Federation Attracts Wide Attention and Wins Many Endorsements

'Labor's fourteen points,' which were unanimously endorsed by the Chicago Federation of Labor at its regular meeting November 17, 1918, have created a sensation in labor and liberal circles all over the country. They have been endorsed by numerous organizations and letters of commendation from societies and individuals have poured into the federation headquarters. This declaration of principles in full follows:

Right to Organize
1. The unqualified right of workers to organize and to deal collectively with employers through such representatives of their unions as they choose.

Democratic Control of Industry
2. Democratic control of industry and commerce for the general good by those who work with hand and brain, and the elimination of autocratic domination of the forces of production and distribution either by selfish private interests or bureaucratic agents of government.

8-Hour Day and Minimum Wage
3. An 8-hour day and a 44-hour week in all branches of industry; with minimum rates of pay which, without the labor of mothers and children, will maintain the worker and his family in health and comfort, and provide a competence for old age, with ample provision for recreation and good citizenship.

Abolition of Unemployment
4. Abolition of unemployment by the creation of opportunity for steady work at standard wages through the stabilization of industry and the establishment, during periods of depression, of government work on housing, road-building, reforestation, reclamation of desert and swamp, and the development of ports and waterways.

Equal Rights for Men and Women
5. Complete equality of men and women in government and industry, with the fullest enfranchisement of women, and equal pay for men, and women doing similar work.

Stop Profiteering
6. Reduction of the cost of living to a just level, immediately and as a permanent policy, by the development of co-operation, and the elimination of

wasteful methods, parasitical middlemen and all profiteering in the creation and distribution of the products of industry and agriculture, in order
that the actual producers may enjoy the fruits of their toil.

Abolish Kaiserism in Education
7. Democratization of education in public schools and universities through
the participation of labor and the organized teachers in the determination
of methods, policies and programs in this fundamental field.

Soldiers' and Sailors' Insurance for All Workers
8. Continuation after the war of soldiers' and sailors' insurance; extension
of such life insurance, by the government without profit, to all men and
women; and the establishment of governmental insurance against accident and illness, and upon all insurable forms of property.

War Debt and Government Expenses
9. Liquidation of the national debt by the application of all inheritances
above a hundred thousand dollars, supplemented as may be necessary by
a direct capital tax upon all persons and corporations where riches have
been gained by war or other profiteering; and payment of the current
expenses of government by graduated income taxes, public profits from
nationally owned utilities and resources, and from a system of taxation of
land values which will stimulate rather than retard production.

Public Ownership and Nationalization of Natural Resources
10. Public ownership and operation of railways, steamships, stock yards,
grain elevators, terminal markets, telegraphs, telephones, and all other
public utilities; and the nationalization and development of basic natural
resources, waterpower and unused land, with the repatriation of large
holdings, to the end that returning soldiers and sailors and dislocated war
workers may find an opportunity for an independent livelihood.

Free Speech, Free Press, Free Assemblage
11. Complete restoration, at the earliest possible moment, of all fundamental
political rights – free-speech, free press, and free assemblage; the removal
of all war-time restraints upon the interchange of ideas and the movement
of people among communities and nations; and the liberation of all
persons held in prison or indicted under charges due to their champion-
ship of the rights of labor or their patriotic insistence upon the rights
guaranteed to them by the constitution.

Labor Representation in the Government
12. Representation of labor, in proportion to its voting strength, in all departments of government and upon all governmental commissions and agen-
cies of demobilization and reconstruction; and recognition of the
principles of trade unionism in the relocation of soldiers, sailors and war
workers in peace pursuits, with adequate provision for the support and
extension of the Department of Labor as the principal agency therefor.

Labor in the Peace Conference
13. Representation of the workers, in proportion to their numbers in the
armies, navies and workshops of the world, at the peace conference and

upon whatever international tribunals may result therefrom, with the labor of this nation represented by the President of the American Federation of Labor and such other delegates as the workers may democratically designate.

An End to Kings and Wars
14. Supplementing the League of Nations, and to make that instrument of international democracy vitally effective for humanity, a league of the workers of all nations pledged and organized to enforce the destruction of autocracy, militarism and economic imperialism throughout the world, and to bring about world-wide disarmament and open diplomacy, to the end that there shall be no more kings and no more wars.

WANT TO JOIN THE NEW PARTY?

Join the Labor Party, fill out and sign this blank, cut it out and mail or bring it to head-quarters of the party at 166 West Washington street.

Application for membership

(Must be filled out by the applicant personally. Write plain and answer all questions.)
PLEDGE: I, the undersigned, recognizing the necessity of Independent political action by the men and women who believe in political, social and industrial democracy, hereby apply for membership in the Labor Party of Cook County. In all my political actions while a member of the Labor Party I agree to be guided by the constitution and platform of that party.

Date ... . 191 ..... .

Name...
Address...........................Ward ....
If member of Labor Union or Organization, so state:
Organization...
Age.............. Country of Birth................... Citizen? – Yes – No –
Proposed by ....

Dues per annum, $4.00. One dollar must accompany this application; 50 cents of which is for dues and 50 cents for subscription to the official party paper, THE NEW MAJORITY, for three months.

Notes

INTRODUCTION

1. Werner Sombart, *Why Is There No Socialism in the United States?* (White Plains, NY: International Arts and Sciences Press, 1976; orig. 1906).
2. There is an extensive range of literature concerning the absence of a working class or third party, far too extensive for consideration here. For a more comprehensive historiography see A.G. Strouthous, 'A Comparative Study of Independent Working-Class Politics: The American Federation of Labor and Third Party Movement in New York, Chicago, and Seattle, 1918–1924' (PhD, London University 1996), pp. 5–8.
3. For a history of German labour and its political party in this period see Carl E. Schorske, *German Social Democracy, 1905–1917: The Development of the Great Schism* (Cambridge, MA: Harvard University Press, 1983; orig. 1955); and for Britain, James Hinton, *Labour and Socialism: A History of the British Labour Movement, 1867–1974* (Brighton: Wheatsheaf Books, 1983).
4. The *Guardian*, 13 June 1996, announced that US union activists were launching a Labor Party *for the first time*: not only proving that interest in a third party remains, but also that such ignorance of the past demonstrates the need for this book.
5. Foner, Philip S., *History of the Labor Movement in the United States Volume 8: Postwar Struggles 1918–20* (New York: International Publishers, 1988).
6. Ira Katznelson and A. Zolberg (eds), *Working-Class Formation: Nineteenth Century Patterns in Western Europe and the United States* (Princeton, NJ: Princeton University Press, 1986), pp. 397–402.

   The literature for and against exceptionalism is too extensive to detail here. See A. G. Strouthous, as note 2 above, pp. 8–9 for further references.
7. Gwendolyn Mink, *Old Labor and New Immigrants in American Political Development* (Ithaca, NY: Cornell University Press, 1986), p. 18.

   The old school of labour history's theory that American trade unions restricted themselves purely to 'job consciousness' is ably illustrated in J.R. Commons, *History of Labor in the United States*, 4 vols (New York: Macmillan, 1935–6) and Selig Perlman, *A Theory of the Labor Movement* (New York: Macmillan, 1923). Marc Karson in his *American Labor Unions and Politics 1900–18* (Boston: Beacon Press, 1958) and Gwendolyn Mink (cited above) continue to reinforce this argument up to the present day.
8. Only one book covers the whole of the period spanned by this study, Nathan Fine, *Labor and Farmer Parties in the United States 1828–1928* (New York: Russell & Russell, 1961). However, a book that covers such a vast sweep of history at a national level is by its very nature a history of national institutions and events.

9.   Much of this history takes the form of unpublished dissertations, many written over 40 or 50 years ago. These include Harry B. Sell, 'The A.F. of L. and the Labor Party Movement of 1918–20' (MA, University of Chicago, 1922); Lawrence Rogin, 'Central Labor Bodies and Independent Political Action in New York City: 1918–1922' (MA, Columbia University, 1931); David Dolnick, 'The Role of Labor in Chicago Politics Since 1919' (MA, Chicago University, 1939); Roger Horowitz, 'The Failure of Independent Political Action: The Labor Party of Cook County, 1919–1920' (BA Essay, University of Chicago, 1982); David Fickes Simonson, 'The Labor Party of Cook County, Illinois, 1918–1919' (MA, University of Chicago, 1959); John Howard Keiser, 'John Fitzpatrick and Progressive Unionism 1915–1925' (PhD, Northwestern University, 1965); Stanley Shapiro, 'Hand and Brain: The Farmer Labor Party of 1920' (PhD, University of California, 1967); Hamilton Cravens, 'A History of the Washington Farmer Labor Party 1918–1924' (MA, University of Washington, 1962); Jonathan Dembo, *Unions and Politics in Washington State 1885–1935* (New York: Garland, 1983).

10.   Richard White, 'Other Wests', Geoffrey C. Ward, *The West* (London: Weidenfeld & Nicolson, 1996), p. 48; For further debate on exceptionalism and working-class history see Rick Halpern and Jonathan Morris (eds), *American Exceptionalism? US Working Class Formation in an International Context* (London: Macmillan, 1996); Seymour Martin Lipset, *American Exceptionalism: A Double Edged Sword* (New York: W. W. Norton, 1996).

11.   Kenneth Campbell MacKay, the major historian of the 1924 La Follette presidential campaign, concentrates on national events and institutions leading him to underestimate the AFL's contribution. Kenneth Campbell MacKay, *The Progressive Movement of 1924* (New York: Octagon Books, 1972, orig. 1947).

12.   See MacKay, see note 11 above.

13.   Zolberg, in Katznelson and Zolberg, see note 6 above, p. 401.

14.   Zolberg, in Katznelson and Zolberg, p. 401.

15.   James E. Cronin, 'Neither Exceptional nor Peculiar: Toward the Comparative Study of Labor in Advanced Society', *International Review of Social History* 38 (1993); Theda Skocpol and Margaret Somers, 'The Uses of Comparative History in Macrosocial Inquiry', *Comparative Studies in Society and History* 22: 2 (1980); Neville Kirk, *Labour and Society in Britain and the USA: Volume 2 Challenge and Accommodation, 1850–1939* (Aldershot: Scolar Press, 1994).

16.   This book is not concerned with the Communists, the Industrial Workers of the World (IWW) or the Red Scare of 1919, except where these matters impact directly on the activities of the AFL and the labour parties. (Of course the employers' and the state's offensive against the working class in this period is part of a theme that permeates this book.) This is not because I think these topics are irrelevant, but because they are, for the most part, beyond the brief of this study. However, these issues, even the Red Scare, were not of central importance to the union activists (excepting those in Seattle) portrayed here. The state mainly persecuted the IWW, immigrants and later the

Communists. State repression is not a plausible explanation for the defeat of the labour party movement. Also these topics are already covered by a more extensive historiography than the subject of this book.

1 FROM RECONSTRUCTION TO LABOUR PARTIES: THE CRUCIBLE OF WAR

1. 'Miners on the War Path', Coal miners' song at the 1919 UMW Cleveland Convention, Heber Blankenhorn Papers, box 4, folder 6, Archives of Labor and Urban Affairs, Walter Reuther Library, Wayne State University, Detroit, Michigan.
2. Bureau of Labor Statistics, US Department of Labor, Government Printing Office, *Monthly Labor Review* 10 (June 1920–December 1920), p. 1506 *passim*.
3. James Weinstein, *The Corporate Ideal in the Liberal State: 1900–1918* (Boston: Beacon Press, 1968), chapter 8, *passim*.
4. W. Jett Lauck, *Political And Industrial Democracy, 1776–1926* (New York: Funk & Wagnall, 1926), pp. 13–15.
5. William E. Forbath, *Law and the Shaping of the American Labor Movement* (Cambridge, MA: Harvard University Press, 1991).
6. Edward Berman, *Labor Disputes and the President of the United States* (New York: Columbia University, 1924), chapter 5 details the WLB.
7. *Pennsylvania Labor Herald*, 22 November 1918, quoted in Joseph McCartin, 'An American Feeling', *Industrial Democracy in America*, eds Nelson Lichtenstein and Howell John Harris (Cambridge University Press, 1993), p. 73. Joseph A. McCartin, 'Labor's Great War: Workers, Unions, and the State, 1916–1920' (PhD, State University of New York at Binghamton, 1990), pp. xxii–xxviii.
8. McCartin, 'An American Feeling', pp. 70–3. Statement dated 12 September 1918, John Fitzpatrick Papers, box 7, folder 50, Chicago Historical Society, Chicago, Illinois (hereafter cited as Fitzpatrick Papers).
9. Lauck, p. 16; Weinstein, pp. 220–36 *passim*; Berman, pp. 138–9; Robert Cuff, *The War Industries Board* (Baltimore, MD: Johns Hopkins University Press, 1973).
10. David Montgomery, 'Industrial Democracy or Democracy in Industry', in Lichtenstein and Harris (eds), p. 36. David Montgomery, *The Fall of the House of Labor: The Workplace, the State, and American Labor Activism (New York, Cambridge University Press, 1987), pp. 417–18.*
11. David Brody, *Labor in Crisis: The Steel Strike of 1919* (Urbana: University of Illinois Press, 1987); Philip S. Foner, *Postwar Struggles, 1918–1920: History of the Labor Movement in the United States*, vol. 8 (New York: International Publishers, 1988); Rick Halpern, *Down on the Killing Floor: Black and White Workers in Chicago's Packinghouses, 1904–54* (Urbana and Chicago: University of Illinois Press, 1997), chapter 2.
12. John Howard Keiser, 'John Fitzpatrick and Progressive Unionism 1915–1925' (PhD, Northwestern University, 1965), p. 28.

13. AFL policy to support the party most favourable to labour. Thus it supported Republicans in some areas and Democrats in others depending on their attitude to labour. This policy of rewarding its friends, and punishing its enemies became known as 'non-partisan'.

14. Sister Marie Eucharia Meehan, CSJ, 'Frank P. Walsh and the American Labor Movement' (PhD, New York University, 1962), *passim*.

15. Keiser, pp. 45, 67–8, 124.

16. Halpern, p. 48; Commission of Inquiry, *Interchurch World Movement, Report on the Steel Strike of 1919* (New York: Harcourt, Brace & Howe, 1920), p. 36; Edward P. Johanningsmeier, *Forging American Communism: The Life of William Z. Foster*, (Princeton, NJ: Princeton University Press, 1994), pp. 155–7.

17. International Association of Machinists to Frank Walsh, 28 November 1918, Frank Walsh Papers, box 7, folder 7, New York Public Library, New York, New York (hereafter cited as Walsh Papers).

18. Harry B. Sell, 'The A.F. of L. and the Labor Party Movement of 1918–20' (MA, University of Chicago, 1922), p. 31.

19. *New Majority*, 4 January 1919.

20. Abraham Epstein, *The Intercollegiate Socialist*, VII: 4 (April–May 1919), pp. 15–16. Epstein states the survey was taken in a leading industrial state in the East, but does not state where.

21. See Chapter 3 for detail of New York Socialists. Weinstein, *The Decline of Socialism in America* (New York: Monthly Review Press, 1967), pp. 326. Evans Clark, 'The 1918 Socialist Vote', *Intercollegiate Socialist* VII: 2 (December–January 1918–19).

22. Melvyn Dubofsky, *When Workers Organize: New York City in the Progressive Era* (Amherst: University of Massachusetts Press, 1968), p. 5.

23. United States Department of Commerce, Bureau of the Census, *Fourteenth Census of the United States,* Vol. IX (1920) (Washington Government Printing Office, 1920), pp. 1026–7 *passim*.

24. *New York Labor Bulletin,* April 1914, p. 1. New York State Department of Labor, *Special Bulletin*, No. 110 (April 1922), pp. 6–31.

25. Dubofsky, p. 2 and chapter 7 *passim*.

26. *Monthly Labor Review* 10 (June 1920), pp. 1506–10.

27. Lawrence Rogin, 'Central Labor Bodies and Independent Political Action in New York City: 1918–1922' (MA, Columbia University, 1931), p. 2.

28. Irwin Yellowitz, *Labor and the Progressive Movement in New York State 1897–1916*, (Ithaca, NY: Cornell University Press, 1965), p. 28.

29. *US Fourteenth Census*, p. 345.

30. James R. Barrett, *Work and Community in the Jungle, Chicago's Packinghouse Workers, 1894–1922* (Urbana: University of Illinois Press, 1987), pp. 19 and 56; *US Fourteenth Census*, p. 345.

31. Robert Ozanne, *A Century of Labour–Management Relations at McCormick and International Harvester* (Madison: University of Wisconsin Press, 1967), pp. 38–9 *passim*. US Department of Labour, *Monthly Labor Review* 12 (January 1921), pp. 168–81; Homer Hoyt, *One Hundred Years of Land Values in Chicago* (Chicago: University of Chicago Press, 1933), p. 205.

32. *US Fourteenth Census*, p. 345.

33. Charles Merriam, *Chicago: A More Intimate View of Urban Politics* (New York: Macmillan, 1929), p. 187; Barret, p.49.
34. Montgomery, *Worker's Control in America* (New York: Cambridge University Press), p. 57.
35. David Fickes Simonson, 'The Labor Party of Cook County, Illinois, 1918–1919' (MA, University of Chicago, 1959), p. 10; Halpern, pp. 53–4; David Brody, *The Butcher Workmen* (Cambridge, MA: Harvard University Press, 1964), pp. 89–91.
36. Margaret Drier Robins to Fitzpatrick, 30 September 1921, Fitzpatrick Papers, box 10, folder 75; Ruth Milkman (ed.), *Women, Work and Protest: A Century of US Women's Labor History* (London: Routledge, 1991), chapter 2 *passim*.
37. Eugene Staley, *History of the Illinois State Federation of Labor* (Chicago: University of Chicago Press, 1930), pp. 206, 315, 563.
38. *Monthly Labor Review* 10 (June 1920), p. 1506.
39. Carlos A. Schwantes, *The Pacific Northwest* (Lincoln: University of Nebraska Press, 1989), p. 192.
40. Robert Friedham, *The Seattle General Strike* (Seattle: University of Washington Press, 1964), p. 23. *Fourteenth Census of the United States*, vol. III, Population 1920, p. 275. By comparison the census recorded 35.4 per cent foreign-born in New York, of which 38.4 per cent were naturalized. The biggest ethnic groupings were not from the UK or Canada, but from Italy and Eastern Europe. In Chicago 109 000 African-Americans made up 4.05 per cent of the population.
41. Friedham, pp. 27, 48, 57, 58.
42. Carlos A. Schwantes, 'Left Wing Unionism in the Pacific Northwest: A Comparative History of Organized Labor and Socialist Politics in Washington and British Columbia, 1885–1917' (PhD, University of Michigan, 1976), pp. 272–4 *passim*; Carlos A. Schwantes, *Radical Heritage: Labor, Socialism, and Reform in Washington and British Columbia, 1885–1917* (Seattle: University of Washington Press, 1979), p. 155; Friedham, pp. 27, 41.
43. Friedham, p. 49; Harvey O'Connor, *Revolution in Seattle* (Seattle: Left Bank Books, 1981; orig. 1964); p. 109.
44. Friedham, pp. 26–7.
45. Friedham, pp. 27, 47–49 *passim*. Friedham describes the Seattle labour movement as unique in failing to note the similarity between 'Duncanism' and 'federated unionism'. Duncan addressed the CFL on federated unionism. Minutes of CFL, 19 January 1919.
46. Kathryn J. Oberdeck, ' "Not Pink Teas": The Seattle Working Class Women's Movement, 1905–1918', *Labor History* 32: 2 (Spring 1991), pp. 204–20 *passim*.
47. *Monthly Labor Review* 10 (June 1920), pp. 1506–9.
48. O'Connor, chapter 6 *passim*.
49. Friedham, chapter 7 *passim*. The consequences of the split between progressives and radicals is detailed in the chapters on Seattle.
50. Friedham, p. 164.
51. Hamilton Cravens, 'A History of the Washington Farmer Labor Party 1918–1924' (MA, University of Washington, 1962), p. 85.

52. Yellowitz, pp. 123–4, 198, 219, 232; Rogin, p. 20.
53. Yellowitz, p. 37.
54. *New York Call*, 7 November 1918.
55. *New York Call*, 7 December 1918; Rogin, pp. 3, 5.
56. Rogin, pp. 8–10.
57. Rogin, p. 8.
58. *Advance*, 27 December 1918.
59. Rogin, p. 14.
60. Roger Horowitz, 'The Failure of Independent Political Action: The Labor Party of Cook County, 1919–1920' (BA Essay, University of Chicago, 1982), p. 17.
61. *Chicago Defender*, 5 April 1919; Horowitz, p. 15.
62. Halpern, p. 66.
63. Simonson, pp. 44, 78; Letter to 'Dear Bill' dated 27 April 1919, *David J. Saposs Papers*, box 1, folder no. 8, State Historical Society, Wisconsin.
64. Minutes of the CFL, Chicago Historical Society, 17 November, 15 December 1918; Eugene M. Tobin, *Organize Or Perish, America's Independent Progressives, 1913–1933* (New York: Greenwood Press, 1986), p. 103.
65. Simonson, p. 13; CFL Minutes, 5 January 1919.
66. Halpern, p. 50.
67. Walsh telegram to Fitzpatrick, Fitzpatrick Papers, 12 March 1919, box 8, folder 57; Correspondence, Walsh and Fitzpatrick, 12 March 1919, Frank Walsh Papers, box 8, folder 2.
68. *Bulletin* of the Chicago Women's Trade Union League, Vol VIII: 1–2, January/February 1919; the *Bulletin*, March 1919, vol. VIII: 3, Chicago WTUL Papers, Chicago Historical Society.
69. CFL Minutes, 15 December 1918.
70. Cravens, p. 37 *passim.*
71. Cravens, pp. 44–9.
72. Cravens, pp. 49–66 *passim.*
73. Cravens, p. 207.
74. O'Connor, p. 207; Hamilton Cravens, 'The Emergence of the Farmer-Labor Party in Washington Politics, 1919–1920', *Pacific Northwest Quarterly* (October 1966), p. 151.
75. Cravens, dissertation, pp. 72–3.
76. Cravens, dissertation, pp. 80– 2.
77. Cravens, 'Emergence of the Farmer Labor Party', p. 151.

2   FALSE DAWN: LABOUR POLITICS IN NEW YORK 1919–20

1. *Justice*, 18 January 1919.
2. Lawrence Rogin, 'Central Labor Bodies and Independent Political Action in New York City: 1918–1922' (MA, Columbia University, 1931), pp. 34–5.
3. *New York Times*, 24 August 1919; *New York Call* (hereafter *Call*), 19 September 1919. In the 1905 mayoral campaign, Hearst was beaten by

only 3474 votes out of a total vote of approximately 609 000. 'But on the basis of the best evidence available, it is clear that the election was stolen from Hearst by the Democratic machine': Philip S. Foner, *The AFL in the Progressive Era 1910–1915* (New York: International Publishers, 1980), p. 81.

4. Selig Perlman, *A Theory of the Labor Movement* (New York: Macmillan, 1928). James O. Morris, *Conflict Within the AFL: A Study of Craft Versus Industrial Unionism, 1901–1938* (Westport, CN: Greenwood Press, 1974). Melvyn Dubofsky, *When Workers Organize: New York City in the Progressive Era* (Amherst: University of Massachusetts Press, 1968).

5. Bureau of Labor Statistics, US Department. of Labor, Government Printing Office, *Monthly Labor Review*, 10 (1920), pp. 1506–13; 12 (1921), pp. 31–2, 222 and 1280–1.

6. *Call*, 2 and 12 January 1919, 11 April 1920. The Marine Affiliate unions were: Master Mates and Pilots Association, Marine Engineers, Steam and Operating Engineers, Lighter Captains, Tidewater Boatmen and Harbor Boatmen.

7. *Call*, 10 April 1920.

8. *Call*, 28 February, 25 April 1920.

9. *New York Times*, 24 August 1920.

10. Secretary's report, New York Women's Trade Union League (NYW-TUL), July 1919, September 1919; President and Organizers report, NYWTUL, October 1919, Papers of the Women's Trade Union League and Its Principal Leaders: Collection IV, New York Women's Trade Union League Minutes and Reports (published for the Schlesinger Library, Radcliffe College, by Research Publications, Woodbridge, Connecticut, 1979) (hereafter cited as WTUL Papers).

11. Minutes of Regular Meeting NYWTUL, 10 November 1919, WTUL Papers, Collection IV.

12. Maud Swartz to Frank Voght, 30 September 1919, NYWTUL Correspondence, WTUL Papers, Collection IV; President to Tuscan Bennett, Connecticut, 9 March 1920, NYWTUL Correspondence, WTUL Papers, Collection IV.

13. *Call*, 12 January 1919.

14. A. Rosebury, *Justice*, 18 January 1919.

15. *Call*, 23 January 1919.

16. 'Proceedings of the 12th Biennial Convention of Cloth Hat and Cap Makers of North America, New York, 1 May 1919 to 8 May 1919', *Headgear Worker*, June 1919, pp. 153–4.

17. Marie Jo Buhle, Paul Buhle, Dan Georgakas (eds), *Encyclopedia of the American Left* (Chicago: St James Press, 1990), pp. 215–16.

18. *Advance*, 16 July 1920.

19. *Advance*, 16 July 1920, 23 July, 13 August 1920; *Call*, 23 July 1920.

20. James Weinstein, *The Decline of Socialism in America* (New York: Monthly Review Press, 1967), table 1, p. 94.

21. *Call*, 3 February 1920.

22. *Call*, 24 February 1920. He gave the example of the Sheet Metal Workers Union Local 28 who overwhelmingly defeated a recommendation from the executive committee not to affiliate to the Labor Party.

23. *Call*, 6 and 24 March, 26 August 1920.

24. *New York Times*, 8 June 1920; *New York State Federation, Proceedings 57th Annual Convention* (Binghamton, 24–26 August 1920).
25. 'Miners on the War Path', undated report on Miners 1919 Convention, Blankenhorn Papers, box 4, folder no. 6, Archives of Labor and Urban Affairs, Walter Reuther Library, Wayne State University, Detroit, Michigan.
26. *Call*, 14 February, 20 March 1920.
27. *Call*, 4 December 1920.
28. *Call*, 5 December 1920.
29. For details of Jews and the New York labour movement see Jacob Rader Marcus, *United States Jewry: The East European Period*, vol. 4 (Detroit, MI: Wayne State University Press, 1993). For the Hebrew Trades see Marcus, pp. 200–2; Rogin, p. 32.
30. Rogin, pp. 33–4.
31. H. Lang to Gompers, 21 October 1920, Letters from Office of President, American Federation of Labor Records: The Samuel Gompers Era (Microfilming Corporation of America, 1981), reel 104.
32. *Call*, 22 May 1920; Rogin, p. 22.
33. *Call*, 28 May 1920. After official support was removed from the New York Labor Party by the CFU, the progressives announced the launching of a Statewide Labor Party. This time they prepared for trouble, having 'enough machinists in attendance at Schenectady to prevent a mob of outsiders from seizing control': *New York Times*, 6 November 1920.
34. *New York Times*, 20 June, 22 October 1920; *Call*, 30 July, 9 August 1920.
35. *Call*, 6 August 1920; Letter from Schneiderman, 19 November 1920, NYWTUL Correspondence, WTUL Papers, Collection IV.
36. *Congressional Quarterly Guide to U.S. Elections*, 1976, p. 286; Harry B. Sell, 'The A.F. of L. and the Labor Party Movement of 1918–20' (MA, University of Chicago, 1922), p. 142.
37. Geneva M. Marsh, 'Campaigning for Senator with Rose Schneiderman', *Life And Labor* (December 1920); Christine A. Lunardini, *From Equal Suffrage to Equal Rights* (New York and London: New York University Press, 1986), p. 129.
38. *Congressional Quarterly Guide to U.S. Elections*, p. 743; David A. Shannon, *The Socialist Party of America* (New York: Macmillan, 1995), p. 158; John Patrick Buckley, *The New York Irish: Their View of American Foreign Policy 1914–1921* (New York: Arno Press, 1976), p. 11, pp. 182–4 *passim*.
39. Rogin, pp. 30, 35–6.
40. Rogin, p. 36.
41. Rogin, pp. 34–5.

3   ONE STEP FORWARD: THE BIRTH OF THE LABOR PARTY, CHICAGO 1919–20

1. Charles Merriam and Harold Gosnell, *Non-Voting: Causes and Methods of Control* (Chicago: University of Chicago Press, 1924), pp. 46–7, 250

passim; Charles Merriam, *Chicago: A More Intimate View of Urban Politics* (New York: Macmillan, 1929).

2. *The New Majority*, 4 January 1919 (hereafter cited as *Majority*). For details of the socialist and progressive press see chapters on New York and Seattle.

3. The *Majority*, 24 April 1920, reported in its first year a print run of 5500. Circulation was spasmodic, increasing to as high as 17 500 during strikes and declining afterwards. *Majority*, 31 July 1920.

4. Roger Horowitz, 'The Failure of Independent Political Action: The Labor Party of Cook County, 1919–1920' (BA Essay, University of Chicago, 1982), p. 1.

5. Hamilton Cravens, 'A History of the Washington Farmer Labor Party 1918–1924' (MA, University of Washington, 1962), *passim*. Richard M. Valelly, *Radicalism in the States: The Minnesota Farmer Labor Party and the American Political Economy* (Chicago: Chicago University Press, 1989), *passim*. Ira Katznelson, *City Trenches: Urban Politics and the Patterning of Class in the US* (New York: Pantheon Books, 1981). For a more detailed discussion of this issue see A. G. Strouthous, 'A Comparative Study of Independent Working-Class Politics: The American Federation of Labor and Third Party Movement in New York, Chicago, and Seattle, 1918–1924' (PhD, London University 1996), pp. 92–4.

6. Commission of Inquiry, *Interchurch World Movement, Report on the Steel Strike of 1919* (New York: Harcourt, Brace & Howe, 1920), p. 36. *Majority*, 4 October 1919; Chicago WTUL, *Bulletin*, VIII: 1–2 (February 1919).

7. *Majority*, 1 March 1919.

8. *Majority*, 24 January, 22, 29 March 1919; 23 October 1920; Philip S. Foner, *Women and The American Labor Movement* (New York: Free Press, 1982), p. 129; *Daily News*, 29 March 1919; Stanley Shapiro, 'Hand and Brain: The Farmer Labor Party of 1920' (PhD, University of California, 1967), p. 117.

9. CFL Minutes, 19 January 1919.

10. *Majority*, 9 October 1920. Buck to Walsh, 2 June 1921, Walsh Papers, box 10, folder June 1921, New York Public Library.

11. *Majority*, 15 February, 29 March 1919.

12. *Majority*, 22 February, 12 April 1919. The *Majority* reported that 25 locals were committed to strike on the mayoral election day. *Majority*, 15 March 1919.

13. *Majority*, 22 February 1919; David Fickes Simonson, 'The Labor Party of Cook County, Illinois, 1918–1919' (MA, University of Chicago, 1959), pp. 26–7.

14. *Majority*, 1 March 1919.

15. *Majority*, 22 February, 1 March 1919.

16. *Majority*, 8, 15 March 1919; Notice of Cook County Labor Party meeting 13 March 1919, Fitzpatrick Papers, box 8, folder 58, Chicago Historical Society; Rick Halpern, *Down on the Killing Floor: Black and White Workers in Chicago's Packinghouses, 1904–54* (Urbana and Chicago: University of Illinois Press, 1997), chapter 2.

17. *Majority*, 15, 29 March 1919.

18. *Majority*, 4 January, 1 February, 29 March 1919; Louise A. Tilly and Patricia Gurin (eds), *Women's Politics and Change* (New York: Russell Sage Foundation, 1990), p. 201.

19. *Majority*, 1, 22 February, 8 March 1919.

20. Morton L. Johnson, the Party's secretary, estimated that 200 000 Chicago citizens entitled to the vote were not registered. He believed that many were the wives, daughters and relatives of working men and that the majority of women who did vote were from other than the working classes. This view is reinforced by Charles Merriam and Harold Gosnell, *Non-Voting: Causes and Methods of Control*, p. 46. *Majority*, 8 March 1919; Tilly and Gurin, p. 160; Simonson, pp. 65–8.

21. Merriam and Gosnell, pp. 29–49; *Chicago Daily News Almanac*, quoted in Simonson, p. 65. (Twenty-four per cent of Fitzpatrick's vote was cast by women: *Majority*, 5 April 1919.)

22. *Majority*, 15 February 1919; Rick Halpern, 'Race, Ethnicity and Union in the Chicago Stockyards, 1917–1922', *International Review Of Social History* 37 (1992), p. 33; Horowitz, pp. 31–2.

23. *Majority*, 8, 14, 22 February, 8 March 1919.

24. *Majority*, 5, 12, 19 July, 4 October 1919.

25. *Majority*, 22, 29 November 1919; 14, 28 February 1920.

26. *Majority*, 19, 26 June, 3, 10 July 1920.

27. *Majority*, 24 July, 23, 30 October 1920; *The Nation*, 4 September 1920, reproduced in the *Majority*, 18 September 1920.

28. *Majority*, 1, 8, 15 February, 13 November 1919; 28 August 1920.

29. Minutes, Typographical Union Local 16, Typographical Union Local 16 Papers, Volume 14, pp. 222–5, Chicago Historical Society; Simonson, pp. 41–3.

30. *Majority*, 8 March 1919; 'Report of Illinois Miners' Convention, Peoria', 23 March 1920, *Majority*, 3 April 1920.

31. *Majority*, 8 February, 1 March, 4 October 1919.

32. *Majority*, 22 March, 5 April 1919, 12 June 1920. (The amount raised by April was $26 783.69.)

33. *Majority*, 15 March, 11 October 1919; CFL Minutes, 5 October 1919; James R. Barrett, *Work and Community in the Jungle, Chicago's Packinghouse Workers, 1894–1922* (Urbana: University of Illinois Press, 1987), p. 209; E. McKillen, 'Chicago Workers and the Struggle to Democratize Diplomacy 1914–24' (PhD, Northwestern University, 1987), p. 176.

34. Hanes Walton Jr, *The Negro in Third Party Politics* (Philadelphia: Dorrance & Co., 1969), p. 48; Charles Merriam and Harold Gosnell, *The American Party System: An Introduction to the Study of Political Parties in the United States* (New York: Macmillan, 1950), pp. 16, 121–5; Dianne M. Pinderhughes, *Race and Ethnicity in Chicago Politics: A Reexamination of Pluralist Theory* (Urbana: University of Illinois Press, 1987), table 4.5, p. 84.

35. Walton, pp. 51–3.

36. Halpern, *Killing Floor*, pp. 51–4; *Majority*, 3 December 1921.

37. Pinderhughes, *Race and Ethnicity*, table 4.1, p. 73. Pinderhughes does not say where the remaining 16 per cent of the black vote went. She states that her figures do not total 100 per cent because of third-party

candidates. In 1919 the Democrat mayoral campaign was split and she makes no mention of this. However, Fitzpatrick did not get a major share of the black 'third-party vote'. The *Majority*, 5 April 1919, gave Fitzpatrick's vote in the predominantly black 2nd ward as 564; Thompson received 15 569.

Defender, 5 April 1919; James R. Grossman, *Land of Hope: Chicago, Black Southerners, and the Great Migration* (Chicago: University of Chicago Press, 1989), pp. 175–6, 231–5; William M. Tuttle Jr, *Race Riot: Chicago in the Red Summer of 1919* (New York: Atheneum, 1970), pp. 202–3; Rick Halpern, *Killing Floor*, chapter 2.

38. *Defender*, 7 September 1918; 6 November 1920.
39. *Defender*, 21 June 1919.
40. *Majority*, 12 July 1919.
41. *Majority*, 9, 16 August 1919.
42. *Defender*, 2, 4, 9 October 1920.
43. *Majority*, 5 April 1919; Simonson, pp. 74–6.
44. Simonson, p. 78.
45. Democratic objections forced Clara Masilotti off the ballot paper, and she ran as a 'write in' candidate. Simonson, pp. 69, 81–4; Kantowicz, p. 142.
46. Olander to Walsh, 27 May 1920, Frank Walsh Papers, box 9, folder 17–31 May 1920. For a description of the Kansas Industrial Relations court, see Henry J. Allen, *The Party Of The Third Part* (New York: Harper & Bro, 1921).
47. *Majority*, 4 December 1920; Edward R. Kantowicz, *Polish-American Politics in Chicago 1888–1940* (Chicago: University of Chicago Press, 1975), pp. 108, 120, 143.
48. Marc Karson, *American Labor Unions and Politics 1900–18* (Boston: Beacon Press, 1958) stresses the conservative influence of Catholic trade unionists on the politics of the AFL.

Harold F. Gosnell, *Machine Politics: The Chicago Model* (University of Illinois Press, 1939), p.101. For details of labour's international politics in Chicago see E. McKillen, cited above.
49. Kantowicz, pp. 26–8.
50. Kantowicz, pp. 43, 50–1, 102, 117–20.
51. Kantowicz, pp. 139, 143.
52. Gosnell, *Machine Politics*, p. 45; Kantowicz, p. 143.
53. E. McKillen, p. 93; *Majority*, 8, 15 March 1919; Walsh to Nockels, 25 March 1919, Walsh Papers, box 8, folder 4.
54. John M. Flynn, Secretary Chicago Local Council of Friends of Irish Freedom, to Fitzpatrick, 9 August 1920, Fitzpatrick Papers, box 9, folder 64, August 1920; McKillen, p. 232.
55. McKillen states (p. 225) that the Irish voted against the Democrats but does not provide direct evidence. Kantowicz, pp. 20, 123.

4   A LONG AND WINDING ROAD: SEATTLE 1918–20

1. Jonathan Dembo, *Unions and Politics in Washington State 1885–1935* (New York: Garland, 1983), pp. 205–8.

2. William John Dickson, 'Labor in Municipal Politics: A Study of Labor's Political Policies and Activities in Seattle' (MA thesis, University of Washington, 1928), p. 19; R. D. Mckenzie, 'Community Forces: A Study of the Non-Partisan Municipal Elections in Seattle', *Journal of Social Forces*, January, March, May (1924), p. 9.

3. Hamilton Cravens, 'A History of The Washington Farmer Labor Party 1918–1924' (MA, University of Washington, 1962), pp. 82–97; Dembo, p. 251.

4. Dembo, pp. 252–4; Cravens, p. 96.

5. Union Record, 3 March 1920 (hereafter cited as *Record*); *Industrial Worker*, Seattle, 9 March 1920; Dickson, p. 53.

6. *Record*, 21 October 1919.

7. On the employers' offensive, Americanization and the workers' response nationally see James R. Green, *The World of the Worker: Labor in Twentieth-Century America* (New York: Hill & Wang, 1989; orig. 1980); Robert K. Murray, *Red Scare: A Study in National Hysteria* (Minneapolis: University of Minneapolis Press, 1955); Robert H. Zieger, *American Workers, American Unions, 1920–1985* (Baltimore, MD: Johns Hopkins University Press, 1986).

8. *Record*, 1, 3, 4, 5, 11 November 1919.

9. *Record*, 12, 13, 14 November 1919; see also Tom Copeland, *The Centralia Tragedy of 1919: Elmer Smith and the Wobblies* (Seattle: University of Washington Press, 1993).

10. *Record*, 21 November 1919; Dana Frank, *Purchasing Power: Consumer Organizing, Gender, and the Seattle Labor Movement, 1919–1929* (New York: Cambridge University Press, 1994), p. 110; Cravens, pp. 91–2.

11. *Record*, 29, 30 November, 3, 6, 11 December 1919.

12. *Record*, 13, 14, 20, 28 January, 10 February 1920.

13. *Record*, 11, 12, 16, 17, 18, 21, 23 February 1920.

14. *Record*, 24, 25, 27 February; 1 March 1920; Frank, p. 18; Harvey O'Connor, *Revolution in Seattle* (Seattle, WA: Left Bank Books, 1981), p. 207.

15. Denzil Cecil Cline, 'The Streetcar Men of Seattle: A Sociological Study' (MA, University of Washington, 1926) pp. 131–2; Mckenzie, p. 23; Dickson, pp. 53–8.

16. *Record*, 4 April, 21 July 1919.

17. *Record*, 26 September, 5, 6, 7 November 1919.

18. *Record*, 20, 27, 29, 30 January, 2, 4, 5, 7, 9 February 1920.

19. Frank, pp. 89–90; *Record*, 21, 23, 26, 28 February 1920.

20. *Record*, 2 July 1920.

21. *Record*, 22, 23, 24, 28 July, 2 August 1920.

22. *Record*, 16, 17, 19, 20, 21, 23 August 1920.

23. *Record*, 30 August, 2, 4, 9 September 1920.

24. *Record*, 15, 24 September 1920.

25. *Record*, 24 September 1920; SCLC Minutes, 15 September, 6, 20, 27 October, 10 November 1920.

26. *Record*, 20, 21 September, 20, 23, 27, 28 October, 1, 2 November 1920.

27. *Record*, 9 September 1920. (The Prohibition Laws allowed several exceptions. Alcoholic content of drinks was restricted to a half per cent.

Individuals could use intoxicating liquor obtained before the law was passed for personal consumption. Non-intoxicating ciders and fruit juices could be prepared at home. Bone Dry Law advocates wanted these concessions removed.) James H. Timberlake, *Prohibition and the Progressive Movement, 1900–1920* (New York: Atheneum, 1970), p. 180.

28. *Record*, 22, 27 October 1920.
29. *Record*, 16, 26 October 1920. For the Japanese response see Frank, pp. 170–1.
30. *Record*, 11, 12, 16 October 1920; Douglas Roscoe Pullen, 'The Administration of Washington State Governor Louis F. Hart, 1919–1925' (PhD, University of Washington, 1974), pp. 238–40.
31. *Record*, 27 October, 1 November 1920.
32. *Record*, 28 September, 1 October, 1 November 1920.
33. *Record*, 29 September, 8, 22, 26 October 1920.
34. Tables 4.1 and 4.2 are compiled from *Abstract of Votes, State of Washington: General Election November 2, 1920* (Washington State: Secretary of State, 1920).
35. Abstracts and Pullen pp. 69–70.
36. Compiled from *Union Record*, 13 November 1920.
37. Norman H. Clark, *The Dry Years: Prohibition and Social Change in Washington* (Seattle: University of Washington Press, 1965), p. 142; Dembo, p. 251; Frank, pp. 17–19; M. L. Krause, 'Prohibition and Reform Tradition in the Washington State Senatorial Election of 1922' (MA, University of Washington, 1963), pp. 61–2.
38. See Dickson, p. 79.
39. Washington State Bureau of Labor, *Twelfth Biennial Report* (1920), p. 1056, quoted in Frank, pp. 101–2; Dickson, p. 79.
40. Jonathan Dembo stresses religious and ethnic divides in Seattle voting patterns. Dembo leans heavily on the work of Denzil Cecil Cline, whose study of 'Streetcar Men in Seattle', a white, mainly Protestant workforce, provides a contemporary analysis of how they voted. Dembo notes that 68 per cent of the streetcar men voted for Duncan, but he ignores the fact that 76.5 per cent of those that actually voted did so for Duncan. Cline's study has little systematic information on ethnicity, religion or attitude. The only substantial references to prejudice is that of Protestant anti-Catholicism. Dembo, p. 256; Cline, pp. 145–8.
41. Cline discovered that there was a constant uniformity of how car men voted, for example, 83 per cent voted for La Follette. The most important insight of Cline's thesis is that union solidarity translated into political commitment. Dembo ignores this central theme and prefers to use the thesis as evidence of anti-Duncan sentiment. Dembo, p. 256; Cline, pp. 132–3.
42. Cline, pp. 150–1.
43. Cline, p. 50.
44. Frank, pp. 17–19.
45. Robert Friedham, *The Seattle General Strike* (Seattle: University of Washington Press, 1964), pp. 159–60.
46. Report of Agent 106, 4 May 1919, Conan Broussain Beck Papers, box 1, folder 1–2, University of Washington, Seattle; Friedham, p. 48.

5 UNITY AND INDEPENDENT POLITICAL ACTION IN NEW YORK 1921–24

1. Nathan Fine, *Labor and Farmer Parties in the United States 1828–1928* (New York: Russell & Russell, 1961), p. 397.
2. Melvyn Dubofsky, *The State and Labor in Modern America* (Chapel Hill: University of North Carolina Press, 1994), pp. 70–1.
3. Walsh to Fine, 27 January 1921, Frank Walsh Papers, box 10, folder January 1921, Manuscripts Room, New York Public Library.
4. *New York Women's Trade Union League Bulletin*, March 1921, in the Papers of the Women's Trade Union League and Its Principal Leaders (Research Publications, Woodbridge, CT, 1979), (hereafter cited as WTUL Papers), Collection IX, WTUL Publications. Secretary's report January 1921; Secretary's report 7 March, WTUL Papers, Collection IV, NYWTUL Minutes and Reports.
5. Annual report for March 1921–22; Minutes of Regular Meeting, 27 June 1922, WTUL Papers, Collection IV, Minutes and Reports; *Call*, 8 September 1921.
6. *New York Times*, 8 September 1921; *Call*, 23 November 1921.
7. David A. Shannon, *The Socialist Party of America* (New York: Macmillan, 1955), p. 165; James Weinstein, *The Decline of Socialism In America* (New York: Monthly Review Press, 1967), p.327.
8. Weinstein, p. 275.
9. *Call*, 27, 28 June 1921.
10. *Call*, 11, 12 July, 22 September 1921.
11. *Call*, 10 October 1921, 4 November 1921.
12. Call, 9, 11, 23 November 1921.
13. *Call*, 24, 28 November 1921.
14. *Call*, 3 February 1922.
15. *Call*, 13 March 1922.
16. *Call*, 2, 25 May, 2, 3 July 1922.
17. *Call*, 7, 12 July 1922.
18. *Call*, 15, 16 July 1922. Minutes of Convention of the Joint Committee for Independent Labor Political Action, New York, 15 July 1922, American Labor Party Minutes, 1922–24 Folder, Tamiment Institute.
19. *Call*, 17, 18 July 1922.
20. *Call*, 12, 15, 17 August, 16 October 1922.
21. *Call*, 17, 18, 20 October, 5 November 1922.
22. *Call*, 20, 26, 31 October, 4, 5, 7 November 1922.
23. Call, 4, 5 November 1922; *Congressional Quarterly Guide to the U.S. Elections*, p. 743; Shannon, p. 158.
24. *Call*, 7 September, 16, 20 October 1922.
25. Call, 9 November, 8 December 1922; *New York Times*, 9 November 1922; *Congressional Quarterly Guide to U.S. Elections*, p. 743.
26. Dubofsky, pp. 97–9; *Call*, 20 February 1922.
27. *Call*, 20, 21, 22, 23 February, 28 November, 6 December 1922.
28. *Call*, 9, 13, 14, 15 December 1922.
29. *Call*, 20, 21 December 1922; Weinstein, p. 272.

30. *Call*, 4, 5, 6 January, 6 April 1923.
31. Minutes of Second Annual Convention of the American Labor Party, New York, 25 February 1923, American Labor Party Minutes; *Call*, 25, 26 February 1923.
32. *Call*, 24 March 1923; Minutes of Second Annual Convention of the American Labor Party, New York, 25 February 1923, American Labor Party Minutes.
33. *Call*, 21 May, 27 June 1923. Minutes of General Council, 21 June 1923, American Labor Party Minutes.
34. *Call*, 30 July 1923.
35. *Labor*, 14 October 1922.
36. *Call*, 7, 28 August 1923; Bernard K. Johnpoll's *Pacifist Progress: Norman Thomas and the Decline of American Socialism* (Westport, CI: Greenwood Press, 1987; orig. 1970), p. 38, cites only financial reasons.
37. *Call*, 24 August 1923. On 28 August 1923 the *Call* announced a change of ownership to 'Labor Press Association Inc.' a joint stock company of trade unions. Progressive unions such as the ILGWU, ACW and teachers held shares. New York State Socialists also had representatives on the board. Norman Thomas became editor-in-chief and Heber Blankenhorn managing editor. The paper appeared under the title of *New York Leader*. Johnpoll, p. 39.
38. *New York Leader*, 1, 4 October 1923.
39. *Leader*, 10, 11, 20 October 1923.
40. *Advance*, 23 July 1920; 26 October 1923; Weinstein, p. 308.
41. *Justice*, 21, 28 September 1923; Edward P. Johanningsmeier, *Forging American Communism: The Life of William Z. Foster* (Princeton, NJ: Princeton University Press, 1994), p. 206.
42. *Leader*, 30, 31 October 1923.
43. *Leader*, 6, 8, 12 November 1923. The new weekly appeared on 19 January 1924.
44. Ibid.
45. *New York Times*, 1, 2 October 1923; Richard M. Valelly, *Radicalism in the States: The Minnesota Farmer Labor Party and the American Political Economy* (Chicago: Chicago University Press, 1989), p. 41.
46. Philip S. Foner, *History of the Labor Movement in the United States Volume 9: The TUEL to the End of the Gompers Era* (New York: International Publishers, 1991), pp. 339–45; Kenneth Campbell MacKay, *The Progressive Movement of 1924* (New York: Octagon Books, 1972), pp. 112–14.
47. Minutes of the General Council, 24 June 1924, American Labor Party Minutes.
48. Organizers report to General Council 30 July 1924, Minutes of the ALP General Council, American Labor Party Minutes.
49. *New Leader*, 12 July 1924.
50. *New Leader*, 19 July 1924; *Times*, 25 July, 6 August, 7, 8 September 1924.
51. Appeal for La Follette campaign from Executive Council, 5 August 1924; press release 17 September 1924, American Federation of Labor Records: The Samuel Gompers Era (cited hereafter as AFL Records), Speeches and Writings, reel 119 (Microfilming Corporation of America, 1981); *New Leader*, 9 August 1924.

52. *New Leader*, 23 August 1924.
53. *Times*, 18, 19, 22, 29 August 1924.
54. *Times*, 29 August, 9, 22 October 1924.
55. *Times*, 31 October 1924.
56. *Times*, 1 November 1924.
57. Gompers' press release, 1 November 1924, AFL Records, Speeches and Writings; *Times*, 12 October 1924; *AFL News*, 25 October 1924; *Times*, 3 November 1924.
58. *Times*, 19 August 1924. See Chapters 6 and 7 of this book for details of AFL action against John Fitzpatrick and James Duncan for opposing AFL political policy.
59. *Times*, 8 October 1924.
60. *Times*, 11, 21 August; 8, 10, 28 September 1924; Johnpoll, p. 45; La Follette Snr, Papers, 1844–1925, box 207, Campaign Folder, Manuscripts Room, Library of Congress, Washington DC.
61. Women's Division Leaflet, La Follette Papers, box 207, Campaign Folder; Schneiderman to Nancy Cook, 18 September 1924; La Follette–Wheeler Campaign Committee to Maud Swartz, 23 October 1924; WTUL Papers, Collection IV, Correspondence.
62. *Times*, 22 October 1924; *Leader*, 18 September 1924.
63. *Times*, 2, 3 November 1924.
64. *Times*, 30 November 1924.
65. Johnpoll, p. 45; *Times*, 30 November 1924; *Leader*, 8 November 1924; Svend Petersen, *A Statistical History of the American Presidential Elections* (Westport, CT: Greenwood Press, 1981), pp. 275–80; MacKay, pp. 219–27.

6 TWO STEPS BACK: RED FLAG TO WHITE FLAG – CHICAGO 1921–24

1. *Report of the Proceedings of the Sixth Biennial International Fur Workers Convention*, 12 May 1924, American Labor Union Constitutions and Proceedings, reel 50, p. 8 (New Jersey: Microfilming Corporation of America, 1977).
2. Fitzpatrick to FLP national committee, 30 October 1920, Fitzpatrick Papers, box 9, folder 66, Chicago Historical Society.
3. Edward P. Johanningsmeier, *Forging American Communism* (Princeton, NJ: Princeton University Press, 1994), pp. 146–7; Letter to National Committee, 2 November 1920, Fitzpatrick Papers, box 9, folder 67; *The New Majority* (hereafter *Majority*), 1 January 1921.
4. CCFLP letter, 15 June 1921, Fitzpatrick Papers, box 10, folder 73.
5. For details of CFL foreign policy see E. McKillen, 'Chicago Workers and the Struggle to Democratize Diplomacy 1914–24' (PhD, Northwestern University, 1987).
6. *Majority*, 8 January, 12, 26 February 1921; CFL Minutes, 6 February 1921.
7. CFL Minutes, 20 March 1921; *Majority*, 19 March 1921.

8. *Majority*, 16 July, 1 October 1921.
9. Gifford Ernest to Executive Committee CCFLP, 5 April 1922, Fitzpatrick Papers, folder 81, box 11; Gifford Ernest to Executive Committee CCFLP, 11 April 1922, Fitzpatrick Papers, folder 81 box 11.
10. *Majority*, 7 January, 29 April 1922; Rick Halpern, *Down on the Killing Floor: Black and White Workers in Chicago's Packinghouses* (Urbana and Chicago: University of Illinois Press, 1997), p. 57.
11. Chicago newspaper reports estimated between 50 000 and 100 000 had demonstrated. *Majority*, 6 May 1922.
12. *Chicago Daily Tribune*, 9 November 1922; J.G. Brown, National Secretary of the FLP, reporting in the *Majority*, 2 December 1922.
13. *Majority*, 14 July 1923. Attendance at CCFLP report November 1923 in *James P. Cannon and the Early Years of American Communism: Selected Writings and Speeches 1920–1928* (New York: Prometheus Research Library, 1992), p. 160.
    The Communists and the forming of the FFLP is detailed in Theodore Draper, *The Roots of American Communism* (New York: Viking Press, 1957) and *James P. Cannon and the Early Years of American Communism*.
14. *Majority, 24* February, 17 March 1923.
15. Report of the FLP of Cook County Quarterly Convention, January 1923 in the *Majority*, 20 January 1923; Letter, 9 November 1921, Jay G. Brown to Otto Branstetter National Secretary of the Socialist Party, Fitzpatrick Papers, box 11, folder 77.
16. *Majority*, 3, 10 November 1923.
17. *Majority*, 1, 8, 22 December 1923.
18. CFL Minutes, 16 December 1923.
19. *New York Leader*, 10 October 1923. Reports on 1923 AFL Annual Convention in the *Majority*, 13, 27 October 1923.
    Walker abandoned the Party before the 3 July 1923 convention. The Illinois State Federation Executive also abandoned the FLP. Gompers was overjoyed and wanted to publicize the decision as widely as possible. Gompers did not have to wait long; Walker launched his attack on the FLP at the October 1923 AFL convention. Minutes, 22 June 1923, 'Conference on Illinois Politics', American Federation of Labor Records: The Samuel Gompers Era, Conferences, reel 122 (Microfilming Corporation of America, 1981) (hereafter cited as AFL Records).
20. Report of the CFL delegation to the Illinois State Convention, *Majority*, 13 October 1923; Keiser, pp. 196–7; Johanningsmeier, pp. 200–1; James P. Cannon, pp. 158–60.
21. The AFL executive stopped paying its half share of Fitzpatrick's salary. The reasons given were financial. Partial payment for the Chicago CFL headquarters was also terminated. Letter, Gompers to Fitzpatrick, 25 April 1923, AFL Records, Vote Books, reel 17.
22. CFL Minutes, 18 May 1924.
23. *Majority*, 7 June, 5 July 1924.
24. Keiser claims that the Labor Party men of Chicago did not support La Follette. The evidence that follows contradicts this assertion. Keiser, p. 147.

25. *Majority*, 26 April, 10, 24 May 1924; CFL Minutes, 17 August 1924.
26. *Majority*, 12 July 1924.
27. *Federation News*, 30 August 1924.
28. Richard Schneirov, *Union Brotherhood, Union Town: The History of the Carpenters Union of Chicago, 1863–1987* (Carbondale: Southern Illinois University Press, 1988), pp. 96–8; *Federation News*. 4, 11, 23 October 1924.
29. Report to CFL 19 October, in *Federation News*, 23 October 1924; *Federation News*, 25 October, 1 November 1924.
30. Financial reports in *Federation News*, 22 November 1924; *Majority*, 5 May 1919.
31. *Federation News*, 1 November 1924.
32. *Tribune*, 2 November 1924; Report of CFL meeting of 7 September 1924 in *Federation News*, 13 September 1924; *Tribune*, 12 October 1924. If there was any serious opposition inside the CFL to the campaign or dragging of feet, the Chicago *Tribune* did not discover it. Unable to point to any serious splits in the unions, it claimed the campaign was supported mainly by the naturalized and needle-trade workers.
33. *Defender*, 26 March 1921; *Majority*, 3 December 1921. For black organizations' attitude to third-party campaigns see Hanes Walton Jr, *The Negro in Third Party Politics* (Philadelphia: Dorrance and Company, 1969), *passim*.
34. *Defender*, 20 September, 4, 18 October 1924; David P. Thelan, *Robert M. La Follette and the Insurgent Spirit* (Boston: Little, Brown, 1976), p. 188.
35. Compiled from *Chicago Tribune*, 6 November 1924.
36. *Congressional Quarterly Guide to U.S. Elections* (Washington, DC: 1976), p. 287.
37. Compiled from *Chicago Tribune*, 6 November 1924.
38. Compiled from *Chicago Tribune*, 6 November 1924.
39. Edward R. Kantowicz, *Polish-American Politics in Chicago 1888–1940* (Chicago: The University of Chicago Press, 1975), pp. 122–4.
40. Kantowicz, pp. 123–4.
41. See discussion of Merriam's study in previous chapter on Chicago.
42. *Tribune*, 14, 17, 26 October 1924.
43. David A. Shannon, *The Socialist Party of America* (New York: MacMillan, 1955), pp. 18–21.
44. *Majority*, 25 March, 22 April 1922; Executive Council Minutes, 10 May 1922, AFL Records, Executive Council Records Minutes, reel 7; Keiser, p. 66.
45. Keiser, p. 66; Johanningsmeier, pp. 182, 218–19.
46. Keiser, p. 104.
47. For a general assessment of La Follette's campaign see Thelan, chapters 8 and 9.
48. Appeal from AFL Non-Partisan Political Campaign Committee, 5 August 1924, AFL Records, Conferences, reel 119.

7 DUNCAN'S LAST STAND: SEATTLE 1921–24

1. William Short's annual report, *Washington State Federation of Labor: Report of the Proceedings, 20th National Convention* (Vancouver, Washington, 11–14 July 1921), pp. 5–7.
2. *Union Record* (hereafter *Record*), 15 July 1921; Hamilton Cravens, 'A History of the Washington Farmer Labor Party 1918–1924' (MA, University of Washington, 1962), pp. 145–8; Harvey O'Connor, *Revolution In Seattle* (Seattle, WA: Left Bank Books, 1981; orig. 1964), pp. 207–9.
3. Cravens, pp. 148–50.
4. Cravens p. 150; Jonathan Dembo, *Unions and Politics in Washington State 1885–1935* (New York: Garland, 1983), pp. 293–4.
5. Cravens, p. 152; Dembo, pp. 294–5.
6. Short, Annual Report, Washington State Federation of Labor, *Report of the Proceedings, 20th Annual Convention*; *Record*, 15 July 1921.
7. *Record*, 18 November 1920.
8. *Record*, 13 and 16 January 1921.
9. *Record*, 13, 14, 20, 22 December 1920.
10. *Record*, 31 January 1921.
11. *Record*, 25, 26 February 1921.
12. Doyle, a painter, was elected business agent by the conservative wing of the council to balance Duncan. O'Connor, p. 111.
13. *Record*, 5, 6, 7, 9 March 1921.
14. *Record*, 4 March, 24 April, 18 July 1922; SCLC Minutes, 3 May 1922; Dembo, p. 305; William John Dickson, 'Labor in Municipal Politics: A Study of Labor's Political Policies and Activities in Seattle' (MA, University of Washington, 1928), p. 136; Mary Joan O'Connell, 'The Seattle Union Record, 1918–1928: A Pioneer Labor Daily' (MA, University of Washington, 1964), pp. 213–14; Denzil Cecil Cline, 'The Streetcar Men of Seattle: A Sociological Study' (MA, University of Washington, 1926), pp. 133–5.
15. *Record*, 4 May 1922.
16. *Record*, 24 April 1922.
17. *Record*, 24 April 1922.
18. Duncan to Short, 29 April 1922, *Record*, 2 May 1922. Letter Short to Duncan, *Record*, 4 May 1922.
19. SCLC Minutes, 10, 17, 24, 31 May 1922; Dembo, p. 316; *Record*, 1 June 1922.
20. *Record*, 5 June 1922.
21. *Record*, 5, 6 June 1922, 10, 13 July 1922.
22. *Record*, 14 July 1922; Dembo, pp. 321–2.
23. *Record*, 13 July 1922; SCLC Minutes, 26 July 1922; Agent 106 Report, 4 May 1919, Conan Broussain Beck Papers (Industrial Espionage Papers), box 1, folder 1–2.
24. SCLC Minutes, 16 August 1922; *Record*, 27 July 1922.
25. SCLC Minutes, 23 August, 6 September 1922; *Record*, 8 September 1922.
26. *Record*, 15, 30 September 1922.

27. *Record*, 2, 17 October 1922; Dembo, p. 330.
28. SCLC Minutes, 11, 18 October 1922; *Record*, 1 November.1922; Cravens, p. 181.
29. *Record*, 9 November 1922; O'Connell, p. 217.
30. Dembo, p. 331; Minutes of Carpenters 131, 14, 28 March, 16 May, 3 October 1922, Carpenters and Joiners Seattle Local 131 Collection, box 1, University of Washington, Seattle.
31. *Record*, 11 November 1922; Dana Frank, *Purchasing Power: Consumer Organizing, Gender, and the Seattle Labor Movement, 1919–1929* (New York: Cambridge University Press 1994), pp. 101–2.
32. Executive Council Minutes, 24 November 1922, 20 February 1923, American Federation of Labor Records: The Samuel Gompers Era, reel 7 (Microfilming Corporation of America: published by the State Historical Society of Wisconsin, Madison, 1981) (cited hereafter as AFL Records); SCLC Minutes, 18 April 1923.
33. SCLC Minutes, 18 April 1923; Executive Council Minutes, 9, 14 May 1923, AFL Records, reel 7.
34. SCLC Minutes, 6 June 1923.
35. Short to Gompers, 25 May 1923; Reply to Gompers written endorsed by SCLC on 6 June 1923. In Gompers, correspondence of 14 June 1923 to the Executive Council, AFL Records, the Vote Books, reel 18.
36. Short to AFL Executive Council, 7 June 1923, in Gompers, correspondence of 14 June 1923 supplied to the Executive Council, AFL Records, the Vote Books, reel 18.
37. Reports from C. O. Young and Short distributed in Gompers, correspondence to AFL executive on 27 June 1923, AFL Records, the Vote Books, reel 18.
38. *Proceedings of 22nd WSFL Annual Convention*, Bellingham, 9–12 July 1923; *Record*, 11 July 1923.
39. *Record*, 12 July 1923; SCLC Minutes, 1 August 1923; Gompers' address to Seattle trade unions, 25 September 1923, AFL Records, Speeches and Writings, reel 118.
40. Gompers' reports to the Executive Council 19 October, 15 November 1923, AFL Records, the Vote Books, reel 18.
41. For details of the FLP after this date see Cravens, p. 198–9 *passim*.
42. Dembo, p. 362.
43. The SCLC supported the AFL's non-partisan campaign and the CPPA, sending delegates to the CPPA and appointing a committee to work with the AFL Non-Partisan Political Campaign Committee; SCLC Minutes, 20, 27 August 1924; *Proceedings of the 23rd Annual Convention of the Washington State Federation of Labor*, Olympia, 14–18 July 1924; *Record*, 15 July 1924.
44. *Record*, 16, July, 21 October 1924.
45. *Record*, 21 October 1924; Cravens, pp. 230–1. Those supporting La Follette included Duncan, Kennedy and Pearl, and others who wanted a revival of the socialists. The Communists were of little importance or influence in Seattle during this period. O'Connor, p. 206.
46. *Record*, 23 July 1924. Founders included L. W. Buck and E. B. Ault. Representatives from unions included the Timber Workers, Machinists

and Bricklayers. Local support came from branches of the Carpenters, Pattern Makers, Electricians, Barbers, and Iron Workers.

47. *Record*, 25 July, 8, 15, 17, 30 September, 8, 16, 22 October 1924; SCLC Minutes, 15, 22 October 1924.

48. *Record*, 4 November 1924.

49. *Record*, 16, 22 October 1924. Morrison's intervention at such a late stage of the campaign undermines the conventional historiography that the AFL did little for the campaign. For example, see Kenneth Campbell MacKay, *The Progressive Movement of 1924* (New York: Octagon Books, 1972; orig. 1947), p. 188.

50. *Record*, 4 November 1924.

51. NB: La Follette percentages are based on the main party vote only and do not include fringe parties. Figures for Washington State and King County from the *Abstract of Votes: State of Washington, General Election 1924* (published by the Secretary of State, Olympia). Figures for Seattle from the *Record*, 6 November 1924.

52. NB: Percentages are based on main parties only. Figures from *Abstract of Votes* (Washington), 1920, 1924; *Record*, 19 February 1920; 6 November 1924.

53. Results on a Seattle-wide basis for the 1920 General Election were not made available.

54. Dembo, table 3, p. 627.

55. *Record*, 6 November 1924.

56. Henry Braine, Secretary of International Union of United Brewery, Flour, Cereal and Soft Drink Workers of America, Local 142, Seattle, to William Short, 11 November 1922 in Correspondence of Washington State Federation, box 13, folder 7–48.

57. For WSFL and SCLC membership see tables 2 and 3 in Dembo, pp. 625–8.

8   CONCLUSION: THE END OF A DREAM

1. *Julius Caesar*, Act IV, scene 3.

2. Gwendolyn Mink, *Old Labor and New Immigrants in American Political Development* (Ithaca, NY: Cornell University Press, 1986), p. 18.

3. The case of the Amalgamated Clothing Workers (ACW) demonstrates this point amply. The failure to relate to the (ACW) is dealt with in Chapter 2.

4. See Chapters 4 and 7.

5. See Chapter 4 for an account of this incident.

6. Frederick C. Howe, *Confessions Of A Reformer* (Kent, OH: Kent State University Press, 1988; orig. 1925), p. 338. Howe noted the massive enthusiasm for La Follette, but observed that people do not always vote as they 'shout', or even vote as they want to vote. He believed that fear was a factor in deciding the final way people voted.

7.   Karl Marx, '*The 18th Brumaire of Louis Napoleon*' *Surveys from Exile: Political Writings, Volume 2* (London: Allen Lane and New Left Review, 1973), p. 146.
8.   Richard White, 'Other Wests', *The West*, ed. Geoffrey C. Ward (London: Weidenfeld & Nicolson, 1996), p. 48.

APPENDIX   LABOR'S FOURTEEN POINTS

1.   *The New Majority*, 4 January 1919.

Index